An Activity-Based Approach to Early Intervention

Third Edition

by

Kristie Pretti-Frontczak, Ph.D.
Department of Educational Foundations
and Special Services
College and Graduate School of Education
Kent State University, Ohio

and

Diane Bricker, Ph.D.
Early Intervention Program
Center on Human Development
College of Education
University of Oregon, Eugene

·P·A·U·L·H·
BROOKES
PUBLISHING CO.®

Baltimore • London • Sydney

Paul H. Brookes Publishing Co.
Post Office Box 10624
Baltimore, Maryland 21285-0624

www.brookespublishing.com

Typeset by Integrated Publishing Solutions, Grand Rapids, Michigan.
Manufactured in the United States of America by
Versa Press, East Peoria, Illinois.

The case studies described in this book are composites based on the authors' actual experiences. Individuals' names have been changed, and identifying details have been altered to protect confidentiality.

Figures 2.1 and 2.2 courtesy of Jennifer Craun. Photographs on page 1 and front cover courtesy of Cort Elgar. Photograph on page 9 courtesy of Mary Louise Hemmeter. Photographs on pages 30, 105, 174, 183, and 203 courtesy of Marcia Molnar. Photographs on pages 155 and 161 courtesy of Christine Balan.

Target goals and objectives in this book are taken from Bricker, D. (Series Ed.). (2002). *Assessment, Evaluation, and Programming System for Infants and Children (AEPS®)*. (2nd ed., Vols. 1–4). Baltimore: Paul H. Brookes Publishing Co. Standards are taken from Ohio Department of Education's Early Learning Content Standards (available from Office of Early Childhood Education, 172 W. High Avenue, Suite 102, New Philadelphia, OH 44663).

Third printing, January 2011

Library of Congress Cataloging-in-Publication Data

Pretti-Frontczak, Kristie
    An activity-based approach to early intervention/by Kristie Pretti-Frontczak and Diane Bricker.—3rd ed.
        p.   cm.
    Rev. ed. of: An activity-based approach to early intervention/by Diane Bricker with Kristie Pretti-Frontczak and Natalya McComas. 2nd ed. ©1998.
    Includes bibliographical references and index.
    ISBN-13: 978-1-55766-736-6 (pbk.)
    ISBN-10: 1-55766-736-5 (pbk.)
    1. Children with disabilities—Education (Preschool)—United States.
    2. Education, Preschool—Activity programs—United States.   3. Child development—United States.   I. Bricker, Diane D.   II. Bricker, Diane D. Activity-based approach to early intervention.   III. Title
    LC4019.2.B74 2004
    371.9'0472—dc22   2004043607

British Library Cataloguing in Publication data are available from the British Library.

Contents

About the Authors

Kristie Pretti-Frontzcak, Ph.D., Associate Professor, Department of Educational Foundations and Special Services, College and Graduate School of Education, 405 White Hall, Kent State University, Kent, Ohio 44242

Dr. Pretti-Frontczak completed her undergraduate work in psychology at Idaho State University and received her master's degree and doctoral degree in early intervention at the University of Oregon. Since then, she has provided extensive professional development regarding activity-based intervention and has conducted a number of studies related to the approach. Dr. Pretti-Frontczak also directs the early childhood intervention specialist program at Kent State University, where she is responsible for preparing preservice personnel to work with children with disabilities ages birth to 8 years and their families. She frequently provides professional development and technical assistance in the United States and Canada to programs interested in the *Assessment, Evaluation, and Programming System for Infants and Children (AEPS®)*, activity-based intervention, and creating legally defensible and meaningful individualized education programs (IEPs). Her lines of research center on the treatment validity of the AEPS; the efficacy of activity-based intervention; the relationship between assessment, IEPs, and curriculum; and documenting effective personnel preparation practices.

Diane Bricker, Ph.D., Professor, Early Intervention Program, Center on Human Development, College of Education, 5253 University of Oregon, Eugene, Oregon 97403

Dr. Bricker completed her undergraduate work at The Ohio State University, her master's degree in special education at the University of Oregon, and her doctoral degree in special education at Vanderbilt University, Peabody College. Her initial work focused on improving the language skills of children with severe disabilities in institutions. That work led to the development of one of the first community-based integrated early intervention programs in the early 1970s. Since then, her work has continued in the area of early intervention. Dr. Bricker has directed a number of national demonstration projects and research efforts focused on examining the efficacy of early intervention; the development of a linked assessment, goal development, intervention, and evaluation system; and the study of a comprehensive, parent-completed screening measure. Dr. Bricker has also directed a graduate training program focused on preparing early interventionists. More than 300 students have received their master's or doctoral degree from this program and have gone on to practice in the field. Dr. Bricker served as Associate Dean for Academic Programs, College of Education, for 8 years. She is currently Professor of Education.

About the Contributor

Natalya McComas, M.S., Early Intervention/Early Childhood Special Education Specialist, Service Coordinator and Consultant, Early Childhood Coordination Agency Referral and Evaluation, College of Education, University of Oregon, 299 E. 18th Avenue, Eugene, Oregon 97401

Ms. McComas completed her undergraduate work in art education and her master's degree in early intervention at the University of Oregon. Since then, she has worked for the university in a variety of roles, including infant/toddler interventionist in a model demonstration program using the activity-based approach; instructor and field placement coordinator for the Early Intervention Personnel Preparation Program; consultant on activity-based intervention to Head Start, Oregon Social Learning Center, and various community-based preschool programs; and co-author of training manuals for the BEST project with Dr. Jennifer Olson at the University of Idaho. Recently, Ms. McComas returned to a direct service role with children from birth to age 6 and their families by working for the Early Childhood Coordination Agency for Referrals, Evaluations and Services (EC CARES), Lane County's early intervention/ early childhood special education agency. In this role, she has had the opportunity to again apply activity-based intervention in a variety of natural settings for children and families. Ms. McComas continues to experiment with ways of applying the approach so that it is meaningful, individualized, and practical for young children and families.

Acknowledgments

Historically, a number of professional colleagues have helped shape the conceptual development of activity-based intervention. William Bricker sparked Diane's thinking toward an approach that would produce better outcomes for young children with severe disabilities. Gisela Chatelanat introduced Piaget and the importance of blending intervention techniques with the developmental process. The Schoggens, Phil and Dikkie, made clear through conversations over the years the importance of environmental context to children's learning. Bob and MaryLynn Cantrell assisted in moving that thinking to intervention efforts with children. Repeated debates with John Filler, Roger Smith, Lizbeth Vincent, and Rick Brinker were also critical in the development of the underlying conceptual framework from which activity-based intervention has evolved.

Since the formal inception of activity-based intervention in the early 1980s, we have profited from the feedback provided by the many students, interventionists, and caregivers who have used activity-based intervention and pointed out what elements and procedures of the approach worked and in which areas change was necessary. Doctoral students who have participated in the University of Oregon's Early Intervention Leadership Training Program since the early 1980s have provided careful analysis of activity-based intervention beginning with the first edition of this book and continuing to this third edition. Their feedback has been valuable in the development of more comprehensive and effective procedures. We appreciate their substantial contributions to the improvement of the approach. Graduate students in the Early Childhood Intervention Program at Kent State University have made significant contributions to this edition. We would like to express our thanks to Denise Barr, Teresa Brown, Nicole Magg, and Amy Senderak.

Several colleagues have also been instrumental in contributing to a better understanding of activity-based intervention. Jane Squires has been steadfast in helping us clarify elements of the approach. We would like to acknowledge the work of Eva Horn and her colleagues for helping to better explain the concept of embedding. We have adopted their terminology throughout this edition in our discussions of learning opportunities. We would also like to thank Jennifer Grisham-Brown, Mary Louise Hemmeter, and Mark Wolery for their willingness to engage in research activities and discussions related to activity-based intervention.

Teams throughout the United States have helped us gain a better understanding of what is clear about the approach and what elements needed further explanation and illustration. In particular, we would like to acknowledge three teams of interventionists from Region XI Educational Service Center in Texas. Under the leadership of Lynn Sullivan, these teams have worked tirelessly to implement activity-based intervention. Much of what we have learned since 1998 is a direct result of our work with them. We would also like to thank two teams of interventionists working for the Council for Economic Opportunities in Greater Cleveland's Head Start Program in Ohio and the teams working for Jessamine Early Learning Village in Wilmore, Kentucky, for their commitment and dedication to improving services for young children with severe disabilities through an activity-based approach. The teams at the Oregon Social Learning Center, Eugene, Oregon, under the leadership of Phil Fisher are also thanked for challenging our thinking about the applicability of an activity-based approach for young children in the foster care system.

Natalya McComas was instrumental in early discussions on the direction and focus of the third edition. Her extensive experience in implementing the approach helped guide the development and explanations of the day-to-day aspects of the approach. In particular, she contributed to the development of Chapter 3 and Chapter 4 appendices and ensured that the overall tone of the third edition conveyed the practical application of key tenets.

We would like to thank the Paul H. Brookes Publishing Co. staff who have been consistently helpful and supportive by working with us to improve the description of activity-based intervention. It is with deep gratitude that we thank our families—Mike, Lonnie, Clint, and Sierra—who have supported our individual and collective efforts to complete this edition.

All of the effort to complete this edition has been driven by the desire to improve our explanation of activity-based intervention that, in turn, we hope and believe, will improve services to young children and their families. We extend our thanks to the many children and families who helped us initially to rethink our approach to intervention and to those who, more recently, have helped shape a more effective intervention process.

To the many students, professionals, and families
who have used the activity-based intervention approach
and who have offered feedback that has been vital
in the development and refinement of this approach

An Activity-Based Approach to Early Intervention

Third Edition

1

Evolution of Activity-Based Intervention

S ince the initiation of early intervention programs in the late 1960s and early 1970s, significant progress has been made in providing quality services to young children with disabilities. Federal- and state-supported education, mental health, and social services programs have been expanded to include services for infants and young children with disabilities and infants and young children who are at risk for disabilities (Bricker, 1989; Huefner, 2000; Odom, 1988). In the brief history of early intervention, program approaches, preparation of personnel, assessment and evaluation instruments, curricular focus, and instructional strategies have changed considerably as a result of clinical experience, consumer feedback, and empirical study. The passage of federal and state legislation during the 1980s has made early intervention a legitimate enterprise that provides services to thousands of families and their infants and young children who have or are at risk for disabilities (Shonkoff & Meisels, 2000; Shonkoff & Phillips, 2000).

Early intervention programs assist in offsetting the potentially negative impact of medical, biological, and environmental conditions associated with increased developmental risk for children (Farran, 2000; Guralnick, 1997; Ramey & Ramey, 1991). Personnel associated with early intervention programs have reason to be proud of the services delivered to participating children and families; however, challenges remain, and further improvement of intervention services is clearly an important goal.

We believe two changes are fundamental to the improvement of services offered in early intervention programs. The first necessary change is the use of systematic approaches to early intervention that link assessment, goal development, intervention, and evaluation processes that should improve the effectiveness and efficiency of current intervention services (Bagnato, Neisworth, & Munson, 1997; Bricker, 1989; Hutinger, 1988). Using a linked systems approach enables personnel to accomplish four essential outcomes:

- To document a child's strengths, interests, and emerging skills and to understand a family's priorities and concerns

- To develop, select, and write meaningful individualized family service plan (IFSP) and/or individualized education program (IEP) goals and objectives for children and families

- To establish individualized intervention content to reach selected goals and objectives

- To monitor children's/families' progress using timely and appropriate methods

A second necessary change fundamental to the improvement of services is the continued shift away from intervention approaches that direct children through a series of fragmented, nonmeaningful teaching routines. Intervention approaches have been developed that capitalize on the use of children's daily interactions with their social and physical environments as the context for providing teaching opportunities. In these approaches, functional goals are selected to enhance children's independence, problem-solving abilities, and adaptability. These approaches respect and incorporate children's motivations and initiations to ensure individualization of instruction and identification of meaningful intervention activities.

This volume contains a comprehensive description of an approach called *activity-based intervention*. Activity-based intervention directly addresses the two changes fundamental to providing quality intervention services for young children by

- Linking assessment, goal development, intervention, and evaluation processes

- Embedding learning opportunities that address functional skills into children's daily activities

Activity-based intervention evolved during the 1980s and was presented as a comprehensive, organized approach in the first edition of this volume, published in 1992. An expanded second edition of the volume appeared in 1998. During the ensuing years, activity-based intervention has been well received by the early intervention community. Activity-based intervention and other so-called "naturalistic" approaches have been seen by many (e.g., Barnett, Bell, & Carey, 1999; Dunst, Hamby, Trivette, Raab, & Bruder, 2000; Rule, Losardo, Dinnebeil, Kaiser, & Rowland, 1998) as an important step forward in assisting young children who have or who are at risk for disabilities to acquire and generalize developmental and educational goals. The first two editions of this volume were instrumental in the adoption of approaches that focus on children's initiations and daily routines by early intervention programs throughout the United States and internationally.

HISTORY OF ACTIVITY-BASED INTERVENTION

Early intervention programs for young children who have or who are at risk for disabilities have emerged as a synthesis of philosophies, curricular approaches, and instructional methodologies (Odom, 1988; Warren & Kaiser, 1988). This synthesis has not occurred without debate (e.g., Atwater, Carta, Schwartz, & McConnell, 1994; Carta, 1995; Carta, Schwartz, Atwater, & McConnell, 1991; Kauffman, 1999; Novick, 1993); however, since their inception, intervention approaches focused on young children at risk and young children with disabilities have evolved from being adult directed and non-ecologically based, to becoming child directed and ecologically sensitive. The following section describes this evolution of activity-based intervention and similar approaches by examining historical and contemporary influences.

Early Influences

The development of the activity-based intervention approach has been greatly influenced by the early work of individuals such as Itard and Seguin, who advocated for making educational interventions relevant and functional (Ball, 1971). Considerable time has elapsed, however, between Seguin's approach and the development of activity-based intervention, and much has transpired.

In the mid-1800s, institutions were developed for people with intellectual disabilities, motor impairments, sensory impairments, and mental illness. Initially, these institutions were developed to help the *deviant* individual become *nondeviant*; thus, only people who were considered able to improve were sent to institutions (Wolfensberger, 1969). It was not until the late 1800s that the purpose of large residential institutions was shifted to permanent repositories for people considered *objectionable and unsavory* (e.g., people with mental retardation). Institutions ceased to provide treatment or educational programs and primarily offered custodial care (MacMillan, 1977). The word *school* was dropped from titles of institutions, and the words *asylum* or *hospital* were substituted. No need was seen for the development of alternative community-based programs for people with moderate to severe disabilities for two reasons: People believed that 1) treatment or education had no effect on these individuals and 2) these individuals posed serious threats to the well-being of other citizens.

Beginning in the 1950s, institutions once again began to change. The motivation for change came from parent groups (e.g., the National Association for Retarded Children, now The Arc), legal action, and a changing perspective about the constancy of the intelligence quotient and the influence of the environment on behavior (Gallagher & Ramey, 1987). Appreciation for the importance of environmental influence helped provide the conceptual base for professionals to advocate for the development of intervention programs to offset or eradicate learning problems seen in people with disabilities. Adding to the conceptual base underlying intervention was an accumulating empirical base that demonstrated that even people with the most severe disabilities are able to learn (Ault, Wolery, Doyle, & Gast, 1989).

From the late 1950s to the early 1960s, students and interpreters of B.F. Skinner began to apply behavior analytical principles (i.e., arranging antecedents, defining responses, and providing immediate consequences) to people with intellectual disabilities and mental illness (Ayllon & Michael, 1959).

Some of this early work was conducted with adults previously thought to be unteachable and uncontrollable. Using behavior analytical principles, investigators were able to teach individuals with severe disabilities to perform a variety of functional behaviors, such as dressing and feeding (Staats, 1964).

Using these same principles, Bijou, Baer, and their colleagues, among others, began working with children in institutional settings (Baer, 1962). This work tended to focus on eliminating unwanted behaviors using structured teaching procedures that emphasized establishing easy-to-discriminate cues (e.g., do this) followed by an adult-modeled response to be imitated by the child.

These early teaching regimes were adult directed and relied on the use of primary rewards (e.g., small sip of juice for the correct imitation). Equally important to note is that much of the educational intervention was conducted in settings and under conditions apart from children's daily activities. For example, instruction would occur in areas away from the child's usual environment (e.g., in research labs), and learning tasks were often discrete skills taken out of context. In the early work of the Brickers (Bricker & Bricker, 1974, 1975), children were repeatedly asked to stand up and sit down, pat the top of their heads, or name unrelated pictures.

It is important to note that the atypical surroundings and activities of residential settings contributed to the focus on nonsituated learning—that is, children living in residential settings were not exposed to and did not have the opportunity to engage in activities similar to those of typically developing children. Institutionalized children often lacked close relationships with adults, were exposed to peers with violent or bizarre behaviors, and received little in the way of cognitive or linguistic stimulation. Investigators working with children in these environments knew that their treatment ran counter to the majority of research findings on young children's adjustment and learning.

Armed with new investigative work that changed perceptions about young children's developmental needs, environmental impact, and the learning potential of children previously thought to be uneducable, researchers began to create the first community-based programs for young children with disabilities. The first center-based programs provided a stunningly positive alternative to the treatment and education of young children who in the past had been relegated to institutions.

Later Influences

A small number of experimental, community-based intervention programs for young children with disabilities began in the early 1970s (see Tjossem, 1976, for a description of many of the most influential early programs). One of these first exploratory projects (initially called the Toddler Research and Intervention Project and later the Infant, Toddler, and Preschool Research and Intervention Project) was located at Peabody College (Bricker & Bricker, 1971).

The initial intervention approach used in the Infant, Toddler, and Preschool Research and Intervention Project was an extension of procedures that had been used by the Brickers with institutionalized people (Bricker & Bricker, 1976). The clinical and educational procedures first used in the program taught children discrete tasks, remained largely adult directed, and relied on tangible rewards. Observations by the intervention and research staff, however, made clear that a highly structured approach often did not produce desired outcomes. For example, the children appeared uninterested in the learning regimes and their rate of learning target skills was often slow and uneven. These observations raised questions and led to a search for strategies that might be more effective with young children.

During the 1970s, three sets of powerful influences changed the Infant, Toddler, and Preschool Research and Intervention Project's intervention philosophy and efforts. Those influences included the work of learning and ecological theorists, investigations of early development, and feedback from the children and families who participated in the project.

Piaget's work, perhaps more than any other, led to a serious rethinking of how to approach young children (Piaget, 1970). One of Piaget's important observations was that young children construct their knowledge through active manipulation of the physical world that then shifts over time to mental manipulations (i.e., thinking). This perspective suggested that children's active involvement (i.e., operating on the environment) is necessary for them to learn. Dewey (1976), as well as other learning theorists, also argued for the importance of children's active involvement for efficient and effective learning to occur. In addition, Dewey emphasized the importance of involving children in activities or tasks that they saw as meaningful, relevant, and enticing. The adoption of conceptual positions that underline the need for young children to be active initiators rather than passive recipients required serious modification of the program's intervention approach.

A second major influence was the investigative work that began in the 1970s, continued into the 1980s, and was focused on studying early developmental processes—in particular, sensorimotor, social, and social-communication development (Bricker & Carlson, 1981). From this investigative work, three major themes emerged. First, children need to attain precursor cognitive and social-communication skills before learning symbolic systems (e.g., language) (Bruner, 1977). That is, early development sets the stage for subsequent development. Second, children influence and are influenced by their social and physical environments (Bronfenbrenner, 1979; Goldberg, 1977). Third, infants' and young children's early development is composed of building functional and useful responses that increasingly permit them to navigate their environment, become independent, and communicate and meet their needs (Greenfield & Smith, 1976). Much of this empirical work made clear the importance of early developmental processes and the "social" nature of young children's development and learning (Uzgiris, 1981).

A third significant influence was feedback from the participating children and families. Fortunately, this program included typically developing children as well as children with disabilities and was probably the first inclusive program for young children with disabilities in the country. The typically developing children taught program staff two valuable lessons. First, children's motivation is critically important. Young children living in reasonable environments are self-directed and frequently object to overt adult management and control. Thus, when faced with an uninteresting, nonmeaningful, adult-directed task, the typically developing children in the program often refused to cooperate and sought ways to free themselves from such unwanted constraints. Second, children considered to be developing typically are often neither engaged by nor interested in pursuing a task or activity because they are provided with a tangible reward; rather, what the typically developing children deemed interesting and meaningful served to involve them and maintain their participation. These observations in concert with the intervention and research staff's growing appreciation of ecological theory (Barker, 1978; Bronfenbrenner, 1979) moved them to better understand the critical nature of the learning context.

Attention was further directed to children's classroom and home ecologies by parental feedback. Parents made clear that their values, wishes, and desires for their children should be seriously considered if program staff wanted their genuine commitment and involvement. Parents wanted to be involved in activities they found valuable and meaningful and did not want to be assigned tasks they deemed of little interest or merit. Over time, feedback from parents and other caregivers produced significant change in the program's approach to assessment, goal development, intervention, and evaluation.

These important influences during the 1970s and early 1980s, as well as others (e.g., situated learning), combined to produce gradual but significant change in the Infant, Toddler, and Preschool Research and Intervention Project's initial intervention efforts. First, the program began a shift from adult-directed and orchestrated activities to those initiated and maintained by children. Second, the curricular focus shifted from learning words, numbers, concepts, and motor behavior to including early sensorimotor, social, and social-communication behavior. Third, based on the program's analysis of the bidirectional effects between children and their environment as well as the importance of the child's larger social context, the Infant, Toddler, and Preschool Research and Intervention Project began a shift from an exclusive focus on children to a focus on children and their environmental surrounds.

Over time, the program also came to align the antecedent response consequence principles with what intervention and research staff had come to learn about children and their early development. Thus, intervention efforts shifted from single, adult-presented antecedents to the use of an array of meaningful antecedents that were connected directly to children's daily interactions and environmental contexts. Target responses were not defined as specific behaviors but rather came to be defined as more general and functional behaviors that could be used across settings, people, and conditions. Finally, consequences, to the extent possible, came to be part of or the result of children's actions or activities. Note that the behavioral learning principles did not change, nor did the program stop using them. Rather, the application of these principles changed. The establishment of appropriate learning conditions, the operational definition of target responses, and the timely delivery of meaningful consequences remains essential to activity-based intervention, and all sound educational practice for that matter (Bricker, 1989; Heward, 2003).

Contemporary Influences

By the early 1980s, the Infant, Toddler, and Preschool Research and Intervention Project's intervention efforts, now located in Oregon, began to resemble activity-based intervention. Two contemporary influences directly shaped the approach into its present form: 1) the need for efficient, contextually based instruction, and 2) language intervention research. In addition, developmentally appropriate practice (DAP) (Bredekamp, 1987; Bredekamp & Copple, 1997), although not a direct influence, supported the adoption of approaches such as activity-based intervention.

From the first intervention efforts, parental feedback has been influential in the evolution of activity-based intervention. As intervention and research staff became more sophisticated about assessment and intervention activities, they became more demanding of parents. It was not unusual to ask parents to conduct daily didactic teaching sessions at home. As parents became bolder in their feedback, they indicated that such requests were often unreasonable given the other daily demands on their time. This feedback, given so consistently over time, demanded that staff rethink what they asked parents to do. On the one hand, repeated practice across settings is essential

for most children to acquire target skills, and thus targeting the home and other locations outside the classroom as teaching sites seemed vitally important. On the other hand, parents do not have unlimited time to work with their children. This dilemma forced the intervention staff to think of ways that teaching could become less an add-on and more a part of children's daily lives. The answer, of course, was to develop an intervention approach that relied, to a great extent, on the use of children's daily and routine activities as the primary vehicle for learning new target goals and objectives. The focus on authentic routine activities is at the heart of activity-based intervention.

A second important formative influence was investigative work focused on language intervention. By the 1980s, a number of investigators were developing instruction techniques focused on teaching functional language or communication skills, as opposed to more didactic or academic approaches (e.g., labeling pictures out of context, being drilled on syntactic structures). These approaches, whether narrow or broad, focused on the importance of teaching functional communication skills in environments that provided children with the necessary motivation for communication to occur (Oliver & Halle, 1982; Warren & Rogers-Warren, 1985).

An early example was the work of MacDonald (1985, 1989) who described a comprehensive system that emphasized the interactive nature of communicative development and competence. Duchan and Weitzner-Lin also presented an approach called *nurturant-naturalistic*, which moved from didactic teaching routines to "nurturant interactions in which the child takes the interactive lead and to naturalistic contexts which the child is likely to encounter in everyday life" (1987, p. 49). Likewise, Synder-McLean and colleagues (1984) introduced an intervention strategy that relied on structuring joint action routines designed to assist children with language impairments in improving their functional communication skills.

In the area of autism, the Koegels (Koegel & Koegel, 1995) devised an approach that they call *natural language teaching,* which included capitalizing on opportunities to respond to natural reinforcers, reinforcing verbal attempts to respond, varying tasks, and taking turns. Warren and Kaiser (1986) broadened the earlier descriptions of incidental and milieu teaching to include the following elements: arranging the environment to encourage child initiations, selecting targets appropriate for children's developmental levels, asking children for elaborations, and reinforcing children's communicative attempts. Our own work in the area of language intervention also assisted in the adoption of intervention approaches that were child initiated, developmentally appropriate, and functional and meaningful from a child's perspective (Bricker & Carlson, 1980, 1981).

Additional support came from the movement toward DAP beginning in the 1980s and continuing today. Although DAP did not directly influence activity-based intervention, the principles underlying DAP evolved in a parallel fashion with reciprocal effects. DAP, as articulated by Bredekamp (1987) and Bredekamp and Copple (1997), and activity-based intervention share many theoretical and philosophical underpinnings (Novick, 1993). Both approaches cite the work of Dewey, Piaget, and Vygotsky as the basis for designing processes and content that match the child's current developmental level. Both approaches maintain that child-directed play activities are preferable to adult-directed, highly structured activities. Activity-based intervention and DAP emphasize a comprehensive curricular approach to enhance children's development across the motor, language, social, and cognitive domains. The importance of teachers and interventionists, and the observations of children at play to determine interests and activities of choice, are highlighted in both DAP principles and an activity-based approach.

Furthermore, neither approach advocates the use of extrinsic rewards; instead, each suggests that children learn through intrinsic rewards provided by the action or activity. Both sources also emphasize the role of the interventionist in using the activity to ensure that active exploration and interaction occur. Activity-based intervention and DAP describe the importance of varying activities and materials and increasing their complexity as children progress. The role of the teacher or interventionist is described in both as a facilitator of engagement and a provider of opportunities for learning. The importance of the family, their input, and their participation in decision making are also considered critical within DAP principles and an activity-based approach.

Despite their many alignments, activity-based intervention and DAP differ in the sense that activity-based intervention provides specific strategies and suggestions for how to intervene with young children whereas DAP provides more general guidelines or recommendations for interacting with young children. For example, within an activity-based approach, specific strategies are given to teams for targeting individualized goals and objectives for children and how to embed learning opportunities related to these targets into a variety of routine and play activities. DAP, in contrast, discusses how to address more global child behaviors and generic strategies for interacting with children. Furthermore, in activity-based intervention, specific strategies and suggestions are provided for conducting comprehensive and systematic assessments that are updated consistently to monitor child progress. Activity-based intervention places considerable emphasis on the fundamental need for accurate and complete assessment and evaluation of children in order to ensure that selected goals and objectives are developmentally and environmentally appropriate. Although Bredekamp and Copple (1997) suggested that assessment is essential, only general assessment guidelines are offered in DAP, and assessments are not used to select individual goals and objectives for children.

COMPARISON OF ACTIVITY-BASED INTERVENTION

Activity-based intervention uses behavioral learning principles to encourage child interactions and participation in meaningful (i.e., authentic) daily activities with the explicit purpose of assisting the child in acquiring, generalizing, and/or strengthening functional goals and objectives. Specifically, activity-based intervention is a child-directed, transactional approach where multiple learning opportunities are embedded into authentic activities and logically occurring antecedents and timely feedback are provided to ensure functional and generative skills are acquired and used by children. The following three scenarios about a nature walk exemplify how activity-based intervention differs from early childhood and adult-directed approaches.

Early Childhood Approach

An early childhood approach would have children discuss, for example, what they are likely to see prior to taking the nature walk. While on the walk, the children are encouraged to explore, ask questions, and even try some "experiments." The interventionist might point out an anthill and suggest that the children watch the insects' activities. The interventionist would encourage, but likely not direct, the children's self-initiated activities. The goals are acquisition of general information, improvement of language and cognitive skills, and encouragement of exploration and innovation. It is unlikely that any child will have specific objectives to be addressed during the walk or that the interventionist will work to develop specific response forms for any of the children. Evaluation of the activity would focus on the children's level of enjoyment and the interventionist's sense of accomplishment.

Adult-Directed Approach

In an adult-directed approach, each child would have a set of specific objectives, and the walk would be used to address the generalization of these skills. Prior to the walk, the children would be engaged in specific instruction to address these objectives. For example, children with an object-labeling goal would be exposed to specific teaching sessions in which the interventionist has pictures of trees, leaves, ants, or clouds. These pictures would be presented to the children repeatedly until they could readily name the pictures. On the walk, the interventionist would locate examples of the target items and ask the children to name the objects (e.g., "What is this?"). The number of correct and incorrect responses would be noted and later transferred to a graph to monitor child progress over time.

Activity-Based Intervention Approach

Using an activity-based intervention approach requires that children have individualized goals and objectives, written as general functional response classes rather than as specific responses. For example, an object-labeling goal might be stated as *Uses words, phrases, or sentences to describe objects, people, or events* as opposed to a more specific goal that might be stated as *Child will label the objects leaf, tree, bug, and path.* Prior to the walk, items that might be encountered on the excursion would be placed around the classroom. As the children use or encounter these items in meaningful interactions, the interventionist would encourage child-directed actions such as counting the leaves, placing them on trees, naming them, or crumpling them. Once on the walk, the interventionist might encourage the children to find leaves to develop opportunities to practice target objectives. For example, if one child picks up a leaf, then the interventionist might draw attention to this as an opportunity to talk about leaves (e.g., color, texture). On returning to the classroom, the interventionist would present examples of items encountered on the walk and record the children's abilities to talk about these items. These data would be used to systematically monitor child progress toward desired goals.

ABOUT THIS VOLUME

Since the publication of the first two editions, the study, refinement, and expansion of the activity-based approach has moved forward at a steady pace. Today, an activity-based approach is seen as 1) a viable option for blending practices from multiple perspectives, 2) reflective of recommended intervention practice, and 3) a means of providing individualized intervention within the context of naturalistic or daily activities. Since 1998, our continued work with interventionists across the country has provided better insight into the critical elements of the approach and better strategies to ensure successful implementation. The impetus for this third edition has been the acquisition of new knowledge and improved practice for employing activity-based intervention. The conceptual and practical knowledge gained since the second edition has been examined, synthesized, and incorporated into this volume.

Although the organization and some of the content contained in this third edition have changed from the first two editions, the major features and elements of this approach remain the same. This volume contains 10 chapters that describe and explain in detail the conceptual framework that underlies activity-based intervention and how to apply the approach. Chapter 1 clarifies terms used throughout the volume and provides a brief history of the evolution of an activity-based approach. Chapter 2 discusses the structural framework, elements, and underlying process of an activity-based approach, whereas Chapter 3 discusses the approach within a linked service delivery system. The organizational structure used to ensure successful application of an activity-based approach is addressed in Chapter 4. Chapter 5 provides examples of an activity-based approach as applied in three broad service delivery models. Chapter 6 describes how the successful implementation of activity-based intervention requires the collaboration of teams composed of direct service delivery personnel, consultants, and caregivers. Critical issues associated with the implementation of activity-based intervention are addressed in Chapter 7. The conceptual foundation for an activity-based approach, including underlying theoretical perspectives, is articulated in Chapter 8. Chapter 9 highlights findings from some of the extensive reviews available on general program effects with populations of young children with disabilities and children who are at risk and a brief review of the studies that have focused directly on evaluating the effects of activity-based intervention. Chapter 10 briefly summarizes the future directions for research, personnel preparation, and day-to-day practices associated with activity-based intervention.

This volume also contains three appendices. The first is the Chapter 3 appendix, which illustrates the relationship between a linked system and an activity-based approach to intervention. The second is the Chapter 4 appendix, which contains multiple completed examples of the organizational structure designed to ensure the successful application of an activity-based approach. The third is the volume appendix, located after Chapter 10. This appendix contains blank, photocopiable forms that are discussed throughout the volume.

The changes in this volume are based on our considerable experience in assisting teachers, therapists, interventionists, aides, and caregivers in learning and using activity-based intervention. These professionals and caregivers have shown us clearly what parts of the approach were understandable and which were problematic for them to implement. We have attempted to remedy the latter through improving descriptions, adding illustrations, and reformatting pieces of the structural framework. We believe that the changes introduced in this volume will enable users of activity-based intervention to grasp the underlying conceptual framework of activity-based intervention and to use the approach effectively in a variety of settings with a range of children and families.

Purpose and Audience

The purpose of this volume is to describe activity-based intervention and provide the necessary structure to enable interventionists and caregivers to use the approach. Although words alone may not be entirely satisfactory when attempting to learn and employ new information, strategies, and skills, the hope is that the detailed descriptions provided in this volume will permit most readers to 1) understand the major assumptions that underlie the approach and the necessary assessment processes, goal setting, and environmental arrangements that provide the guiding structure; and 2) incorporate into their teaching repertoires the essential elements that define activity-based intervention.

For several reasons, we believe that the individuals for whom this volume is intended will vary in their ability to understand and incorporate activity-based intervention. Some readers will be experienced in using child-directed techniques and find adoption of the approach relatively straightforward. Other caregivers, interventionists, and consultants may have been educated in adult-directed approaches and will find it challenging to learn to become observers of, and responders to, children. Often, ingrained habits are difficult to relinquish even with the intent to do so. For example, adults who direct children through individual activities as well as through the entire school/home day may find it difficult to permit children to engage frequently in self-directed activities or may find it challenging to use routines and daily activities as teaching vehicles.

We have also noted that many are eager to learn the concrete elements of an approach and are less interested in the conceptual base and underlying structure of the approach. These individuals may be tempted to focus on Chapters 4 and 5 and avoid Chapters 2, 3, 8, and 9. We believe the material presented across chapters is essential to the effective and generalized application of activity-based intervention. When we observe a teacher, therapist, interventionist, or caregiver having significant problems in applying the approach, we find that these individuals often have a limited appreciation of the conceptual base of the approach or have little or no knowledge about the framework and structure that underlie the approach. As with so much of life, understanding the underlying fundamentals is essential to effective application and absolutely vital to diagnosing and remedying problems.

Definition of Terms and Concepts

To help ensure clarity of the material presented in this volume, it is useful to define several terms that appear throughout the chapters. The terms *early intervention, early childhood special education,* and *early childhood intervention* are used interchangeably. These terms refer to a field of study and a method of intervention focused on children who have or who are at risk for disabilities from birth through preschool and their families. Although the principles and strategies contained in an activity-based approach may be appropriate for other groups, the examples and research base described in this volume address systems and programs that target children from birth through 5 years of age, including children served in community-based and inclusive programs.

The term *interventionist* is used to represent the array of professionals and paraprofessionals who deliver services to young children who participate in early intervention/early childhood special education and early childhood education programs. We find the term *teacher* to be overly limiting when the team of professionals who work in early intervention programs includes speech-language pathologists, occupational therapists, physical therapists, psychologists, and medical personnel as well as early childhood teachers, aides, and parents. The term *interventionist* is intended to include all of the professionals and paraprofessionals associated with early intervention, early childhood special education, and early childhood education programs.

We agree with the federal mandate that children with disabilities and their families require a team of professionals to offer the array of needed services specified in the IEP/IFSP. We therefore use the term *team* to refer to the group of professionals, paraprofessionals, and parents/caregivers who work together to deliver the needed services. In addition, we use the terms *interventionists* and *teams* interchangeably throughout the volume. Finally, the term *caregiver* is used throughout this volume to describe individuals who provide primary care to young children (e.g., parents, foster parents, grandparents, other extended family members, child care providers, neighbors).

SUMMARY

This chapter sets a context for understanding activity-based intervention by reviewing its evolution since the early 1970s, describes the content and organization of the third edition, and provides clarification on terms used throughout the third edition. Appreciating the evolution of activity-based intervention should assist the reader in better understanding the approach. Activity-based intervention has evolved from earlier traditions and perspectives that did not produce optimal outcomes for children with disabilities. Initial efforts to educate young children with disabilities were too invasive and too structured. As a result, the field has moved steadily toward developing and adopting strategies and content that capitalize on children's motivation and the use of daily activities to embed authentic learning opportunities. The activity-based intervention approach has organized our past learning and current knowledge into a cohesive system designed to produce optimal growth in young children with developmental problems.

REFERENCES

Atwater, J., Carta, J., Schwartz, I., & McConnell, S. (1994). Blending developmentally appropriate practice and early childhood special education: Redefining best practice to meet the needs of all children. In B. Mallory & R. New (Eds.), *Diversity and developmentally appropriate practices* (pp. 185–201). New York: Teachers College Press.

Ault, M., Wolery, M., Doyle, P., & Gast, D. (1989). Review of comparative studies in the instruction of students with moderate to severe handicaps. *Exceptional Children, 55*(4), 346–356.

Ayllon, T., & Michael, J. (1959). The psychiatric nurse as a behavioral engineer. *Journal of the Experimental Analysis of Behavior, 2,* 323–334.

Baer, D. (1962). Laboratory control of thumbsucking by withdrawal and representation of reinforcement. *Journal of the Experimental Analysis of Behavior, 5,* 525–528.

Bagnato, S.J., Neisworth, J.T., & Munson, S.M. (1997). *LINKing assessment and early intervention: An authentic curriculum-based approach.* Baltimore: Paul H. Brookes Publishing Co.

Ball, T. (1971). *Itard, Seguin, and Kephart: Sensory education: A learning interpretation.* Columbus, OH: Charles E. Merrill.

Barker, R. (1978). *Habitats, environments, and human behavior.* San Francisco: Jossey-Bass.

Barnett, D., Bell, S., & Carey, K. (1999). *Principles and techniques for observing. Designing preschool interventions: A practitioner's guide.* New York: The Guilford Press.

Bredekamp, S. (Ed.). (1987). *Developmentally appropriate practice in early childhood programs serving children from birth through age 8.* Washington, DC: National Association for the Education of Young Children.

Bredekamp, S., & Copple, C. (Eds.). (1997). *Developmentally appropriate practice in early childhood programs* (Rev. ed.). Washington, DC: National Association for the Education of Young Children.

Bricker, D. (1989). *Early intervention for at-risk and handicapped infants, toddlers and preschool children.* Palo Alto, CA: VORT Corp.

Bricker, D., & Bricker, W. (1971). *Toddler research and intervention project report: Year 1* (IMRID Behavioral Science Monograph No. 20). Nashville: George Peabody College, Institute on Mental Retardation and Intellectual Development.

Bricker, D., & Carlson, L. (1980). An intervention approach for communicatively handicapped infants and young children. In D. Bricker (Ed.), *Language intervention with children.* San Francisco: Jossey-Bass.

Bricker, D., & Carlson, L. (1981). Issues in early language intervention. In R. Schiefelbusch & D. Bricker (Eds.), *Early language: Acquisition and intervention* (pp. 477–515). Baltimore: University Park Press.

Bricker, W., & Bricker, D. (1974). An early language training strategy. In R. Schiefelbusch & L. Lloyd (Eds.), *Language perspective: Acquisition, retardation, and intervention* (pp. 431–468). Baltimore: University Park Press.

Bricker, W., & Bricker, D. (1975). Mental retardation and complex human behavior. In J. Kauffman & J. Payne (Eds.), *Mental retardation* (pp. 190–224). Columbus, OH: Charles E. Merrill.

Bricker, W., & Bricker, D. (1976). The infant, toddler, and preschool research project. In T. Tjossem (Ed.), *Intervention strategies for high risk infants and young children.* Baltimore: University Park Press.

Bronfenbrenner, U. (1979). *The ecology of human development: Experiments by nature and design.* Cambridge, MA: Harvard University Press.

Bruner, J. (1977). Early social interaction and language acquisition. In H. Schaffer (Ed.), *Studies in mother–infant interaction* (pp. 271–289). San Diego: Academic Press.

Carta, J. (1995). Developmentally appropriate practice: A critical analysis as applied to young children with disabilities. *Focus on Exceptional Children, 27*(6), 1–14.

Carta, J., Schwartz, I., Atwater, J., & McConnell, S. (1991). Developmentally appropriate practice: Appraising its usefulness for young children with disabilities. *Topics in Early Childhood Special Education, 11*(1), 1–20.

Dewey, J. (1976). *Experience and education.* London: Colliers MacMillan.

Duchan, J., & Weitzner-Lin, B. (1987). Nurturant-naturalistic intervention for language impaired children. *Asha, 29*(7), 45–49.

Dunst, C., Hamby, D., Trivette, C., Raab, M., & Bruder, M. (2000). Everyday family and community life and children's naturally occurring learning opportunities. *Journal of Early Intervention, 23*(3), 151–164.

Farran, D. (2000). Another decade of intervention for children who are low income or disabled: What do we do now? In J.P. Shonkoff & S.J. Meisels (Eds.), *Handbook of early childhood intervention* (2nd ed., pp. 510–548). New York: Cambridge University Press.

Gallagher, J.J., & Ramey, C.T. (1987). *The malleability of children.* Baltimore: Paul H. Brookes Publishing Co.

Goldberg, S. (1977). Social competence in infancy: A model of parent–infant interaction. *Merrill-Palmer Quarterly, 23,* 163–177.

Greenfield, P., & Smith, J. (1976). *Structuring and communication in early language development*. San Diego: Academic Press.

Guralnick, M.J. (Ed.). (1997). *The effectiveness of early intervention*. Baltimore: Paul H. Brookes Publishing Co.

Heward, W. (2003). Ten faulty notions about teaching and learning that hinder the effectiveness of special education. *Journal of Special Education, 36*(4), 186–205.

Huefner, D. (2000). *Getting comfortable with special education law: A framework for working with children with disabilities*. Norwood, MA: Christopher-Gordon.

Hutinger, P. (1988). Linking screening, identification, and assessment with curriculum. In J. Jordan, J. Gallagher, P. Hutinger, & M. Karnes (Eds.), *Early childhood special education: Birth to three* (pp. 29–66). Reston, VA: Council for Exceptional Children.

Kauffman, J. (1999). Commentary: Today's special education and its message for tomorrow. *Journal of Special Education, 32*(4), 244–254.

Koegel, R.L., & Koegel, L.K. (1995). *Teaching children with autism: Strategies for initiating positive interactions and improving learning opportunities*. Baltimore: Paul H. Brookes Publishing Co.

MacDonald, J. (1985). Language through conversation: A model for intervention with language delayed persons. In S. Warren & A. Rogers-Warren (Eds.), *Teaching functional language* (pp. 89–122). Baltimore: University Park Press.

MacDonald, J. (1989). *Becoming partners with children*. San Antonio, TX: Special Press.

MacMillan, D. (1977). *Mental retardation in school and society*. Boston: Little, Brown and Co. Adult Trade Division.

Novick, R. (1993). Activity-based intervention and developmentally appropriate practice: Points of convergence. *Topics in Early Childhood Special Education, 13*(4), 403–417.

Odom, S.L. (1988). Research in early childhood special education: Methodologies and paradigms. In S.L. Odom & M.B. Karnes (Eds.), *Early intervention for infants and children with handicaps: An empirical base* (pp. 1–21). Baltimore: Paul H. Brookes Publishing Co.

Oliver, C., & Halle, J. (1982). Language training in the everyday environment: Teaching functional sign use to a retarded child. *Journal of The Association for the Severely Handicapped, 8,* 50–62.

Piaget, J. (1970). Piaget's theory. In P. Mussen (Ed.), *Carmichael's manual of child psychology* (Vol. 1, pp. 703–732). New York: John Wiley & Sons.

Ramey, C., & Ramey, S. (1991). Effective early intervention. *Mental Retardation, 30,* 337–345.

Rule, S., Losardo, A., Dinnebeil, L., Kaiser, A., & Rowland, C. (1998). Translating research on naturalistic instruction into practice. *Journal of Early Intervention, 21*(4), 283–293.

Shonkoff, J.P., & Meisels, S.J. (2000). Early childhood intervention: The evolution of a concept. In J.P. Shonkoff & S.J. Meisels (Eds.), *Handbook of early childhood intervention* (pp. 3–31). New York: Cambridge University Press.

Shonkoff, J.P., & Phillips, D.A. (Eds.), (2000). *From neurons to neighborhoods*. Washington, DC: National Academies Press.

Snyder-McLean, L., Solomonson, B., McLean, J., & Sack, S. (1984). Structuring joint action routines. *Seminars in Speech and Language, 5*(3), 213–228.

Staats, A. (1964). *Human learning*. New York: Holt, Rinehart & Winston.

Tjossem, T. (Ed.). (1976). *Intervention strategies for high risk infants and young children*. Baltimore: University Park Press.

Uzgiris, I. (1981). Experience in the social context. In R. Schiefelbusch & D. Bricker (Eds.), *Early language: Acquisition and intervention*. Baltimore: University Park Press.

Warren, S., & Kaiser, A. (1986). Incidental language teaching: A critical review. *Journal of Speech and Hearing Disorders, 51,* 291–299.

Warren, S., & Kaiser, A. (1988). Research in early language intervention. In S. Odom & M. Karnes (Eds.), *Early intervention for infants and children with handicaps: An empirical base* (pp. 89–108). Baltimore: Paul H. Brookes Publishing Co.

Warren, S., & Rogers-Warren, A. (Eds.). (1985). *Teaching functional language.* Baltimore: University Park Press.

Wolfensberger, W. (1969). The origin and nature of our institutional models. In R. Kugel & W. Wolfensberger (Eds.), *Changing patterns in residential services for the mentally retarded* (pp. 59–72). Washington, DC: President's Committee on Mental Retardation.

2

Description of Activity-Based Intervention

A main purpose of intervention for young children with disabilities or children who are at risk for disabilities is to assist them in the acquisition and generalization of critical developmental skills so that they can, to the extent possible, achieve independent functioning across environments. This purpose requires intervention efforts focused on helping children reach their individual learning and developmental goals and objectives. This chapter provides a description of activity-based intervention—an approach that is specifically designed to help children reach their individual goals within the context of daily activities. In effect, the driving force behind activity-based intervention is the attainment of functional skills that can be used across environments and situations.

To maximize opportunities for children to acquire their individual goals, activity-based intervention maps intervention efforts onto or integrates them into daily interactions that children experience. The contribution of the approach is that it makes explicit use of children's daily environmental transactions and that it provides a structure for doing so. Figure 2.1 illustrates how daily interactions between children and their social and physical environment appear to provide much of the information and feedback necessary for children to learn.

In the first frame of the figure, Tobia looks at a book and says, "Horsie!" Her mother, who is nearby, asks her to repeat what she said, and Tobia again says "Horsie." In the second frame, Tobia's mother looks to see what Tobia is referring to and states, "Oh, where do you see a horsie?" Tobia responds, "Here . . . lookie," while pointing to a picture of a horse in the book. Tobia's mother affirms her understanding by saying, "Oh, I see the horse." She then expands on Tobia's comment by saying, "It's brown." Tobia looks again at the picture and asks, "Brown?" In the third frame, Tobia's mother joins her on the carpet and points to the picture of the horse. She says, "Yes, the horse is brown. The horse also has a brown mane." Again, the mother's introduction of new words and ideas not only maintains Tobia's original interest in the horse but also expands her observation to other attributes of the horse. In response to her mother's comment, Tobia asks, "Mane?" and her mother responds, "Yes, the hair on the horse's neck is called a mane." Tobia repeats a portion of her mother's comment by saying, "Mane." In the fourth frame, her mother expands on her attention to the horse's mane by asking, "Do you have a mane?" Tobia responds, "No, I have hair." The mother affirms Tobia's response by saying, "You're right. Horses have manes, and people have hair." Tobia again repeats part of her mother's comment by saying, "I have brown hair."

The target goals listed in this chapter are taken from Bricker, D., Pretti-Frontczak, K., Johnson, J., and Straka, E. (2002). In D. Bricker (Series Ed.), *Assessment, Evaluation, and Programming System for Infants and Children (AEPS®): Vol. 1. Administration guide* (2nd ed.). Baltimore: Paul H. Brookes Publishing Co. The reader is referred to this source for more information.

Figure 2.1. Illustration of how daily interactions between children and their social and physical environments provide the information and feedback necessary for learning.

A review of the interaction between Tobia and her mother suggests several interesting features. First, the interactions were at least equally initiated and directed by the child. Tobia's mother followed her child's lead and provided information and feedback that appeared to meet her child's need. Second, the transactions between mother and daughter were a meaningful sequence of reciprocal exchanges that were appropriate to Tobia's level of development. Third, the interactions had some novel characteristics—that is, they were not static but evolved and changed in meaningful ways. Fourth, if both partners are responsive, then the interaction is somewhat obligatory yet positive.

Activity-based intervention is designed to capitalize on daily interactions such as those between Tobia and her mother. The following vignettes of Joel, Alyson, and De'Shawn provide further examples of activity-based intervention used in daily interactions.

JOEL

Joel, who is 11 months old, is side-stepping down the length of the couch when he notices a favorite ball that is just beyond his reach. He points to the ball and asks, "Ba?" His father passes by, and Joel looks at him and then back to the ball, again pointing and asking, "Ba?"

His father stops, leans over him, and says, "Ball. You want the ball?"

Joel says, "Ba," and his father responds, "Do you want to play with the ball?"

Joel first looks at his father, then at the ball, then back to his father and says, "Ba." His father picks up the ball and places it on the couch beside Joel. The toddler reaches to pick up the ball.

His father holds out his hands and says, "Throw the ball to me." Joel releases the ball, laughs, and waves his arms. His father laughs and picks up the ball and holds it out to Joel. "Do you want the ball? Come and get it."

Joel says, "Ba," and takes several steps to his father.

His father, still holding out the ball, says, "Here's the ball."

ALYSON

Five-month-old Alyson is in an infant seat on the kitchen counter while her older brother puts away groceries. She waves her arms and coos. Her brother leans toward her and imitates her cooing sound. He then picks up a paper bag to discard it, and the crackling paper attracts Alyson's attention. She looks intently at the paper and waves her arms again. Her brother shakes the paper bag, and she immediately quiets and stares at the paper bag. Her brother then places the paper bag within easy reach. Alyson reaches for the paper bag, grasps it, and moves it to her mouth. Her brother says, "That's a noisy paper bag." He then guides her hand away from her mouth and moves her arm to shake the paper bag. As the bag moves, the crackling sound occurs, and Alyson stops her activity. After a few seconds, her brother gently shakes her arm again, causing the paper to make the crackling noise. Alyson pauses but soon independently shakes her arm to produce the crackling noise.

DE'SHAWN

De'Shawn (5 years old) walks into his house in tears. His grandmother asks him what happened. He sniffles that his playmate took his toy truck. His grandmother comforts him and then asks, "What should we do about it?" De'Shawn shrugs his shoulders. His grandmother says, "Could you ask Hayden to share the truck? Or could we find another truck for you?"

De'Shawn runs to his bedroom but soon yells to his grandmother, "I can't find a truck!"

His grandmother replies, "Where did you look?"

"I looked in my toy box," says De'Shawn.

"Where else can you look?" asks his grandmother.

In a few minutes, De'Shawn stands before his grandmother with a red fire truck in his hands and explains, "It was under my bed."

In these scenarios, Tobia, Joel, Alyson, and De'Shawn were permitted to initiate and lead the activities. The sequence of events for these four children was logical and continuous, and the interaction was meaningful to both partners in each situation. Activity-based intervention promotes the use of daily child interactions and activities; however, the approach is selective about the nature and type of interactions and activities it uses because not all daily interactions that occur are meaningful or relevant to children.

Now consider the following vignettes for Lori and Tomaselo.

LORI

Lori, a 16-month-old child with Down syndrome, is crawling toward a toy on the floor. Her mother intercedes, picks her up, and seats her in a small chair at a table. Her mother sits across the table and says, "Come on, Lori, let's find the toys." She goes on to explain that it's Lori's job to find hidden objects today. To begin, she holds a small rattle for Lori to see. Lori looks at the rattle and then reaches for it. Without letting Lori touch the rattle, her mother removes the rattle and, while Lori is watching, places it under a small cloth and says, "Lori, find the rattle." Lori looks away, and her mother prompts a response by shaking the cloth. Lori looks at the cloth and picks it up. Lori shakes the cloth and places it on her head to play Peekaboo. Her mother says, "Lori, look for the rattle," and removes the cloth from Lori's head. Lori sweeps the rattle on the floor with her arm.

TOMASELO

Tomaselo, a 5-year-old with spina bifida and developmental delays, is sitting in his father's lap. His father says, "Hey, it's time to work on naming colors." He has a set of small cards, each containing a swatch of color. He shows Tomaselo the first card and asks, "What color is this?"

Tomaselo looks at the card and says, "Red."

"Great," says his father, "That's right." Turning the next card, his father asks again, "What color is this?"

"Red," says Tomaselo.

"No," his father says, "this is green. Say green."

"Green," Tomaselo says as he looks at his dog across the room.

"Okay," says his father. He turns the next card and asks, "What color is this?"

Tomaselo looks at his father and, without conviction, says, "Green."

In contrast to the earlier scenarios, Lori's and Tomaselo's caregivers initiated and directed the interactions. Although the caregivers' intent was understandable and the children were responsive, repeated observation of such transactions raises questions about the effectiveness of intervention activities that do not appear to recognize the child's motivation or the relevance of the activities for the child. Consider the following changed scenarios for Lori and her mother and Tomaselo and his father.

LORI

Lori is crawling toward a small doll on the floor. Her mother knows that the doll is a favorite toy. As Lori moves to the toy, her mother drops a towel over the doll. Lori stops crawling, sits back, and looks at her mother who says, "Lori, where is the doll?" Lori looks at the towel, and her mother says, "Find the doll." Lori lifts the towel, picks up and cuddles the doll, and smiles at her mother. Her mother says, "You found your doll. Can you say doll?"

Lori says, "Da," and points to her doll.

TOMASELO

Tomaselo is getting dressed, and his father says, "What color shirt do you want to wear today? You can wear a red one or a green one." Tomaselo points to the green shirt, and his father says, "What color is this shirt?" Tomaselo looks at the shirt but does not reply. His father says, "This is green. Can you say green?"

Tomaselo says "green" while pointing to the shirt. His father helps him put on the shirt while asking again the color of the shirt.

The previous examples described interactions between children and their caregivers that were either adult directed or child directed. The next two examples depict transactions that occur between groups of children and their interventionists that can also be classified as child directed (Morehead Preschool) or adult directed (Pleasant Hill Preschool).

MOREHEAD PRESCHOOL

Morehead Preschool is a child-directed program where teachers follow children's lead, create multiple and varied learning opportunities, and attend to the various developmental levels of the children. For example, at opening group time the teacher asks the children, "What songs shall we sing today?" The children offer a number of requests. The teacher lists the requested songs on the board and says, "You have selected six songs. How shall we decide which songs to sing today?" The children and teacher discuss prioritizing the songs. They decide that because there are too many songs for one day, they will sing half of the songs that day and the other half the next day. As illustrated in Figure 2.2, the teacher encourages the children to suggest which songs will be sung, thus building on their interests and following their lead. Furthermore, the teacher creates multiple learning opportunities to address literacy, mathematics, problem solving, social communication, and social goals. Finally, the teacher allows the children to participate at their developmental level (e.g., by maintaining proximity, watching others, holding song cards, answering questions, offering opinions).

PLEASANT HILL PRESCHOOL

Pleasant Hill Preschool uses an adult-directed approach, and group time begins with the teacher asking the children to sit quietly in their assigned places. Once accomplished, the teacher describes which centers are open that day and reminds students of classroom rules. The teacher then reviews the days of the week (e.g., children are asked what day of the week it is and what the weather is like). One child is asked to select the correct "day" card and place it on the board. Another child is asked to select the correct "weather" card and do likewise. Then, the teacher says she would like everyone to sing a song about rainy weather. During the teacher-selected and teacher-directed activities, the children have little opportunity to indicate their interests.

These two examples, as shown in Figure 2.2 and the previous vignette, are offered to distinguish between situations in which children's interests are followed and shaped into important learning opportunities and situations in which the adult selects and directs activities to enhance children's learning. Despite the move to "naturalistic" approaches as recommended practice (Hanson & Bruder, 2001), our observations of programs serving young children show that much of the intervention work conducted with children with disabilities remains primarily adult selected and adult directed. One is likely to see scenarios such as those initially portrayed for Lori, Tomaselo, and Pleasant Hill Preschool. The approach described in this volume offers an alternative to these scenarios.

Activity-based intervention is designed to capture the essence of learning represented by the transactions that occurred between Tobia, Joel, Alyson, De'Shawn, and their caregivers and the children and teacher at Morehead Preschool. This approach capitalizes on children's motivation and the use of activities that are authentic (i.e., meaningful) and relevant to children. The following section describes the framework underlying the approach including the purpose, focus, elements, and underlying process that results in a comprehensive approach for working with young children and their families.

ACTIVITY-BASED APPROACH TO INTERVENTION

The purpose of an activity-based approach is to assist young children with disabilities or children who are at risk for disabilities to learn and to use important developmental skills. The foundation of the approach is the daily transactions that occur between infants and young children and their physical and social environments. These daily transactions account for the primary means by which children learn. Within an activity-based approach, learning opportunities that address children's educational and therapeutic goals and objectives are specifically embedded into authentic child-directed, routine, and planned activities. These authentic (i.e., meaningful) activities provide a range of practice opportunities for young children. Furthermore, an activity-based approach has a comprehensive framework that enables the user to capitalize on child–environment transactions and maximize development and

Teacher: What songs should we sing today?

Children: The Wheels on the Bus! Head, Shoulders, Knees, and Toes!
The Itsy, Bitsy Spider! Old McDonald Had a Farm!
If You're Happy and You Know It! The ABCs!

Teacher: (Lists the songs on the board.) You have selected six songs.
How should we decide which songs to sing today?

Children: Let's vote! Sing my song! Sing all the songs!

Teacher: Why don't we sing half today, which is Monday, and the other half
tomorrow, which is what?

Children: Tuesday!

Figure 2.2. Illustration of a group activity conducted at Morehead Preschool, a child-directed program.

learning. The activity-based intervention framework is presented in Figure 2.3 and includes the purpose, focus, elements, and underlying process.

The purpose of activity-based intervention is to promote the acquisition and generalization of functional and developmentally appropriate skills in young children. To meet this purpose, the daily transactions that occur between young children and their physical and social environment are capitalized on to offer multiple and varied learning opportunities. Learning opportunities, in turn, elicit functional and generative responses from children, which are then supported by timely and integral feedback/consequences. The focus of an activity-based approach is on daily transactions. The approach is composed of four elements:

1. Child-directed, routine, and planned activities

2. Multiple and varied learning opportunities

3. Functional and generative goals

4. Timely and integral feedback or consequences

The underlying process associated with activity-based intervention is the embedding of learning opportunities into authentic activities. Embedding refers to a process of addressing children's target goals and objectives during daily activities in a manner that expands, modifies, or is integral to the activity in a meaningful way.

In the next section, the concept of child–environment transactions is addressed, followed by a discussion of each element of activity-based intervention. Finally, the process of embedding learning opportunities that integrates the elements into a comprehensive approach is described.

Purpose:	To enhance children's learning and use of important developmental skills			
Focus:	Child-environment transactions during authentic activities			
Elements:	1	2	3	4
	Child-directed, routine, and planned activities	Multiple and varied learning opportunities	Functional and generative goals	Timely and integral feedback or consequences
Underlying process:	Embedding is a process that occurs across daily activities (child-directed, routine, and planned), offering multiple and varied learning opportunities that in turn elicit desired responses from children (i.e., demonstrating functional and generative skills) that are supported by timely and integral feedback or consequences that are directly related to or contingent on children's behaviors.			

Figure 2.3. The activity-based approach to intervention framework including the purpose, focus, elements, and underlying process.

Child–Environment Transactions

Understanding transactional exchanges between children and their environments is fundamental to the application of activity-based intervention. Transactional implies a bidirectionality of effect (Sameroff & Chandler, 1975; Sameroff & Fiese, 2000; Warren, Yoder, & Leew, 2002). For example, the infant Alyson coos, and her brother responds by imitating her vocalization. Her brother's imitation may, in turn, affect the nature of her next vocalization. The vocal exchanges or transactions that occur are likely to change over time (e.g., they may become longer or more varied, a new element may be introduced).

JOEL

Joel points and says, "Dat?"

His father follows his point and says, "That's your car. Do you want your car?"

Joel nods his head and says, "Ka." During the next transaction with his father, Joel points and uses the new consonant–vowel combination *ka*.

The transactions between Joel and his father illustrate the bidirectionality of effect and how the interaction is changed over time. Child–environment transactions are at the heart of learning and can be used to produce change in children's behavioral repertoires. To obtain desired change and growth, intervention efforts should focus on activities and events that are authentic to children. In this sense, authentic refers to transactions or exchanges that are salient and relevant for children as well as integral to the ongoing flow of daily activities. The transactions that occurred between Alyson and her brother and Joel and his father offer examples of authentic transactions, whereas nonauthentic exchanges are contrived, artificial, isolated, and not meaningful for children. For example, asking a child to label flashcard pictures in an effort to teach him or her labels for objects is less authentic than answering a child's question about a toy of interest. Likewise, having a child practice walking on a balance beam to improve body awareness and balance is less authentic than encouraging the child to play on equipment at the park. Learning to produce vowel–consonant combinations in isolation is likely less authentic than learning to produce them in words that, when used, produce desired effects (e.g., a child says "mo" to get more juice). Learning about object permanence when a child drops toys from a high chair may be more meaningful (i.e., authentic) and relevant than having an adult move objects from a child's line of vision and instruct the child to find the object.

Whenever possible, caregivers and interventionists should strive to make child–environment transaction as authentic as possible. This often means learning about and designing intervention around individual children's strengths, interests, and needs, which is primarily accomplished by considering the four elements of an activity-based approach. Each of the elements is described next. Note how the four elements build on one another into a comprehensive approach.

Element 1: Child-Directed, Routine, and Planned Activities

Within an activity-based approach, three general types of activities are used as the context for child–environment transactions. Each of the activities allows for multiple and varied learning opportunities. Learning opportunities (described in the next section), in turn, allow children to acquire and use functional and meaningful skills. The three types of activities are child directed, routine, and planned.

Child-Directed Activities

Child-directed actions, play, or activities refer to those that are initiated or guided by the child. For example, when Peter chooses to ride his tricycle or chooses to play in the sandbox without prompting, he is engaging in child-directed activities. Having children assemble for group time is generally an adult-directed rather than a child-directed activity; however, child-directed actions can occur during group time. For example, the children can select the number and types of songs they sing, or the children can be allowed to sit in places and positions that are comfortable for them rather than having all children sit in chairs. Allowing children to guide or direct the flow of activities or events is possible even when an adult is also involved in arranging and facilitating an activity.

Child-directed activities capitalize on children's motivation and interests and have been shown to enhance learning in a range of populations and environments (e.g., Goetz, Gee, & Sailor, 1983; Griffin, 2000; Mahoney & Weller, 1980; Stremel-Campbell & Campbell, 1985). Adults who use child-directed activities 1) follow children's leads, 2) build on children's interests, and 3) match their responses or transactional exchanges to those initiated by children.

Child-directed activities are usually relevant and authentic for children. If children introduce and remain engaged in an activity, it is likely that they are motivated to do so because the activity is relevant, meaningful, and reinforcing to them (making the activity by definition authentic). Furthermore, when children are motivated and interested in a given activity, maintaining involvement does not require the use of primary or artificial rewards. For example, reaching for and grasping a desired toy is sufficiently rewarding for most children to practice and maintain their reaching and grasping behavior.

Following children's leads, in practice, translates into adults capitalizing on children's interests to guide the acquisition and generalization of important developmental skills. Transactions such as those initiated by Alyson and Joel permit parents to take advantage of their child's motivation and interests (e.g., Joel's father took advantage of his son's interest in a ball to teach him a word). In the description of Morehead Preschool and the illustration in Figure 2.2, child initiations were possible by permitting children to suggest songs or variations on usual songs. Using other examples, Lori's mother could have followed her child's direction by playing Peekaboo. The goal of working on object constancy would be maintained, but the activity choice would be child directed.

Not all child-directed activities necessarily move children toward the acquisition and use of target goals and objectives. For example, Eddie, a child with autism, may direct much of his activity to repetitive actions. The challenge for interventionists and caregivers is to gradually shift or expand Eddie's responses to address his target goal: *Eddie will use functionally appropriate actions with objects.* If Eddie's choice of activities is to repeatedly spin the wheels of a toy truck, his mother might prompt Eddie to place the toy's wheels on the floor and push the toy forward, producing a functional and appropriate response with the toy.

Routine Activities

A routine activity refers to the daily or regular occurrences of necessary events required to negotiate one's day-to-day existence. Eating, dressing, bathing, and traveling are all examples of routine activities. Everyone is faced with a daily or periodic regime of activities that must, for the most part, be accomplished. Using these routine activities to embed learning opportunities can significantly expand the potential number of opportunities for children to practice their goals and objectives. For example, Hayden's communication goal is to use two word utterances to describe objects, people, and/or events. During the daily routines of meal and bath times, Hayden's caregivers can repeatedly address this functional and generative skill by modeling two word utterances that describe (e.g., *my towel, cold water, all done, wash more*).

Another of Hayden's goals is to undress himself. The routine of getting ready for bed could be used as an ideal time to address this goal by asking Hayden to take off his socks, shoes, shirt, and pants in order to undress for bed. Furthermore, this goal could be practiced each time Hayden removes his sweater or jacket when coming indoors.

In addition to increasing the number of practice opportunities, routine activities meet the definition of being authentic, and their use enhances the targeting of functional goals. The goals targeted for Hayden are functional and will assist him in becoming independent. Identifying opportunities for children to learn target goals in routine activities likely provides a significant increase in the number of available opportunities for the acquisition and maintenance of important developmental skills.

Planned Activities

Planned activities refer to designed events that occur with adult guidance; for example, 3-year-old Francine goes to the park with her mother to play, or Ms. Limon gathers the preschoolers around her to read them a story about a zebra. Thoughtfully designed planned activities can be used to provide multiple and varied learning opportunities for children to practice target goals. Successful planned activities require knowledge about individual children's present level of performance (including strengths and interests), advanced planning, and awareness of children's target goals. Planned activities should be constructed in such a manner as to create multiple and varied opportunities for children to practice target goals. Francine has two goals: *Initiate and complete age-appropriate activities,* and *Manipulate objects with both hands.* With advance planning, comprehensive information about Francine, and knowledge of her target goals, opportunities to practice these prioritized skills can be incorporated into a variety of activities, such as making cookie dough, conducting a science experiment on the playground, or engaging in an art project with other children. In addition, her parents can provide opportunities at home by encouraging her to color pictures in a coloring book or put puzzles together.

To the extent possible, planned activities should offer multiple and varied opportunities for children to engage in authentic activities. Planned activities should also be of interest to children and offered or structured in ways children find appealing while allowing interventionists to address target goals.

Element 2: Multiple and Varied Learning Opportunities

The nature and frequency of learning opportunities offered to children is important. Children must be able to practice new skills across a range of settings, people, and conditions. Events do not replicate exactly; therefore, children must learn how to adapt to changing conditions (Stokes & Baer, 1977). For example, one must be able to open doors that are small, large, or heavy, when it is raining or the wind is blowing, and while talking or carrying a package. Such commonplace realities strongly mitigate against teaching children highly predictable routines conducted under static conditions if, indeed, the goal is to help children acquire flexible repertoires that assist them in adapting to changing environmental conditions. Thus, learning opportunities should be provided across child-directed, routine, and planned activities.

Adequate numbers of learning opportunities must also be available if children are to acquire and generalize important developmental skills. Unfortunately, a number of studies have reported that limited opportunities are provided for children to practice individual target goals (e.g., Fleming, Wolery, Weinzierl, Venn, & Schroeder, 1991; Pretti-Frontczak & Bricker, 2001; Schwartz, Carta, & Grant, 1996). Sufficient learning opportunities related to children's individual target goals are unlikely to occur incidentally or without adult intervention and advanced planning. Procedures for ensuring adequate learning opportunities are discussed in Chapters 4 and 5.

Learning opportunities need to be relevant or meaningful to children for them to benefit from the learning opportunity. Useful learning opportunities should match the child's current developmental abilities, be tailored to his or her interests, and prompt the child to practice target goals within the context of authentic activities or transactions. For example, if a child is learning to use both hands to manipulate objects, it is unlikely he or she will benefit from repeated attempts by an interventionist to cut out shapes unless 1) the child has the necessary prerequisite skills (e.g., ability to grasp, follow simple directions, sit upright); 2) the child is interested in cutting; and 3) joint attention is secured (e.g., having an adult assist the child in cutting using a hand-over-hand teaching strategy while the child is looking out the window will likely not result in acquisition and use of both hands to manipulate objects). Ensuring meaningful opportunities requires teams to engage in ongoing observations of children.

Element 3: Functional and Generative Goals

Transactions and the learning opportunities embedded in them should focus on behaviors that expand children's communicative, motor, adaptive, social, and problem-solving skills. Learning opportunities that elicit critical developmental skills are likely to assist in improving and expanding children's repertoires. Fundamental to the activity-based intervention approach is targeting educational and therapeutic goals and objectives that are functional and generative (i.e., represent broad classes of behavior and can be generalized across settings, conditions, and people).

Functional goals permit children to negotiate their physical and social environments in an independent manner satisfying to themselves and others. We use the term *functional* to refer to skills that are useful to children. For example, it is generally functional (i.e., useful) for children to learn how to open doors, turn on faucets, and flush toilets. Labeling days of the week may not have direct relevance to very young children's daily activities and, therefore, may not be a functional target (it may become more relevant as the children become older). Learning to name pictures in a book may be less useful to children than learning to label objects being used in play. Learning to initiate social interactions with peers (e.g., greeting, giving a peer a toy) is likely more useful for most children than learning to sing "I'm a Little Teapot." Engaging in "fun" activities such as singing songs should be encouraged; however, caregivers and interventionists should consider the value of an activity for expanding and enhancing children's development, in particular, as related to acquiring functional skills.

Goals should be generative as well as functional. *Generative* refers to two important perspectives. First, generative refers to selecting targets that can be used across settings, people, events, and objects. In most cases, children need to learn that the word *dog* refers to a class of objects, pictures, toys, and living animals rather than just the family pet. For the word *dog* to be generative, children must use it appropriately across a broad range of exemplars. For a pincer grasp to be generative, children must be able to use the response across settings (e.g., at the meal table, on the floor, at the bathroom sink), objects (e.g., Cheerios, beads, animal crackers, coins), and under a variety of conditions (e.g., when objects are hard, soft, wet, or dry).

The second perspective associated with generative refers to the need to assist children in learning how to make response modifications as settings, objects, people, and conditions change. A functional goal is following directions; however, for a response to be generative, children should be able to vary their responses to follow directions offered by teachers and parents. Children should also have a range of substitutable responses. For example, when asked, "Where is Daddy?" the child might appropriately point to or go to

Daddy (if he is in the room), say "daddy" while looking at his or her father, or indicate with a headshake that he or she does not know.

Overall, goals need to be a priority to the family, deemed developmentally and individually appropriate, and considered critical for the child's participation in daily activities. Goals targeted for intervention should also represent underlying processes that promote a child's access to and participation in the general curriculum and/or family routines. Furthermore, teams need to understand whether the goal of intervention centers on acquisition or use of the target skill(s)—both of which may require differentiated intervention efforts. Finally, teams should understand the differences between the targeting of general curricular outcomes for all children and individualized goals for particular children.

Goals targeted for individual children (often written on the individualized family service plan [IFSP] or individualized education program [IEP]) should be aligned with the child's present level of functioning and identified needs. The target goals should also promote independence and participation across a wide range of activities. In many instances, teams will identify more skills as potential intervention targets than can be reasonably addressed—thus, the need arises for teams to prioritize goals. When prioritizing, teams should select goals that 1) are not likely to develop without intervention, 2) significantly enhance a child's behavioral repertoire, 3) enable the child to be involved in the general curriculum/daily activities, and 4) match a child's developmental level of performance. For example, learning to make requests has the potential of enhancing a child's behavioral repertoire more than learning to label pictures on flashcards. By learning to make requests, children are able to get their needs met, interact with adults and peers, and engage in age-appropriate activities and play, whereas labeling pictures on flashcards is limited to a single activity that is not as likely to be interesting to the child or to promote independence and problem solving.

Activity-based intervention is designed to help young children acquire and use functional and generative goals. This approach does not focus on teaching children to respond to specific cues under specific conditions; instead, the approach focuses on developing generalized motor, social, adaptive, communication, and problem-solving skills that are modifiable across conditions.

Element 4: Timely and Integral Feedback or Consequences

Having children participate in child-directed, routine, and planned activities will not necessarily produce desired changes. Such activities and the provision of learning opportunities should provide a rich and meaningful context for intervention, but a final critical element is required. Without timely and appropriate feedback or consequences, children may not acquire or use target goals. The type of feedback or consequences, however, must meet two important criteria. First, the feedback/consequences provided to children should be timely, and second, the feedback/consequences should be, to the extent possible, associated with, connected to, or a logical outcome of the activity, action, or response.

There is a vast literature on the need for feedback/consequences to occur in a timely manner if efficient and effective learning is to occur (e.g., Duncan, Kemple, & Smith, 2000). The need to tie feedback/consequences to child behaviors may be particularly important for young children and for children with learning disabilities. If a toddler points at a cup, says "ju," and receives the cup within a brief time span, he or she may quickly learn what response generally gets a cup of juice; however, if pointing and vocalizating never gets him or her juice, the toddler will likely try some other response (e.g., screaming). If considerable time passes between the child's response and receiving the juice, it may take many more transactions before the toddler learns that a point and a vocalization gets juice. To the extent possible, interventionists and caregivers should provide immediate feedback/consequences so the child can discern the relationship between the response and subsequent feedback/consequences.

A second criteria associated with the delivery of feedback/consequences in an activity-based approach is to make it directly integral to or a logical outcome of the response. For example, the feedback/consequence associated with walking is that a child moves to a desired location or leaves an undesirable situation. The fact that the child can retrieve a desired toy by walking to it should negate the use of an artificial consequence (e.g., saying "Good walking"). Using or building in integral feedback/consequences also helps ensure it is timely. The action or connected feedback/consequences associated with turning a light switch in a dark room is that a person can see immediately, or turning a faucet generally produces water for a person to drink immediately. Using feedback or consequences that occur as a direct result of an action or response is greatly enhanced by using authentic transactions.

Figures 2.4 and 2.5 illustrate the fact that activity-based intervention is not designed to teach children specific responses in relation to specific cues. Rather, the approach is designed to offer children varied and multiple learning opportunities across activities. The main purpose of an activity-based approach is to have children associate classes of learning opportunities with classes of responses. So, too, with feedback/consequences, the goal is not to develop specific or one-to-one correspondences between responses and consequences but for children to effectively manage the range of feedback they may receive. The toddler who points for juice may receive his or her juice in a cup or glass, may be given a sip from someone else's glass, or may be given milk instead. Figure 2.4 also illustrates the range and variety of feedback or consequences that can be provided. A second example of how

Child-directed, routine, and planned activities	Multiple and varied learning opportunities	Functional and generative goals	Timely and integral feedback or consequences
Free play	Puzzles and blocks (favorite toys of the child) are made available in the classroom and at home.	Child fits puzzle pieces together or stacks blocks.	Child completes puzzle or tower.
Center time	Dress-up clothes, art aprons, and doll clothes with zippers, buttons, and ties are made available throughout the classroom.	Child buttons chef jacket and ties apron.	Child continues playing and wearing selected clothing.
Bath time	Caregiver asks the child to rub the soap bar on a washcloth.	Child rubs soap onto washcloth.	Mom comments on how clean the child is getting.
Snack	Teacher gives the child a cup and a small pitcher of juice.	Child pours juice into cup.	Child drinks juice and is no longer thirsty.
Arrival	Upon arrival at school, the child is required to take off his coat and get lunch out of his backpack.	Child unzips coat and unzips back-pack.	Teacher smiles and nods.
Small group activity	Child joins a small group playing with playdough.	Child rolls, ham-mers, and cuts playdough.	Peer points to different shapes and labels.
After-school activity	Caregiver puts out coloring books, storybooks, and art materials for an afternoon activity.	Child colors pages with crayons, turns pages in a book, and cuts out shapes.	Art project gets completed and shared with others.
Science and discovery table	Child is encouraged to transfer and measure different substances at the discovery table.	Child pours sand from a cup into a tub.	Tub gets filled with sand.

Figure 2.4. Example of activities in which multiple and varied learning opportunities can be provided to address the functional and generative target goal of *Manipulating objects with both hands* and examples of timely and integral feedback or consequences designed to enhance learning.

Child-directed, routine, and planned activities	Multiple and varied learning opportunities	Functional and generative goals	Timely and integral feedback and consequences
Free play	Playing with toy in highchair and dropping it to the floor	Looks at caregiver, points to the toy on the floor	Caregiver retrieves toy
Dressing/ diapering	Getting diaper changed	Looks at caregiver and smiles	Caregiver smiles back
Circle time	Sitting on caregiver's lap reading stories	Places caregiver's hands together to signify the desire to play Pat-a-cake	Caregiver sings and does hand motions

Figure 2.5. Example of three activities in which multiple and varied learning opportunities can be provided to address the functional and generative target goal of *Initiating interaction with familiar adults* and examples of timely and integral feedback or consequences designed to enhance learning.

the four elements build on one another into a comprehensive approach is provided in Figure 2.5.

Underlying Process: Embedding Learning Opportunities

The underlying process associated with activity-based intervention is the embedding of learning opportunities into authentic activities. Embedding refers to a process of addressing children's target goals during daily activities and events in a manner that expands, modifies, or is integral to the activity or event in a meaningful way. The process of embedding learning opportunities that address children's target goals is conceptually straightforward; however, the application of the process can be challenging (Grisham-Brown, Pretti-Frontczak, Hemmeter, & Ridgley, 2002; Pretti-Frontczak & Bricker, 2000).

The successful creation and embedding of meaningful learning opportunities requires that interventionists and caregivers engage in the following practices: 1) conduct comprehensive and ongoing assessments; 2) create multiple and varied learning opportunities during child-directed, routine, and planned activities; 3) target functional and generative goals; and 4) systematically monitor the effects of intervention. These practices are discussed at length in Chapter 5.

SUMMARY

Addressing important developmental targets, focusing on child–environment transactions, incorporating the four elements, and embedding learning opportunities provides the framework for activity-based intervention. This approach can be used in a variety of settings and under a variety of conditions by a range of direct service delivery personnel, consultants, and caregivers. The approach can be successfully used when working with individual children as well as groups of children with diverse repertoires and backgrounds. The flexibility of activity-based intervention permits broad application to infants and young children with disabilities or children who are at risk for mild, moderate, or severe disabilities. In addition, activity-based intervention can be successfully used with groups of children with varying developmental levels, economic backgrounds, experiences, values, and cultures.

An activity-based approach relies to a great extent on child-directed and routine activities that are not predetermined but rather instigated by children in particular environments. Child-directed activities allow children to engage in activities that are familiar and appealing and likely reflect the family's values (e.g., the types of toys and books available to the child in the home). So, too, the use of routine activities lends itself well to the incorporation of the child's learning into activities the family members have chosen as essential parts of their lives. Finally, planned activities can also be chosen or designed to reflect family experiences, cultures, and values. The introduction of a zoo activity might make little sense to young children who have never visited a zoo, whereas planning an activity focused on domestic animals may be more meaningful. Fundamental to the successful implementation of activity-based intervention is the tailoring of activities to the children and their goals that, in turn, permits respect for diversity.

REFERENCES

Bricker, D., Pretti-Frontczak, K., Johnson J., & Straka, E. (2002). In D. Bricker (Series Ed.), *Assessment, Evaluation, and Programming System for Infants and Children (AEPS): Vol. 1. Administration guide* (2nd ed.). (2002). Baltimore: Paul H. Brookes Publishing Co.

Duncan, T., Kemple, K., & Smith, T. (2000). Reinforcement in developmentally appropriate early childhood classrooms. *Childhood Education, 76*(4), 194–203.

Fleming, L., Wolery, M., Weinzierl, C., Venn, M., & Schroeder, C. (1991). Model for assessing and adapting teachers' roles in mainstreamed preschool settings. *Topics in Early Childhood Special Education, 11*(1), 85–98.

Goetz, L., Gee, K., & Sailor, W. (1983). Using a behavior chain interruption strategy to teach communication skills to students with severe disabilities. *Journal of The Association for Persons with Severe Handicaps, 10*(1), 21–30.

Griffin, E. (2000). *Narrowing the gap in reading: Instructional promise and peril.* Paper presented at the annual meeting of the American Educational Research Association, New Orleans.

Grisham-Brown, J.L., Pretti-Frontczak, K.L., Hemmeter, M.L., & Ridgley, R. (2002). Teaching IEP goals and objectives in the context of classroom routines and activities. *Young Exceptional Children, 6*(1), 18–27.

Hanson, M., & Bruder, M., (2001). Early intervention: Promises to keep. *Infants and Young Children, 13*(3), 47–58.

Mahoney, G., & Weller, E. (1980). An ecological approach to language intervention. In D. Bricker (Ed.), *Language resource book* (pp. 17–32). San Francisco: Jossey-Bass.

Pretti-Frontczak, K., & Bricker, D. (2000). Enhancing the quality of IEP goals and objectives. *Journal of Early Intervention, 23*(2), 92–105.

Pretti-Frontczak, K., & Bricker, D. (2001). Use of embedding strategies during daily activities by early childhood education and early childhood special education teachers. *Infant-Toddler Intervention: The Transciplinary Journal, 11*(2), 111–128.

Sameroff, A., & Chandler, M. (1975). Reproductive risk and the continuum of caretaking casualty. In F. Horowitz, E. Hetherington, S. Scarr-Salapatek, & G. Siegel (Eds.), *Review of child development research* (Vol. 4, pp. 187–244). Chicago: University of Chicago Press.

Sameroff, A., & Fiese, B. (2000). Transactional regulation: The developmental ecology of early intervention. In J. Skonkoff & S. Meisels (Eds.), *Handbook of early childhood intervention* (pp. 135–159). New York: Cambridge University Press.

Schwartz, I., Carta, J., & Grant, S. (1996). Examining the use of recommended language intervention practices in early childhood special education classrooms. *Topics in Early Childhood Special Education, 16*(2), 251–272.

Stokes, T., & Baer, D. (1977). An implicit technology of generalization. *Journal of Applied Behavioral Analysis, 10,* 349–367.

Stremel-Campbell, K., & Campbell, R. (1985). Training techniques that may facilitate generalization. In S. Warren & A. Rogers-Warren (Eds.), *Teaching functional language* (pp. 251–285). Baltimore: University Park Press.

Warren, S., Yoder, P., & Leew, S. (2002). Promoting social-communicative development in infants and toddlers. In S.F. Warren & J. Reichle (Series Eds.) & H. Goldstein, L.A. Kaczmarek, & K.M. English (Vol. Eds.), *Communication and language intervention series: Vol 10. Promoting social communication: Children with developmental disabilities from birth to adolescence* (pp. 121–149). Baltimore: Paul H. Brookes Publishing Co.

3

Activity-Based Intervention and a Linked System

Activity-based intervention is a comprehensive approach that is most successful when conceptualized and implemented within a linked system composed of four interrelated and fundamental processes: assessment, goal development, intervention, and evaluation (Bagnato & Neisworth, 1991; Bagnato, Neisworth & Munson, 1997; Bricker, 1989, 1996a, 1996b, 2002). The purpose of this chapter is to describe the four essential processes of a linked system and to describe the relationship between the processes and an activity-based approach. Figure 3.1 presents a linked system framework that incorporates the four processes and depicts their putative cyclical relationship. The interrelated and cyclical nature of a linked system permits an efficient and focused approach that maximizes the probability of promoting positive outcomes for children and their families. Furthermore, it is important to recognize that although activity-based intervention focuses directly on the intervention process of a linked system, the approach cannot be fully implemented without attention to all of the processes.

The first process of a linked system is assessment. Assessment refers to "an ongoing collaborative process of systematic observations and analysis" (Greenspan & Meisels, 1995, p. 23). The purpose of assessment is to collect objective information that permits identifying children's strengths, interests, and emerging skills and provides the necessary information to develop individualized family service plan (IFSP)/individualized education program (IEP) goals and objectives and subsequent intervention content.

The second process is goal development. The purpose of goal development is to individualize and prioritize a set of goals and objectives that are developmentally appropriate, functional, and important behaviors that will advance children's behavioral repertoires. The development of high-quality, developmentally appropriate, and functional goals is dependent on comprehensive information gathering during the assessment process.

The third process is intervention. The purpose of intervention is to assist children in acquiring and using prioritized individualized goals and objectives. Specifically, activity-based intervention is designed to assist caregivers and interventionists in using daily activities as the context for delivering specially designed instruction that will produce desired change in children.

Evaluation is the fourth process of a linked system and refers to documenting key behaviors in which children's previous performance in an area is compared with later performances. Some states use the term *evaluation* to describe the process for determining eligibility for services, but our use of the term refers to ongoing monitoring or data collection. Evaluation data should be used to monitor and alter assessment procedures, target goals, and intervention efforts to better meet the needs of children, families, and programs.

Employing a linked system permits 1) efficient use of personnel and other resources, 2) accountability in terms of program impact over time, and

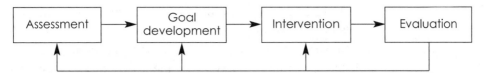

Figure 3.1. The four processes of a linked system framework.

3) individualization through the design of programs specific to the needs of children and their families. Furthermore, a linked system provides the necessary context for the implementation of activity-based intervention. The successful application of activity-based intervention is dependent on the use of an assessment tool that yields information that can be translated into appropriate goals and objectives for children. The approach is also dependent on targeting goals and objectives that are functional and developmentally appropriate and that can be addressed within daily activities. Finally, the approach requires careful and continuous evaluation of children's performance over time.

ACTIVITY-BASED INTERVENTION
AND THE ASSESSMENT PROCESS

When using an activity-based approach, it is critical to obtain information regarding children's strengths, interests, and emerging skills. Meaningful intervention efforts can be designed and monitored only through ongoing observations and conversations with people who interact frequently with the child. It is therefore essential that assessment information provide a continuous, accurate, and comprehensive profile of children's behavioral repertoires. Many formal and informal procedures have been developed to guide teams in observing and documenting children's behaviors across a wide variety of settings. Formal procedures may include completing norm-referenced and/or standardized tests (e.g., Bayley Scales of Infant Development [Bayley, 1993], Battelle Developmental Inventory [Newborg, Stock, & Wnek, 1998]), criterion-referenced or curriculum-based measures (e.g., Assessment, Evaluation, and Programming System for Infants and Children [AEPS®; Bricker, 2002], Hawaii Early Learning Profile [HELP; VORT Corporation, 1995]), or conducting structured interviews with caregivers (e.g., Vineland Adaptive Behavior Scales [Sparrow, Balla, & Cicchetti, 1984]). Informal procedures may include observations of young children during daily activities, completion of program-created checklists, the collection of anecdotal notes, or conversations with caregivers and other team members.

In particular, when selecting or creating a measure designed to assess children's behaviors, it is important for teams to ensure that the purpose for which the measure was designed matches how it will be used (e.g., Bagnato

& Neisworth, 1991; Bagnato et al., 1997; Bricker, 1996a, 1996b; McLean, Wolery, & Bailey, 2004). Various measures have been developed for use with young children. In particular, measures have been developed for screening, determining eligibility, planning intervention, and program evaluation. Although some test developers and publishers suggest that a measure can be used for multiple purposes (e.g., screening and diagnosis), in most cases a single measure can be successfully used for only one purpose (e.g., Pellegrino, Chudowsky, & Glaser, 2001).

Screening measures are designed to sort children into one of two categories: those whose development appears okay and those whose development is suspect. Screening measures, in most cases, are used with large groups of children, thus requiring that the measures be administered quickly and economically. Given these conditions, screening measures make relatively gross discriminations about children (i.e., further testing is or is not needed).

Eligibility measures are usually standardized and norm referenced and are used by teams to determine a child's performance in relation to a normative sample. These measures are typically administered by trained professionals (e.g., speech-language pathologist, psychologist, occupational therapist, physical therapist), and are often administered under controlled conditions using standardized materials and procedures. Results from diagnostic measures often provide a summary of children's development in one or more areas and document the child's level of delay and areas of need.

Programmatic measures (i.e., criterion referenced, curriculum based, curriculum embedded) compare children's performances with established criteria and can be administered using nonstandardized procedures. These measures often encourage family involvement and are specifically designed to assist teams in describing a child's level of functioning; selecting, prioritizing, and writing appropriate goals; designing appropriate intervention content; and monitoring child progress.

Program evaluation measures can provide comparative data at weekly, quarterly, annual, or longer intervals. Depending on the evaluative purpose, formal (norm-referenced or programmatic measures) or informal measures (e.g., anecdotal notes, portfolios) can be used to monitor child, family, or program outcomes.

When measures are used indiscriminately (i.e., used for the wrong purpose or without consideration of the intended purpose), problems may arise. A frequent and unfortunate problem is the use of screening or diagnostic measures for unintended purposes (e.g., to generate IFSP/IEP goals). The use of measures that do not yield intervention-relevant content can lead to the development of IFSP/IEP goals and objectives that are developmentally inappropriate, create intervention efforts that are not directly related to the child's individual needs, or allow small changes in behavior to go undetected (Bagnato et al., 1997; Notari & Bricker, 1990; Notari & Drinkwater, 1991; Pretti-Frontczak & Bricker, 2000). For a more detailed description of different assessment tools and their intended purposes, see McLean, Wolery, and Bailey (2004).

The successful application of activity-based intervention is dependent on the use of a programmatic measure that yields information necessary for the development of functional and generative skills and appropriate intervention content. Curriculum-based measures (CBMs) are defined as "a form of criterion-referenced measurement wherein curricular objectives act as the criteria for the identification of instructional targets and for the assessment of status and progress" (Bagnato & Neisworth, 1991, p. 87). CBMs have several advantages in comparison with standardized norm-referenced assessments when linking assessment and goal development to intervention. In general, CBMs such as the AEPS (Bricker, 2002) are composed of items directly relevant to the development of high-quality and individually appropriate goals. Some CBMs are also comprehensive in that their content addresses all major developmental domains (e.g., motor, communication, social development). In addition, CBM items can be modified to meet children's individual needs and can be observed across settings, time, materials, and people. The appendix to this chapter contains an example of how to use CBM results to develop individual child goals.

ACTIVITY-BASED INTERVENTION AND THE GOAL DEVELOPMENT PROCESS

Activity-based intervention addresses children's individual needs by embedding multiple and varied learning opportunities into their daily activities and by providing timely feedback/consequences designed to promote children's acquisition and use of functional and generative skills. Fundamental to the successful application of this approach is the development of children's goals that provide direction and guidance for the design and implementation of intervention.

When developing IFSPs/IEPs, teams should follow federal and state mandates. For example, the Individuals with Disabilities Education Act of 1990 (IDEA; PL 101-476) and Individuals with Disabilities Education Act Amendments of 1997 (PL 105-17) specify that teams develop IEP intervention targets as measurable annual goals and short-term objectives or benchmarks and IFSP intervention targets as outcomes. How the terms *goals, objectives,* and *benchmarks* are used across states and written sources varies. Throughout this volume, *goals* are defined as measurable skills targeted for a child to acquire

or master within approximately 1 year. Goals often address general or broad classes of behaviors, are needed by children across settings, and demonstrate their independence in performing the target skill(s). Goals are composed of a set of more specific skills often referred to as objectives or benchmarks.

Objectives or *benchmarks,* as defined in this volume, represent intermediate or measurable steps toward the goal as well as earlier milestones or building blocks of a goal. Target objectives or benchmarks should be related to the annual goal and serve as an indicator of a child's progress towards attaining the annual goal (e.g., Michnowicz, McConnell, Peterson, & Odom, 1995; Notari & Bricker, 1990; Notari & Drinkwater, 1991; Tymitz, 1980). Objectives or benchmarks occasionally need to be further delineated into simpler or smaller components referred to as *program steps.* Last, throughout this volume, the term *target skills* is used generically to refer to behaviors (i.e., goals, objectives/benchmarks, or program steps) selected for children to learn, strengthen, and/or use as part of their functional behavioral repertoire.

The primary method of ensuring a wise choice of specific intervention activities is through the development of high-quality individual goals for children. If skills targeted for intervention are well chosen and operationally defined, intervention efforts become clear and the selection of teaching strategies or capitalization on learning opportunities, as well as the reinforcement of child-directed and child-initiated activities, become straightforward. Developmentally appropriate and functional goals help ensure that interventionists and caregivers can select with confidence intervention activities that ensure the learning of target skills. Intervention efforts may not be effective if children's goals are not of high quality. The criteria used to write high-quality goals are addressed in the appendix to this chapter.

ACTIVITY-BASED INTERVENTION
AND THE INTERVENTION PROCESS

Intervention refers to the planning and executing of actions by caregivers and professionals designed to assist children in the acquisition and use of target skills. In an activity-based approach, intervention is conceptualized as the intentional and incidental actions and responses by adults and peers as well as the arrangement of the physical environment that provide guidance and practice opportunities for children to learn target skills.

Intervention efforts during the early childhood years are intended to occur during daily activities. Selection of daily activities and events should be guided by children's individual interests and needs and should ensure that all children 1) have access to the general curriculum, 2) make progress within the general curriculum, and 3) accomplish or achieve their individualized skills.

To ensure appropriate intervention efforts within daily activities or events, teams employing an activity-based approach should 1) derive content for intervention from children's performance on CBMs, 2) target functional and generative skills, 3) incorporate a variety of evidence-based instructional procedures designed to meet children's individual needs, and 4) systematically monitor children's progress to ensure that effective intervention is consistently provided. Furthermore, to ensure that children make desired progress toward target skills, an organizational structure should be present that directs teams to develop activities that provide frequent opportunities for practicing and learning target skills. Creating and maintaining such a structure requires ongoing, consistent, and thoughtful planning among team members. The literature on quality practices cites the importance of planning to ensure successful intervention and, in particular, individualized instruction for young children with disabilities (e.g., Bennett, DeLuca, & Bruns, 1997; Fleming & Wolery, 1991; Hoyson, Jamieson, Strain, & Smith, 1998; McDonnell, Brownell, & Wolery, 2001; Salisbury, Mangino, Petrigala, Rainforth, & Syryca, 1994). Adequate planning time is necessary for teams to successfully use activity-based intervention (e.g., Grisham-Brown & Pretti-Frontczak, 2003). Chapters 4 and 5 provide a comprehensive discussion of the application of an activity-based approach to intervention.

ACTIVITY-BASED INTERVENTION
AND THE EVALUATION PROCESS

Evaluation is a cyclical process that involves making decisions regarding what to observe, when to observe, who to observe, where to observe, and how to document observations. When considering the type of evaluative data desired, it is important to determine how the data will be used (e.g., as a description of the child's performance or an evaluation of their progress over time). Evaluation data are comparative in that children's individual or group performances are compared to either their previous performance or to some other criterion such as norms for a specific chronological age. Typically, teams document a child's progress on target IFSP/IEP skills, monitor a child's progress in the general curriculum, and determine whether broad program goals are being met.

To successfully use an activity-based approach, teams will need to collect weekly, quarterly, and annual evaluation data to ensure effective intervention over time. Weekly data collection permits monitoring children's performance during daily activities and routine events. Data should be collected weekly regarding children's progress toward target skills (i.e., typically those targeted on the IFSP/IEP for individualized intervention). The weekly data that are collected regarding both a child's performance and progress should be systematically summarized and reviewed by team members to make sound decisions regarding intervention efforts.

Weekly data collection is necessary to ensure that children are making adequate progress toward specific target skills. If goals and objectives are of high quality (i.e., functional, generalizable, addressable, and measurable), it should be a straightforward process for teams to collect systematic information on children's progress. The collection of weekly data is necessary to make timely and informed decisions about the effectiveness of intervention for individual children.

Weekly data collection should focus on the acquisition and use of target skills that are designed to move children toward individual target goals; therefore, these data often do not address children's progress on more global outcomes or their progress toward skills associated with the general curriculum. In addition, weekly data are often difficult to combine across children, making them inappropriate for examining group effects or program efficacy. The collection of more global evaluation data three to four times per year can provide useful feedback on children's progress toward goals selected from a programmatic measure (e.g., AEPS [Bricker, 2002]) and/or from the program's general curriculum. In addition, quarterly data may permit examining group effects and/or program outcomes.

Teams should also be prepared to collect annual data regarding children's progress and program outcomes. The collection of annual data can be an extension of the quarterly data collection procedures if teams decide to use the same measure. For example, if a programmatic measure is administered to children quarterly, these data can also be used for annual evaluations. Teams should develop strategies to keep their data collection activities focused and efficient. Additional data collection strategies and suggestions are discussed in Chapter 5.

SUMMARY

This chapter describes a linked system framework that provides the broader context for situating activity-based intervention. The linked system framework encompasses four essential processes: assessment, goal development, intervention, and evaluation. These four processes are critical to the delivery of effective services for young children and an activity-based approach in particular. The chapter appendix illustrates the link between assessment and goal development within an activity-based approach. The illustration is continued in Chapters 4 and 5, in which the practices deemed necessary for applying an activity-based approach within a linked system are discussed.

REFERENCES

Bagnato, S., & Neisworth, J. (1991). *Assessment for early intervention: Best practices for professionals.* New York: The Guilford Press.

Bagnato, S.J., Neisworth, J.T., & Munson, S.M. (1997). *LINKing assessment and early intervention: An authentic curriculum-based approach.* Baltimore: Paul H. Brookes Publishing Co.

Bayley, N. (1993). *Bayley Scale of Infant Development–II.* San Antonio, TX: Psychological Corporation.

Bennett, T., DeLuca, D., & Bruns, D. (1997). Putting inclusion into practice: Perspectives of teachers and parents. *Exceptional Children, 64*(1), 115–131.

Bricker, D. (1989). *Early intervention for at-risk and handicapped infants, toddlers, and preschool children.* Palo Alto, CA: VORT Corp.

Bricker, D. (1996a). Assessment for IFSP development and intervention planning. In S. Meisels & E. Fenichel (Eds.), *New visions for the developmental assessment of infants and toddlers* (pp. 169–192). Washington, DC: ZERO TO THREE, National Center for Infants, Toddlers, and Families.

Bricker, D. (1996b). Using assessment outcomes for intervention planning: A necessary relationship. In M. Brambring, H. Rauh, & A. Beelmann (Eds.), *Early childhood intervention theory, evaluation, and practice* (pp. 305–328). Berlin/New York: Aldine de Gruyter.

Bricker, D. (Series Ed.). (2002). *Assessment, Evaluation, and Programming System for Infants and Children* (2nd ed., Vols. 1–4). Baltimore: Paul H. Brookes Publishing Co.

Fleming, L., & Wolery, M. (1991). Model for assessing and adapting teachers' roles in mainstreamed preschool settings. *Topics in Early Childhood Special Education, 11*(1), 85–98.

Greenspan, S., & Meisels, S. (1995). A new vision for the assessment of young children. *Exceptional Parent, 25*(2), 23–25.

Grisham-Brown, J., & Pretti-Frontczak, K. (2003). Using planning time to individualize instruction for preschoolers with special needs. *Journal of Early Intervention, 26*,(1), 31–46.

Hoyson, M., Jamieson, B., Strain, P., & Smith, B. (1998). Duck, duck—colors and words: Early childhood inclusion. *Teaching Exceptional Children, 30*(4), 66–71.

Individuals with Disabilities Education Act Amendments of 1997, PL 105-17, 20 U.S.C. §§ 1400 *et seq.*.

Individuals with Disabilities Education Act of 1990, PL 101-476, 20 U.S.C. §§ 1400 *et seq.*

McDonnell, A., Brownell, K., & Wolery, M. (2001). Teachers' views concerning individualized intervention and support roles within developmentally appropriate preschools. *Journal of Early Intervention, 24*(1), 67–83.

McLean, M., Wolery, M., & Bailey, D. (Eds.). (2004). *Assessing infants and preschoolers with special needs* (2nd ed.). Columbus, OH: Charles E. Merrill.

Michnowicz, L., McConnell, S., Peterson, C., & Odom, S. (1995). Social goals and objectives of preschool IEPs: A content analysis. *Journal of Early Intervention, 19*(4), 273–282.

Newborg, J., Stock, J.R., & Wnek, J. (1998). *Battelle Developmental Inventory Complete Version.* Chicago: Riverside Publishing.

Notari, A., & Bricker, D. (1990). The utility of a curriculum-based assessment instrument in the development of individualized education plans for infants and young children. *Journal of Early Intervention, 14*(2), 117–132.

Notari, A., & Drinkwater, S. (1991). Best practices for writing child outcomes: An evaluation of two methods. *Topics in Early Childhood Special Education, 11*(3), 92–106.

Pellegrino, J., Chudowsky, M., & Glaser, R. (Eds.). (2001). *Knowing what students know: The Science and design of educational assessment.* Washington, DC: National Academy Press.

Pretti-Frontczak, K., & Bricker, D. (2000). Enhancing the quality of IEP goals and objectives. *Journal of Early Intervention, 23*(2), 92–105.

Salisbury, C., Mangino, M., Petrigala, M., Rainforth, B., & Syryca, S. (1994). Innovative practices: Promoting the instructional inclusion of young children with disabilities in the primary grades. *Journal of Early Intervention, 18*(3), 311–322.

Sparrow, S.S., Balla, D.A., & Cicchetti, D.V. (1984). *Vineland Adaptive Behavior Scales.* Circle Pines, MN: American Guidance Service.

Tymitz, B. (1980). Instructional aspects of the IEP: An analysis of teachers' skills and needs. *Educational Technology, 9*(20), 13–20.

VORT Corporation. (1995). *Hawaii Early Learning Profile (HELP).* Palo Alto, CA: Author.

Linking Assessment and Goal Development

The purpose of this appendix is to illustrate how teams can use information gathered during the assessment process to develop meaningful goals within an activity-based approach. The assessment process includes administration of a curriculum-based measure (CBM) and assessing family resources, priorities, and concerns. Assessment information is summarized to determine children's strengths and emerging skills as well as to identify priority needs. Priority needs serve as the basis for developing individualized goals that then become the focus of intentional intervention efforts and that require systematic monitoring.

As stated previously, implementation of an activity-based approach is dependent on the targeting of meaningful goals. Procedures for developing goals can vary across states/regions and the age of the child (i.e., developing an individualized family service plan [IFSP] rather than an individualized education program [IEP]). Readers are encouraged to review examples provided in the Assessment, Evaluation, and Programming System for Infants and Toddlers, Second Edition (AEPS; Bricker, 2002), regarding a five-step process (and variation of that process) for developing both IFSP outcomes and IEP goals from assessment results. The following example illustrates how results from the AEPS Test were used to guide a team in selecting and writing meaningful goals for a specific child.

The AEPS Test was selected by the team in this example because of three features that make it useful for developing children's IFSP/IEP goals and objectives. First, most items from the AEPS Test are written to reflect conceptual or generative response classes rather than specific responses (e.g., target stacking a variety of objects such as books, clothes, carpet squares, and cups versus stacking three 1-inch cubes). Second, many AEPS Test items are composed of skills essential for young children to function independently and to cope with environmental demands (e.g., moving around their environment, expressing their wants and needs). Third, the AEPS Test contains prototype goals that can serve as guides or models for writing children's individualized goals and objectives.

SERINA JOHNSON

Serina Johnson is 4-year-old girl eligible for early childhood special education (ECSE) services under the category of general developmental delay. Serina attends a neighborhood preschool program 3 days per week, where she receives ECSE services including occupational and speech-language therapy. To develop an appropriate IEP that recognizes her strengths, addresses her needs, and considers her family's priorities, a coordinated assessment was undertaken.

Gathering Information

To begin, the team, composed of Serina's parents, the ECSE classroom-based teacher, classroom assistant, and therapists, administers the AEPS Test and AEPS Family Report and reviews relevant documents (e.g., recent tests conducted, medical summaries). This comprehensive approach to gathering assessment information is designed to assist the team in developing meaningful goals that, in turn, will guide intervention.

Serina's team gathers information by observing her during daily activities at home, at school, and within the community. At school, team members use the AEPS assessment activity plans to guide the presentation of a number of planned activities. AEPS assessment activity plans are designed to help teams obtain an accurate and complete picture of a child's functional repertoire (e.g., what skills he or she has and how these skills are used) in an efficient manner. The team chooses three AEPS assessment activities and sets up stations around the classroom. Serina and other children are encouraged to participate in the planned activities. As Serina participates in activities at the different stations, the teacher, therapists, and assistants note her performance in terms of skills she demonstrates, skills that are emerging or for which she needs assistance to perform, and skills she does not yet demonstrate.

Team members also talk to people familiar with Serina (e.g., her grandparents, her child care providers) and her parents complete the AEPS Family Report, which provides information about the family's daily routines and, in particular, Serina's participation in those daily and community routines. The Family Report allows caregivers the opportunity to record a child's strengths, interests, and emerging skills across areas of development.

Summarizing Information

Following administration of the AEPS Test, completion of the AEPS Family Report, and review of existing and relevant documents, the team summarizes the assessment information. In general, teams are encouraged to summarize assessment results in several ways (e.g., numerically, visually, narratively). When summarizing assessment information, teams are encouraged to focus on a child's strengths, interests, and emerging skills. Teams should identify patterns in the demonstration of skills (e.g., with or without assistance, consistently or inconsistently, in certain locations) and identify the relationship between the child's performances across areas of development (e.g., teams may look for a common feature that impedes the child from performing related tasks).

Serina's team reviews the information they gathered and summarizes their findings in three ways. First, they calculate an area percent score for each of the six developmental areas of the AEPS. Area percent scores represent the percentage of items the child can perform independently/consistently and those items they are beginning to demonstrate or can demonstrate with assistance across the six areas assessed (e.g., gross motor, adaptive, social). Second, they summarize the information visually by completing the AEPS Child Progress Record. The Child Progress Record was developed to monitor individual children's progress over time and provides teams with a visual record of the child's accomplishments, current targets, and future targets (Bricker, 2002). Third, the team summarizes information narratively by noting Serina's strengths, interests, and needs. Narrative summaries should be jargon free, objective, and descriptive, and should indicate how the child's disability affects his or her access to and participation in daily activities.

Selecting Individualized Education Program Goals

Skills selected for intervention should meet at least four quality criteria: 1) functional, 2) generative, 3) measurable, and 4) able to be addressed within daily activities (Pretti-Frontczak & Bricker, 2000). Serina's team uses the Revised Goals and Objectives Rating Instrument (adapted from Notari-Syverson & Shuster, 1995) to ensure that potential goals selected from assessment results meet the quality criteria. (See http://fpsrv.dl.kent.edu/play/Information/Measures/gori.pdf for a copy of the Revised Goals and Objectives Rating Instrument.) For example, the team identified cutting paper in two and cutting out shapes with straight lines as a need. Using the Revised Goals and Objectives Rating Instrument, the team notes that this skill did not meet all of the quality criteria to be selected as an IEP goal. The team then decides that manipulating objects with both hands (a broader skill that includes cutting out shapes with straight lines) does meet the four quality criteria listed on the Revised Goals and Objectives Rating Instrument, and, therefore, the broader skill is considered as a potential target for intervention. In all, the team identifies seven skills that meet the quality criteria and serve as potential intervention targets:

- Manipulates toys and materials with both hands

- Draws simple shapes and letters

- Eats and prepares (e.g., taking the wrapper off of foods, removing the peel from fruits) more types of foods

- Follows directions

- Talks more and increases intelligibility

- Plays with other children

- Plays with toys and materials

Prioritizing Individualized Education Program Goals

After the team selects potential intervention targets (i.e., goals and objectives) and ensures the target skills meet quality criteria, they determine which skills are of highest priority and require specialized services. The team prioritizes by reviewing Serina's strengths and needs and by answering a series of questions:

- Do all team members understand the nature of the target skills?

- Are the skills deemed to be a priority by all team members?

- Will intentional and individualized instruction be provided for the child to acquire and use the skills?

- Are the target skills developmentally and individually appropriate?

- Are the skills necessary for the child's participation in the general curriculum (i.e., daily activities) or necessary for the completion of most daily routines?

- Are the skills related to or aligned with the general curriculum and state standards for all children and/or do they represent the critical function of the standard versus a restatement of the standard?

Table A3.1 contains a summary of potential IEP goals and the team's rationale for inclusion or exclusion.

The prioritization process resulted in the following skills selected to serve as IEP goals:

- Manipulates toys and materials using both hands (e.g., cutting, drawing, zipping, pouring)

- Plays with toys and materials (i.e., functional use and representational use)

- Talks more and is intelligible to others (i.e., uses words to greet, inform, and request)

Table A3.1. Summary of potential individualized education program (IEP) goals and rationale for inclusion or exclusion

Potential IEP goals	Rationale for inclusion or exclusion on IEP
Manipulates toys and materials with both hands	This goal remains a priority for Serina's IEP because she needs the skill during most daily activities and individualized intervention is needed for her to acquire the skill.
Draws simple shapes and letters	It is not necessary to target this goal on Serina's IEP because the team can address drawing simple shapes and letters as a part of targeting the manipulation of toys and materials.
Eats and prepares more types of foods	It is not necessary to target this goal on Serina's IEP because the team feels that learning to eat more types of food will come with time and does not require individualized intervention. Furthermore, by addressing the skill of manipulating materials, the team is addressing Serina's need to be more independent with preparing foods.
Follows directions	It is not necessary to target this goal on Serina's IEP because the skill is required by all children in the preschool and is addressed within the context of the general curriculum, not through individualized intervention efforts.
Talks more and increases intelligibility	This goal is a high priority that requires individualized intervention and will therefore be included on Serina's IEP.
Plays with other children	This goal is not necessary to target on Serina's IEP because the team feels the skill will emerge as Serina improves her ability to play with toys/materials and to be understood by others. Serina also receives exposure to play with others at the preschool.
Plays with toys and materials	This goal remains a priority for Serina's IEP because she needs skills to increase her participation in activities with other children, and individualized intervention is needed for her to acquire the skill.

Writing IEP Goals and Objectives/Benchmarks

Serina's team lists the priority skills and writes them as IEP goals and associated objectives or benchmarks that meet their state's and agency's rules and regulations. The team used the AEPS goal/objective examples for writing Serina's IEP. The AEPS goal/objective examples are designed to assist teams in writing meaningful goals/objectives and subsequent intervention (see Chapters 4 and 5). Serina's team uses the examples from the AEPS as a starting point. They modify and individualize the examples using a straightforward ABC formula, in which *A* represents an antecedent, *B* represents the child's target behavior, and *C* represents the criterion or level of acceptable performance. Figure A3.1 provides a comparison of AEPS goals/objectives examples and how the team individualizes them for Serina. The individualized goals and objectives/benchmarks are then used to guide intervention efforts.

Linking assessment information and goal development is a critical aspect of an activity-based approach to intervention. This appendix illustrates how a team conducts a comprehensive assessment and uses that information to develop functional and generative goals. Chapter 5 continues the example of Serina Johnson and her team as they plan individualized intervention and monitor her performance over time on target goals.

AEPS goal/objective examples	IEP goals and objectives/benchmarks for Serina
Level II, Fine Motor Area *Strand A, Goal 1.0*	*Goal 1.0*
The child will use two hands to manipulate objects, each hand performing different movements (e.g., tie shoes, button clothing, cut out shapes with curved lines).	During daily activities, Serina will manipulate a variety of objects, toys, or materials that require use of both hands at the same time, while performing different movements. She will manipulate three different objects, toys, or materials once a day for 2 weeks. For example, Serina will tie shoes, button clothing, thread and zip a zipper, and/or cut out shapes with curved lines.
Level II, Fine Motor Area *Strand A, Objective 1.1*	*Benchmark 1.1*
The child will perform any two-handed task holding an object with one hand while the other hand manipulates (e.g., holds paper while drawing, steadies container while removing playdough).	During daily activities, Serina will perform any two-handed task using one hand to hold or steady an object, toy, or material while using the other hand to manipulate the object, toy, or material or perform a movement. She will perform three different two-handed tasks per day for 2 weeks. For example, Serina will hold a piece of paper and draw with a crayon, hold paper and cut paper in half, hold a bowl and spoon up food or liquid, spread food with a knife, zip a zipper, or turn the pages of a book.
Level I, Fine Motor Area *Strand A, Goal 3.0*	*Benchmark 1.2*
The child will grasp hand-size object (e.g., bath toy, block, rattle) with either hand using the ends of thumb, index, and second fingers; object is held by the fingers and does not rest in palm.	During daily activities, Serina will grasp hand-size objects with either hand using the ends of her thumb, index, and second fingers. Objects need to be held by the fingers and not rest in her palm. She will grasp three different hand-size objects each day for 2 weeks. For example, Serina will grasp bath toys, blocks, crackers, playdough pieces, large/fat crayons, or markers.

Figure A3.1. AEPS goal/objective examples and how they were revised to serve as Serina's target IEP goals and objectives/benchmarks.

AEPS goal/objective examples	IEP goals and objectives/benchmarks for Serina
Level II, Social Communication *Strand A, Goal 1.0*	*Goal 2.0*
The child will use words, phrases, or sentences to do the following: • Express anticipated outcomes • Describe imaginary objects, events, or people • Label own or others' affect/emotions • Describe past events • Make commands to and requests of others • Obtain information • Inform	Using a variety of one and two words, Serina will **request** objects, people, or materials, **inform** others, and **greet** others during daily activities. Two different adults will understand what she says three times a day for 2 weeks. *Across Goal 2.0 and associated objectives, to be understood by other adults means that when Serina says words to request, inform, and/or greet, adults will hear Serina produce target final consonant sounds and/or produce target initial consonant sounds without making substitutions. The final consonant target sounds are /p, b, t, d, k/ and the initial consonant target sounds are /k, l, g, f, v, ch, j, th/.*
Level II, Social Communication *Strand A, Objective 1.5*	*Objective 2.1*
The child will use words, phrases, or sentences to make commands to and requests of others (e.g., the child says, "Give me the red one"). Errors in syntax are acceptable.	Using a variety of one and two words, Serina will **request** objects, people, or materials from others (adults or peers) during daily activities. Two different adults will understand what she says three times a day for 2 weeks. For example, Serina will say words/phrases such as "Up," "Give toy," or "More food."
Level II, Social Communication *Strand A, Objective 1.7*	*Objective 2.2*
The child will use words, phrases, or sentences to describe objects, actions, and events and to inform others about plans, intentions, and experiences (e.g., the child calls to a parent, "I'm going outside"). Errors in syntax are acceptable.	Using a variety of one and two words, Serina will **inform** others (adults or peers) about daily activities. Two different adults will understand what she says three times a day for 2 weeks. For example, Serina will say words/phrases such as "Cat," "Milk," or "Big book."
Level II, Social Area *Strand A, Objective 1.4*	*Objective 2.3*
The child will greet others with whom he or she is familiar by vocalizing, verbalizing, hugging, patting, touching, or smiling.	Using a variety of one and two words, Serina will **greet** others (adults or peers). Two different adults will understand what she says three times a day for 2 weeks. For example, Serina will say "Hey," "Hi Marley," "Hi Beth," "Hi Kate," or "Good Morning."

continued

Figure A3.1.   *(continued)*

AEPS goal/objective examples	IEP goals and objectives/benchmarks for Serina
Level I, Cognitive Area *Strand F, Objective 1.1*	*Goal 3.0*
When playing, the child will use representational actions with objects (e.g., pretend to write with stick, feed doll with crayon, pretend to drink out of a block).	During a variety of daily activities, Serina will use one object to represent another object (e.g., use a stick as a pencil, a crayon as a bottle, a block as a telephone). She will use representational actions with three different objects daily for 2 weeks.
Level I, Cognitive Area *Strand F, Objective 1.2*	*Benchmark 3.1*
When playing, the child will use functionally appropriate actions with objects (e.g., hold a telephone to ear, comb hair with comb).	During a variety of daily activities, Serina will act on objects using functionally or socially appropriate actions (i.e., actions for which the object was intended or designed). She will use functionally or socially appropriate actions with three different objects daily for 2 weeks. For example, Serina will hold a play telephone to ear, or put comb to head and attempt to comb hair.

REFERENCES

Bricker, D. (Series Ed.). (2002). *Assessment, Evaluation, and Programming System for Infants and Children* (2nd ed., Vols. 1–4). Baltimore: Paul H. Brookes Publishing Co.

Bricker, D. (Series Ed.) (2002). *Assessment, Evaluation, and Programming System for Infants and Children: Child Progress Record* (2nd ed.). Baltimore: Paul H. Brookes Publishing Co.

Bricker, D. (Series Ed.). (2002). *Assessment, Evaluation, and Programming System for Infants and Children: Family Report* (2nd ed.). Baltimore: Paul H. Brookes Publishing Co.

Notari-Syverson, A., & Shuster, S. (1995). Putting real life skills into IEP/IFSPs for infants and young children. *Teaching Exceptional Children, 27*(2), 29–32.

Pretti-Frontczak, K., & Bricker, D. (2000). Enhancing the quality of IEP goals and objectives. *Journal of Early Intervention, 23*(2), 92–105.

4

Organizational Structure of an Activity-Based Approach

As outlined in federal legislation and recommended practice, individualized family service plans (IFSPs) and individualized education programs (IEPs) are designed to serve as a guide or map for intervention (Bricker, 2002; Pretti-Frontczak & Bricker, 2000). Because these individualized plans are not designed to serve as day-to-day treatment or lesson plans, teams need to develop other mechanisms to ensure that children are provided with multiple and varied learning opportunities. Learning opportunities should be designed to address children's individual needs within the context of child–environment transactions. At first glance, an activity-based approach may appear to only permit children to initiate activities of interest or to only engage in "fun" activities. Using fun and interesting activities is only one aspect of a more complex approach. The approach actually requires an underlying structure that directs the work of professional team members and caregivers. The underlying organizational structure of activity-based intervention is illustrated through the use of three forms: intervention guides, embedding schedules, and activity plans.

Intervention guides require teams to consider the major parameters that will direct intervention efforts. When completed, these documents expand the information contained in the IFSP/IEP and ensure that a child's needs are addressed within daily activities. *Embedding schedules* alert teams to when, where, and how target skills can be addressed and further ensure that multiple and varied learning opportunities are provided within daily activities. Finally, *activity plans* present formal descriptions of daily activities (child directed, routine, or planned) that can be used with team planning to embed opportunities for children to practice their target goals and objectives. Intervention guide, embedding schedule, and activity plan forms, or variations of them, provide the necessary organizational structure for ensuring that daily activities promote learning of important developmental skills and lead to positive changes. This chapter provides a description of these forms and the process for their completion.

Activity-based intervention focuses on child–environment transactions that occur during daily activities. Furthermore, within an activity-based approach the child's active participation is critical to the learning process. Activities in and of themselves do not guarantee children will practice or make desired progress toward their individual goals, even when the activities are attractive to them. Likewise, a child's active participation in an event may not lead to positive changes in development. Rather, a structure must be present that directs teams to develop activities that provide ample opportunities for children to practice and learn target skills.

Each part of the organizational structure assists teams in moving from the overall guide for intervention (i.e., IFSP/IEP) to the day-to-day practices that will promote learning and development. Specifically, the intervention guide expands on the IFSP/IEP by identifying what to teach, how to teach, where to teach, and how to determine if teaching was effective. Embedding schedules pull information from the intervention guide and put the information in the context of daily activities or routines (e.g., how the team will embed learning opportunities for a target goal during dressing, travel, and meals). Finally, activity plans ensure that multiple and varied learning opportunities are created for either multiple goals and/or multiple children.

Each part of the organizational structure is described in the following sections. Completed examples of each of the forms (i.e., intervention guides, embedding schedules, and activity plans) are contained in the chapter appendix. The completed forms are designed to show teams how the organizational structure ensures the successful application of an activity-based approach across a variety of service delivery models. Furthermore, blank samples of the three forms are contained in the book appendix following Chapter 10. Teams are encouraged to reproduce and/or modify the forms to assist them in implementing the approach.

INTERVENTION GUIDES

Intervention guides systematically direct teams in planning intervention and recording the intervention content and process. Prior to planning activities or using routine events or child-directed actions effectively, the team should develop intervention guides for each child's set of target goals. Intervention guides provide direction and criteria for teaching target goals and for making decisions based on data. Initially, intervention guides may appear to be extra paperwork. In practice, however, teams will discover the benefits of the organization and the structure that intervention guides can provide. Because intervention guides are designed for teams to use following the completion of the IFSP/IEP, they can extend and continue conversations regarding such issues as

- Necessary accommodations, modifications, and intervention strategies
- Where learning opportunities will occur (i.e., during which activities)
- How often learning opportunities will be provided
- Who will be responsible for providing learning opportunities and monitoring children's progress over time

Intervention guides can take on a variety of formats but should include the following information

1. Identifying information such as the child's name, intervention team member names, and dates for initiation and completion of intervention efforts related to a particular goal

2. Target goals, objectives/benchmarks (can be drawn directly from IEPs), and/or program steps

3. How the form is linked to state standards or IFSP outcomes

4. Multiple and varied learning opportunities, functional and generative goals, and timely and integral feedback or consequences

5. Accommodations, modifications, and intervention strategies necessary for the child to participate in social and physical aspects of his or her environment

6. Data collection procedures (can be drawn directly from IEPs)

7. Decision rules regarding how to interpret the child's progress over time and make subsequent decisions (Bricker, 2002)

Basic Information

Intervention guides should include a section for the child's name, the team members responsible for implementing intervention, and the timeline for which intervention will be provided. Dates for initiation and completion help teams devise realistic intervention efforts that are in line with existing resources. The date for completion will vary depending on the child and the number or type of skills targeted for a particular goal.

Goal, Objectives/Benchmarks, Program Steps

In the Goal, Objectives/Benchmarks, Program Steps section of the intervention guide, teams can note the target goal and the associated objectives/ benchmarks that come directly from a child's IFSP/IEP. Teams can also include program steps in this section. Program steps are simpler or smaller components of an objective/benchmark and may be necessary when creating intervention guides for children with moderate to more severe disabilities. For example, a program step for the objective of grasping objects might be "extending the arm from the body and/or opening the palm." Typically, a separate intervention guide is created for each goal and its associated objectives/benchmarks and program steps.

State Standards or IFSP Outcomes

Accountability movements have increased the need to align intervention efforts with the child's documented needs and subsequent services. In the State Standards or IFSP Outcomes section of the intervention guide, teams should list the state/local/agency standards[1] that are aligned with a child's

---

[1]States and agencies are increasingly developing standards for young children that vary greatly in terms of content, organization, and numbers. Although it is beyond the scope of this volume to show how various standards align with children's individual goals, teams should become familiar with their state's/agency's standards and ensure that intervention efforts are aligned with broader outcomes for all children.

target goal and objectives/benchmarks. For example, if the skill of "Manipulates objects with both hands" is targeted, the team could show how targeting the goal addresses or aligns with a number of state standards such as "Manipulates familiar objects to accomplish a purpose or complete a task or solve a problem" or "Explores by manipulating materials using simple equipment (e.g., magnets and magnifiers)."[2] Goals targeted for intervention should be based on the child's identified needs in gaining access to and making progress in the general curriculum.

Section three of the intervention guide also allows teams to show the alignment between target goals and IFSP outcomes. In many states, IFSP outcomes are written as broad statements in the family's own words and may require measurable goals and objectives to accompany the outcome to adequately guide intervention efforts. For example, if an IFSP outcome is "We want our child to be happy and to develop friendships," the team may need to develop associated measurable and meaningful skills that indicate how this broad IFSP outcome will be achieved. Figures A4.1 and A4.2 in the chapter appendix illustrate the process of aligning IFSP outcomes or state standards respectively, with functional and generative goals targeted for intervention.

Multiple and Varied Learning Opportunities, Functional and Generative Goals, Timely and Integral Feedback or Consequences

At the heart of ensuring multiple and varied learning opportunities is the selection and use of appropriate antecedents. Antecedents refer to any event, action, or condition that is designed, selected, or has occurred with the intent of providing a learning opportunity. Adults (e.g., teachers, caregivers, therapists), peers/siblings, or the physical environment (e.g., object, event, picture/sign/word) can provide antecedents. At times, antecedents will also originate from within the child (e.g., hunger, interest in a toy). Antecedents range from simple (e.g., teacher provides hand-over-hand physical assistance, model of target skill) to more complex (e.g., progressive time delay, mand-model), and from nondirective (e.g., placing a toy out of reach) to directive (e.g., making a request, giving a direction). Multiple antecedents should be selected and used for each target goal (and associated objectives/benchmarks and program steps) and noted on the intervention guide. The purpose of noting antecedents on the intervention guide is to ensure that multiple and varied learning opportunities are provided consistently across daily activities and across team members.

---

[2]All examples of state standards in Chapters 4 and 5 and the appendix to Chapter 4 are taken directly from the Ohio Department of Education's Early Learning Content Standards.

A learning opportunity is created when at least two conditions are in place. First, antecedents related to one or more of the target goals occur. In other words, the antecedent has the potential of allowing the child to practice, perform, or attempt to produce one or more target goals. Second, the antecedents should have the potential of allowing the child to continue an action or maintain the child's inferred intent or interest within the activity or with materials that are present. If an antecedent modifies or extends the child's action or attention, it must not shift the child's behavior or focus away from his or her inferred intent or interest. In other words, an antecedent should not require the child to shift attention away from what he or she is interested or engaged in. The following scenario illustrates how different antecedents do or do not create learning opportunities related to a child's target goal of signing MORE.

Marcy sits at a child-size table with six other children. Each child has a place setting, and extra food is located on the counter behind the table. The adults in the room sit at the table with the children, walk around the room, or get more food or drink. Marcy sits at the opposite end of the table from an adult and the extra food and drink. As she finishes her last cracker, she holds up her plate and looks toward the box of crackers on the shelf and then at Brian who is sitting next to her. If Marcy observes Brian sign MORE and receive more food to eat, a learning opportunity is created. The antecedent of Brian signing MORE provides a learning opportunity because 1) it is related to Marcy's target goal, and 2) Marcy's attention is on Brian. If, instead, an adult asks Marcy if she wants more to drink, a learning opportunity may not be created. Even though the antecedent of the adult asking Marcy if she wants more to drink may encourage Marcy to demonstrate her target goal (i.e., to sign MORE), the focus on asking for more to drink instead of eat may cause Marcy to shift her interest or intent of getting more to eat to getting more to drink. Marcy's interest or intent is inferred from observable actions (i.e., holding an empty plate up and looking at the box of crackers). The possible shift in her attention is likely to reduce the chance that Marcy will sign MORE.

Functional and generative goals, as described in Chapter 3, often include associated objectives/benchmarks and at times, program steps. These goals, objectives/benchmarks, and program steps are referred to as *target behaviors* on an intervention guide. Target behaviors or responses are the desired skills teams select for a child to acquire and use during daily activities and interactions. It is also important for teams to list *nontarget behaviors* or the responses a child is likely to perform following the presentation of an antecedent that are not the actual goals, objectives/benchmarks, or program steps the team is teaching. For example, a teacher asks Mateo to take off his coat. Target responses may include taking off the coat or asking the teacher for help. Nontarget responses may include no response from Mateo or Mateo walking away without taking off his coat. It is important to consider both target and nontarget child responses so that timely and integral feedback/consequences can be provided for all child responses (i.e., encouraging target behaviors to occur again or consistently and diminishing the occurrence of nontarget behaviors).

Feedback and consequences include adult (e.g., teacher, caregiver, therapist) behaviors; peer/sibling behaviors; and/or physical environmental objects, events, pictures, signs, or words that support a child's responses (e.g., smiles, affirmations, getting needs or wants met). To the extent possible, as discussed in Chapter 2, feedback and consequences should be timely and integral. Timeliness is important so children can discern the relationship between their responses and subsequent consequences. Integrality suggests a logical or inherent relationship between the feedback or consequence and the outcome of the activity, action, or child's response. Noting the type of feedback/consequence on the intervention guide for both target and nontarget behaviors ensures team consistency.

Accommodations, Modifications, and Intervention Strategies

In the Accommodations, Modifications, and Intervention Strategies section of the intervention guide, teams indicate the accommodations, modifications, and intervention strategies a child may require to participate in or benefit from interactions during daily activities. For example, teams can list specific accommodations and modifications to the physical and social aspects of the classroom, home, and community environments that have a direct impact on the child's ability to participate in daily activities. Accommodations and modifications may be temporary or permanent in nature and may include the following:

- Pace (e.g., extended wait or performance time, number of transitions)
- Presentation of information (e.g., verbal, visual, modeling, tactile)
- How directions are provided (e.g., oral and written, number of steps, visual cues/aids)
- Environmental arrangement (e.g., placement of objects/toys, distraction reductions, unobstructed view)
- Type of materials (e.g., adaptive equipment, size of print, augmentative and alternative communication device, various textures, computers)
- Social supports (e.g., peer tutoring, cooperative learning groups, conflict resolution skills)
- Reinforcement or motivation considerations (e.g., intrinsic, extrinsic, verbal, nonverbal, child choice/preference)
- Self-management strategies (e.g., picture schedule)
- Assessment and testing considerations (e.g., type of questions, testing environment, length of time, grading)

Teams can include intervention strategies and suggestions in this section of the form. It is important that teams discuss and track the impact different strategies have on promoting children's acquisition and use of target skills. The intervention guide provides a means of communicating with one another regarding strategies that may be effective and that can be used across activities.

Activity-based intervention is designed for use with a variety of teaching strategies and relies heavily on the use of nondirective strategies. Although the use of massed trials and drill is not incompatible with activity-based intervention, this approach recommends that interventionists and caregivers use, to the extent possible, intervention strategies that are responsive to a child's initiations and that are compatible with daily routines and meaningful planned activities. A brief description of seven such strategies—forgetfulness, novelty, visible but unreachable, change in expectations, piece by piece, assistance, and interruption or delay—is provided next.

Forgetfulness

The strategy of "forgetting" can be used by interventionists and caregivers to encourage action and problem solving by children. It is an effective strategy for determining what children know and can do. Forgetting can occur when the adult fails to provide the necessary equipment or materials or overlooks a familiar or important component of a routine or activity. Examples include not having a primary food such as peanut butter for making peanut butter and jelly sandwiches at snack time, not having paintbrushes available for a painting activity, or not recalling a word or phrase to a familiar story or song. When forgetfulness occurs, children should recognize the missing element and convey this information by asking questions, searching for materials, or engaging in other appropriate problem-solving actions.

Novelty

Children are generally enticed by new toys or activities. The careful introduction of novelty may stimulate desirable reactions from children. For infants and children with severe disabilities, this strategy may be more effective if the novelty is introduced within the context of a routine or familiar activity; for example, a new action or change in words could be added to a familiar game such as Duck, Duck, Goose. The game could be slightly altered by changing the words to Cat, Cat, Mouse. For older or more capable children, examples might include bringing in a classroom pet, taking a new path from the bus to the classroom, or adding laminated shapes on the floor where children line up for transitions. For most infants and young children, the introduction of novelty is most effective if the change is not dramatically discrepant from their expectations. For example, a team member who makes major changes to his or her appearance, such as cutting very long hair to a very short style, may present a form of novelty that is initially reacted to with crying and stranger anxiety. Adding materials to a sensory table that are foreign to children is another example of novelty that may initially be ineffective because the children are not interested or do not understand how to use the materials.

Visible But Unreachable

A strategy that requires only simple environmental manipulation is placing objects so that they are visible but unreachable. Placing objects within children's sight but out of their reach can facilitate the development of social, communication, and problem-solving behaviors. Families often use this strategy without thinking of its use as an intervention strategy. For example, they may place a favorite food such as cookies or a favorite toy such as a talking doll on a shelf out of reach. By sheer desire alone, children are motivated to figure out how to get that food item or object. When using this strategy, it is important that the child is able to see the object and that a peer or adult is available to retrieve the object unless independent problem solving is being sought.

Placing objects out of reach is often an effective strategy to use with children who are learning early communication skills. A simple strategy that a team can use often is to place food items in the center of the table before or after a serving is provided. Placement of foods in the center of the table before serving them allows the adult to name the items and wait for children to request them. Returning foods to the center of the table after one serving also allows children to see and request more of the food item.

Change in Expectations

Omitting or changing a familiar step or element in a well-practiced or routine activity is a strategy known as *change in expectations*. Many changes may appear comical to children. For example, an adult who tries to draw or write with an upside-down pencil using the eraser as the lead may seem silly. The purpose of a change in expectations like this is twofold: 1) children's recognition of change provides information about their discrimination and memory abilities, and 2) such changes provide ideal situations for evoking a variety of communication and problem-solving responses (e.g., the child verbalizes a protest, the child turns the pencil so that the pointed end is down). Children with severe disabilities can often recognize changes, such as putting a mitten on a foot, and communicate this recognition. The alert team member can often shape these communicative responses into functional behaviors.

Piece by Piece

Another often easy-to-execute nondirective intervention strategy can be used when activities require materials that have many pieces. The interventionist can ration access to a multipiece project by retaining pieces so that the child must request materials repeatedly, piece by piece. For example, when working on a puzzle, pieces can be handed out as a child asks for them. Labeling of the piece or action can be encouraged or required. This strategy may be used effectively when children use paint, glue, paper, crayons, blocks, or other small items. Meals with foods such as cereal, raisins, or fruit or vegetable slices/pieces also present opportunities for employing this strategy.

Team members should be alert, however, to the introduction of too many disruptions. For example, having a child request each puzzle piece may interrupt the continuity of the activity and interfere with its meaningfulness for the child. The interventionist should balance providing opportunities to practice skills with the children's needs to become actively and genuinely involved in the activity.

Assistance

An effective strategy for teams to consider is assistance. To get materials or to perform some part of the activity, the child will need some form of assistance from an adult or peer. This strategy can be effective in the development of a range of skills in the adaptive, fine motor, gross motor, and communication areas. For example, placing materials in a clear container with a lid that the child cannot remove sets the stage for the child to seek assistance. Once the child has asked for help or presented the container to someone with an expectant look, the lid is loosened. The child can then practice grasping the lid and rotating his or her other wrist to complete the opening of the container and retrieve the material. Other examples include 1) wind-up toys that require an adult to start each time they cease their action; 2) tightening faucet knobs so that children must ask for assistance to turn them; 3) adding new dress-up clothes and accessories (purses, wallets) that have buttons, snaps, and laces that are too difficult for children to open.

Interruption or Delay

Interruption requires that a member of the team stop the child from continuing a chain of behaviors. For example, during a tooth-brushing routine, the caregiver interrupts the child when he or she starts to put toothpaste on the toothbrush. The caregiver holds the tube of toothpaste and asks, "What do you need?" The child will have to indicate what is needed to complete the behavior chain. This strategy has been effective with individuals with severe

disabilities (Carter & Gurnsell, 2001; Goetz, Gee, & Sailor, 1983; Roberts-Pennell & Sigafoos, 1999; Romer, Cullinan, & Schoenberg, 1994).

The delay strategy introduces a pause, or small delay, in an activity in order to prompt a response from the child. For example, an adult who is teaching a child to imitate a word may pause after saying the word and wait for the child to imitate. Delaying fits easily into many activities, and time delay has been shown to be effective in increasing the initiation of requests by children (e.g., Daugherty, Grisham-Brown, & Hemmeter, 2001; Schuster & Morse, 1998; Wolery, 1992; Wolery, Anthony, Caldwell, Snyder, & Morgante, 2002).

Two points should be emphasized when using these nondirective intervention strategies. First, as discussed previously, children's goals should guide teams. The strategies should be used only when they assist in helping children reach their designated goals. Employing these strategies without careful integration with children's overall intervention guide will likely yield unsatisfactory outcomes. Second, nondirective intervention strategies should be used in a thoughtful and sensitive manner. The overuse of any strategy will likely produce an undesired outcome. For example, if interruptions or delays are overused, then children may experience frustration that leads to the onset of an emotional outburst. Activity-based intervention encourages the use of these strategies with careful monitoring of their effectiveness.

Data Collection Procedures

IFSPs/IEPs require teams to note how and when data regarding children's performance on target skills will be collected, reviewed, and shared with caregivers. Intervention guides are designed to further specify how child progress data will be collected and used in making decisions. To begin, teams should decide *who* is going to collect data on different target skills. For example, will the parent, occupational therapist, preschool teacher, or early interventionist collect data or will more than one of them collect data? Next, teams should decide *where* to collect the data (i.e., in which settings or during which activities). For example, will data be collected at home or at school? If necessary, a team may want to specify the activity where they will collect data. For example, data may be collected in the classroom during snack, on the playground, or during circle time activities. Once the location is selected, teams should determine *when* to collect data based on the criteria portion of the child's IFSP/IEP goals and objectives/benchmarks. When to collect data includes how often the data will be collected (daily, weekly, monthly) and/or the specific days. Finally, teams should discuss *how* to monitor progress on the child's goal, objective/benchmark, and/or program step. Three general methods are available for teams to use when collecting data: written descriptions, permanent records, and counts or tallies. Methods for documenting child progress are discussed further in Chapter 5.

Decision Rules

Intervention guides can also be used to help teams make intervention decisions about child progress toward target skills. When children are not making expected progress, teams should consider changing 1) which goals are targeted; 2) which antecedents and/or feedback/consequences are selected; 3) which accommodations, modifications, or intervention strategies are provided; 4) how often learning opportunities are provided; and/or 5) where learning opportunities occur. Teams should indicate the rule or rules they think are appropriate for each child based on the data collected.

Making the process of developing intervention guides more efficient is important for most teams. For example, when children have similar target skills, the same or a slightly modified intervention guide can be used with multiple children. Even if minor to moderate variations are required for children, the team may be able to use the essence of an intervention guide for several children. For example, the goal may remain the same for two children, but the consequences or evaluation procedures for each child may be different.

Intervention guides are important to the successful implementation of an activity-based approach as they provide the structure that assists teams in planning the intervention necessary to promote children's progress toward target goals. Once intervention guides are completed for each priority, the team is ready to develop embedding schedules for addressing target goals during a variety of daily activities.

EMBEDDING SCHEDULES

Using children's routine and daily activities for intervention is generally more effective than creating a set of specific teaching sessions. Embedding schedules can be used to help ensure children's daily activities are used to address target skills. Embedding schedules are the second part of the organizational structure of an activity-based approach. Teams need to consider the following when creating embedding schedules to address target skills. First, consider whether the schedule is for one child (e.g., receiving home-based services or itinerant services in a community-based program or child care center) or for a group of children (i.e., receiving services within the same playgroup or center-based program). Second, consider how the schedule will be designed (e.g., by activity, by routine, by state standard, by personnel). Third, consider the type of information that will be placed within the intersect boxes of the schedule (e.g., possible teacher behaviors, desired child responses, data related to child performance).

Regardless of the environment for which the schedule is created (home, school, community), the number of children, or the information that will be shared in the intersect boxes, embedding schedules should contain basic information regarding the child or children's names, team members responsible for embedding learning opportunities, and the dates the schedule will be used. Once the basic information has been noted, the team creates the schedule itself, which is a grid or series of rows and columns that can be used and reused as children's target goals and intervention strategies change. Traditionally, embedding schedules are created with the child or children's goals listed across the top of the schedule and the sequence of daily activities listed down the left hand column. As with intervention guides, blank reproducible embedding schedules are contained in the book appendix following Chapter 10.

After the grid is created, teams determine what information to place in the intersect boxes. Teams may pull information from the intervention guide (i.e., antecedents and consequences, examples of target behaviors) and place it in the intersect boxes. For example, if a child's target goal is to manipulate objects with both hands, the team would take the antecedents selected on the intervention guide to create learning opportunities (i.e., placing objects to be manipulated within the child's reach, prompting the child to manipulate objects, modeling how to manipulate objects) and/or feedback/ consequences designed to promote and enhance learning and place the information in the intersect boxes with different daily activities. When deciding which activity to use as the context for embedding learning opportunities, teams consider which activities provide authentic situations for the child to practice/perform target goals (e.g., arrival, snack, art, discovery table). Therefore, in this example, the antecedent "model how to manipulate objects" could occur at arrival as peers and adults model how to unzip coats and backpacks. Given the growing popularity and utility of embedding schedules to address children's target goals, a number of variations have emerged (e.g., Grisham-Brown, Pretti-Frontczak, Hemmeter, & Ridgley, 2002; Hemmeter & Grisham-Brown, 1997; Raver, 2003). Figures A4.3–A4.8 in the chapter appendix provide descriptions and examples of these variations.

The creation of embedding schedules should not preclude variations and spontaneity in the type and sequence of activities used for intervention. If, for example, children introduce a change, or an unplanned event occurs that can be used to foster the development of target goals and objectives, then team members should not be reluctant to deviate from the schedule. When developing and using embedding schedules, it is critical that all team members be familiar with children's target goals. Knowledge of target goals allows interventionists to follow children's leads and interests, even when these actions deviate from planned events, and ensures multiple opportunities for practice of target goals. Teams implementing activity-based intervention are encouraged to experiment with the embedding schedule forms provided. The examples contained in the chapter appendix and Chapter 5 should be viewed as catalysts for such discussions.

ACTIVITY PLANS

The third component to the organizational structure of the activity-based approach is the design and use of activity plans. Activity plans represent a formal mechanism for ensuring that antecedents and consequences related to target goals are embedded within daily activities in order to maximize learning experiences. Activity plans are generally created for planned activities (i.e., designed events that require adult planning, preparation, and guidance), though they can be created for child-directed and routine activities (e.g., snack, dressing, bathing). Examples of planned activities can include taking field trips, completing art or science projects, and participating in circle time events. Planned activities can be created for children when receiving home-based services but are generally created for children receiving services in community-based or center-based programs.

Activity plans benefit teams in at least two ways. First, a team that plans activities may discover opportunities to address children's target skills that were not obvious or apparent prior to the planning. Second, teams may enhance their cooperation, collaboration, and use of limited resources. The activity plans described here are composed of nine elements; however, not all activity plans require the completion of all nine elements: 1) activity name, 2) materials, 3) environmental arrangement, 4) sequence of steps, 5) embedded learning opportunities, 6) planned variations, 7) vocabulary, 8) peer interaction opportunities, and 9) caregiver involvement.

Activity Name

The name of the activity should be noted on each plan (e.g., blocks, dinosaur eggs, butterfly blot prints, puzzles, meals, pet store). Ideas for activities can be selected from curricula or curricular guides—such as the Assessment, Evaluation, and Programming System for Infants and Children (AEPS; Bricker, 2002); The Creative Curriculum for Infants and Toddlers (Dombro, Colker, & Trister Dodge, 1997); and More Mudpies to Magnets: Science for Young Children (Sherwood, Williams, & Rockwell, 1990)—or from the team's experiences.

Materials

An important consideration when planning activities is the selection of materials. Four criteria can assist teams in selecting materials:

1. Materials are relevant to daily activities

2. Materials are multidimensional

3. Materials are developmentally appropriate

4. Materials enhance learning opportunities and generalization of skills

Materials that are relevant to daily activities are accessible and part of the child's environment (e.g., when in the kitchen, use bowls, pots, and pans). They should acknowledge children's interests and life experiences. For children living near the ocean, using sand, seashells, rocks, beach grass, or driftwood sticks can provide practice with counting, categorizing objects, and printing names in the sand.

Multidimensional materials are ones that can be used in a variety of ways. Balls are an excellent example because they come in different sizes and textures and can be used to kick, roll, throw, bounce, or toss. Materials such as balls often spark a child's interest to use the material in both predictable and unpredictable ways. Popsicle sticks are another example of a multi-dimensional material because children can use Popsicle sticks as a tool, to make a picture frame, to count, to color, or to spread glue.

Teams should be aware of children's individual developmental abilities when selecting materials so children are able to interact with the materials successfully. Knowing the general developmental stages that children progress is important in selecting materials that will challenge and assist them at each stage. For example, knowing that children start with sensory exploration of materials and progress to functional and imaginary use of materials will help teams select materials that allow children to safely explore the materials/ objects with their senses (i.e., using their eyes, ears, mouth, hands, and nose). For example, 12- to 18-month-old babies will likely remove pieces of a simple three-piece puzzle and taste them or clap two of the pieces together before putting the pieces back in the puzzle. Returning the pieces may require adult modeling or direction. Older children may remove and replace the pieces in the puzzle and may advance to imaginary play with the puzzle pieces. They may remove the fire truck puzzle piece and pretend to drive it to a fire before returning it to the puzzle. Another child may take out an animal puzzle piece and make animal sounds, feed the animal, and pretend to brush its hair. A whole scenario of taking care of the animal may occur before the child inserts the piece back into the puzzle. Finally, materials should be chosen that increase learning opportunities and facilitate generalization. The use of materials that are incorporated into a variety of activities, situations, and settings offers slightly different learning experiences with the use of the same or similar skills.

Environmental Arrangement

Arranging the environment for an activity is important for several reasons. First, some activities may require the team to assemble or purchase materials ahead of time. For example, a team may want to collect large appliance-size boxes for children to reenact one of their favorite stories. The team will need to find the boxes and alter the room to accommodate the boxes. Second, some activities may require extensive shifts in the physical environment (e.g., arranging an obstacle course, changing a dramatic play area from house-keeping to a winter sports shop). Third, appropriate amounts of materials and sufficient space should be available to accommodate children during specific activities. Teams must decide how many children can reasonably and safely play in each activity area. Teams must also ensure children's equipment (e.g., wheelchairs, walkers, orthopedic chairs, communication devices) can be accommodated easily in the area and is available for children who rely on the equipment for participation. Finally, how the environment is arranged should keep transitions and wait time for children to a minimum.

Sequence of Steps

Most activities follow a sequence of steps and contain events associated with a beginning (e.g., getting materials, moving to a particular location, describing what to do), middle (e.g., manipulating of objects, accomplishing a task, participating in a project), and end (e.g., cleaning up materials, reviewing what was accomplished, transitioning to another area or event). Teams need to understand how to maximize and use each part of an activity to create learning opportunities that address children's target skills.

The beginning of an activity can create numerous opportunities to address children's target skills. For example, having children get needed materials creates opportunities for children to practice such skills as 1) following multiple-step directions, 2) finding objects in usual locations, 3) walking across different surfaces, 4) problem solving, and 5) demonstrating an understanding of spatial relations such as *behind* and *next to*. Once materials have been obtained, discussing directions associated with the activity and moving to the location where the activity will be conducted can create additional learning opportunities.

The middle portion of an activity often provides the most obvious and varied learning opportunities for target skills. This portion of an activity reviews the primary events expected to occur and initiated by the children leading to the completion of the activity. Thinking through the actual steps of an activity should help teams ensure a match among children's interests, abilities, and needs.

The ending of an activity, like the beginning and middle, can provide numerous learning opportunities to practice different skills. Well-planned clean-up procedures and a recall or summarization of the activity can provide practice on skills from different developmental areas (e.g., fine motor, gross motor, social, cognitive). Recalling or summarizing the activity involves a discussion between children and adults about what happened or what was learned during the activity.

Embedded Learning Opportunities

As stated in Chapter 2, the purpose of activity-based intervention is to promote the acquisition and generalization of functional and developmentally appropriate skills in young children. To meet this purpose, the daily transactions that occur between young children and their physical and social environment are used to offer multiple and varied learning opportunities. Embedding refers to a process of addressing children's target skills during daily activities in a manner that expands, modifies, or is integral to the activity in a meaningful way. Activity plans help to ensure that teams consider all the skills that can be addressed during a given activity and help to ensure sufficient learning opportunities are created when they design activities.

The Embedded Learning Opportunities section of the activity plan allows teams to highlight goals targeted for individual children as well as broader outcomes targeted for all children by conducting the activity. Individual goals can be taken directly from children's IFSPs/IEPs or intervention guides, and broader outcomes can be taken from agency (e.g., Head Start Outcomes Framework) or state standards.

After reviewing the materials, environmental arrangement, and sequence of events, teams should be able to note specific and general goals/outcomes that will be addressed by children's participation within the activity. For example, in an activity that involves several children singing familiar songs and playing musical instruments, teams can address skills from across the curriculum, target individual children's goals, and ensure that multiple children participate differently within the same activity. In this example, some children may participate by watching and listening while others participate by singing, asking questions verbally or by using sign language, dancing, or playing a musical instrument. It is critical, particularly in center-based programs, that children with a wide variety of skills and abilities are able to participate fully in classroom activities. In addition, it is important to examine families' daily routines (e.g., bathing, dressing) to ensure learning opportunities are embedded throughout.

Planned Variations

Activities can easily be reused and enhanced by variations to them. Variations seek to build on the basic structure of an activity by introducing one or more changes that can be used if children display little interest in the original planned activity or to expand the activity in a meaningful way. Many variables affect children's interest, and any well-planned or favorite activity may become unappealing on a particular day. Variations also allow for enhancing the number and type of opportunities available to embed learning opportunities related to individual goals or broader curricular outcomes. For example, if a teacher plans an obstacle course and the children do not show interest in the activity, the teacher can try a planned variation of a musical parade which would allow for similar learning opportunities to be embedded (e.g., both activities address mobility, balance, coordination, following directions, participation with others, opportunities to inform/request, opportunities to express ideas, anticipation).

Vocabulary

For most teams, the use of developmentally appropriate language with children is common practice. The challenge is to keep in mind children's specific vocabulary goals and objectives/benchmarks. The vocabulary included in activities should serve two purposes. First, the items should represent a range of words/signs used to convey thoughts, wants, needs, and descriptions of objects and events. Second, the selected items should be based on children's assessment information and include familiar and new words/signs to build children's vocabulary. A speech-language pathologist can assist in selecting vocabulary items that target particular sounds that children need practice producing. Depending on the words/signs selected for the activity, teams may need to review their materials list. Perhaps a particular material must be included in an activity to ensure that the interventionist targets identified words, signs, or sounds. Commercially available curricula often contain associated materials lists or word lists that teams can use when developing activity plans, for example, AEPS (Bricker, 2002), The Complete Resource Book: An Early Childhood Curriculum with over 2000 Activities and Ideas (Schiller & Hastings, 1998), The Creative Curriculum for Preschool (Trister Dodge et al., 2002), and Learning Center: Open-Ended Activities (Wilmes & Wilmes, 1991).

Peer Interaction Opportunities

Creating and maintaining successful (i.e., positive and constructive) interactions between children with different developmental levels, skills, and interests requires thoughtful planning and adult guidance (Bricker, 1995; Odom & Brown, 1993; Turnbull & Turbiville, 1995). When children's social skills are delayed in their development, they are likely to 1) not initiate interactions, 2) not maintain the interaction, and/or 3) not make attempts that lead to unsuccessful interactions and reactions from their peers. Children need adults to assist in the development of their peer interaction skills. Planning opportunities for children to practice social skills in activities helps ensure that children will learn critical social skills.

Joseph and Strain (2003) reviewed several curricula for promoting children's skills (e.g., Incredible Years Child Training Program—Dina Dinosaur

Social Skills and Problem Solving Curriculum [Webster-Stratton, 1990], First Step to Success [Walker, Kavanaugh, Stiller, Golly, Severson, & Feil, 1997]) that teams may find helpful as they specifically address children's social skill needs during daily activities. Examples of peer interaction opportunities that may be noted on an activity plan include having peers serve as positive models of language and social behavior, encouraging children to observe and comment on one another's actions/work, and assisting children to share and exchange objects used in play.

Caregiver Involvement

Caregivers are vital members of the team; therefore, it is important to involve them in activity planning, implementation, and evaluation. Suggestions and involvement from parents/caregivers enable teams to plan activities with an eye toward family priorities and concerns while utilizing families' strengths and resources. Seeking parent involvement will likely result in planning activities that are meaningful to children while broadening opportunities for family and professional team members to work together.

How to obtain family involvement and participation can present challenges. Several strategies, however, exist including

1. Asking the families to share information regarding their daily routine and their child's interests (e.g., caregivers complete AEPS Family Report)

2. Sharing information regarding their child's individual needs

3. Sending home information about activities their children are participating in at school

4. Providing written or verbal information about how families can incorporate or extend activities into the home routine or following a home visit

5. Inviting families to the classroom to share their skills and interests with children during the activity

6. Asking families for assistance with contributing materials or other resources that enable a range of activities to be presented to their children

7. Asking families to assist with data collection efforts to determine the success of the planned activities in promoting and embedding learning opportunities

These strategies can enhance the team's efforts to involve families in all phases of intervention efforts.

SUMMARY

An activity-based approach requires an underlying structure to direct the work of professional team members and caregivers. The underlying structure described here is guided by the use of intervention guides, embedding schedules, and activity plans. Without using an underlying structure, teams would not have an organized way to use activity-based intervention and to address children's goals and objectives during daily activities and routines. Teams who use activity-based intervention should employ organized and systematic procedures to ensure optimal learning conditions are arranged for children. The chapter appendix provides additional examples/variations of intervention guides, embedding schedules, and activity plans.

REFERENCES

Bricker, D. (1995). The challenge of inclusion. *Journal of Early Intervention, 19*(3), 179–194.

Bricker, D. (Series Ed.). (2002). *Assessment, Evaluation, and Programming System for Infants and Children* (2nd ed., Vols. 1–4). Baltimore: Paul H. Brookes Publishing Co.

Carter, M., & Gurnsell, J. (2001). The behavior chain interrupted strategy: A review of research and discussion of future directions. *Journal of The Association for Persons with Severe Handicaps, 26*, 37–49.

Daugherty, S., Grisham-Brown, J., & Hemmeter, M.L. (2001). The effects of embedded skill instruction on the acquisition of target and non-target skills with preschoolers with developmental delays. *Topics in Early Childhood Special Education, 21*, 231–221.

Dombro, A., Colker, L., & Trister Dodge, D. (1997). *The Creative Curriculum for Infants and Toddlers.* Washington, DC: Teaching Strategies.

Goetz, L., Gee, K., & Sailor, W. (1983). Crossmodel transfer of stimulus control: Preparing students with severe multiple disabilities for audiological assessment. *Journal of The Association for Persons with Severe Handicaps, 8*(4), 3–13.

Grisham-Brown, J., Pretti-Frontczak, K., Hemmeter, M.L., & Ridgley, R. (2002). Teaching IEP goals and objectives in the context of classroom routines and activities. *Young Exceptional Children, 6*(1), 18–27.

Hemmeter, M., & Grisham-Brown, J. (1997). Developing children's language skills in inclusive early childhood classrooms. *Dimensions in Early Childhood, 25*(3), 6–13.

Joseph, G.E., & Strain, P.S. (2003). Comprehensive evidence-based social-emotional curricula for young children: An analysis of efficacious adoption potential. *Topics in Early Childhood Special Education, 23*(2), 62–73.

Odom, S.L., & Brown, W.H. (1993). Social interaction skills interventions for young children with disabilities in integrated settings. In C.A. Peck, S.L. Odom, & D.D. Bricker (Eds.), *Integrating young children with disabilities into community programs: Ecological perspectives on research and implementation* (pp. 39–64). Baltimore: Paul H. Brookes Publishing Co.

Pretti-Frontczak, K., & Bricker, D. (2000). Enhancing the quality of IEP goals and objectives. *Journal of Early Intervention, 23*(2), 92–105.

Raver, S. (2003). Keeping track: Using routine-based instruction and monitoring. *Young Exceptional Children, 6*(3), 12–20.

Roberts-Pennell, D., & Sigafoos, J. (1999). Teaching young children with develop-
    mental disabilities to request more play using the behaviour chain interruption
    strategy. *Journal of Applied Research in Intellectual Disabilities, 12,* 100–112.

Romer, L.T., Cullinan, T., & Schoenberg, B. (1994). General case training of request-
    ing: A demonstration and analysis. *Education and Training in Mental Retardation, 29,*
    57–68.

Schiller, P., & Hastings, K. (1998). *The Complete Resource Book: An Early Childhood Cur-
    riculum with over 2000 Activities and Ideas.* Beltsville, MD: Gryphon House.

Sherwood, E., Williams, R., & Rockwell, R. (1990). *More Mudpies to Magnets: Science for
    Young Children.* Beltsville, MD: Gryphon House.

Schuster, J., & Morse, T. (1998). Constant time delay with chained tasks: A review of
    the literature. *Education and Treatment of Children, 21*(1), 74–107.

Turnbull, A., & Turbiville, V. (1995). Why must inclusion be such a challenge? *Jour-
    nal of Early Intervention, 19*(3), 200–202.

Walker, H., Kavanaugh, K., Stiller, B., Golly, A., Severson, H.H., & Feil, E. (1997).
    First Step to Success. Longmont, CO: Sopris West.

Webster-Stratton, C. (1990). *Incredible Years Child Training Program—Dina Dinosaur
    Social Skills and Problem-Solving Curriculum.* Seattle, WA: Incredible Years.

Wilmes, D., & Wilmes, L. (1991). *Learning Center: Open-Ended Activities.* Elgin, IL:
    Building Blocks.

Wolery, M. (1992). Constant time delay with discrete responses: A review of effec-
    tiveness and demographic, procedural, and methodological parameters. *Research in
    Developmental Disabilities, 13*(3), 239–266.

Wolery, M., Anthony, L., Caldwell, N., Snyder, E., & Morgante, J. (2002). Embedding
    and distributing constant time delay in circle time and transitions. *Topics in Early
    Childhood Special Education, 22*(1), 14–26.

Examples of Organizational Structure Forms

This appendix contains a series of completed intervention guide, embedding schedule, and activity plan forms. These completed examples are designed to show readers multiple and varied ways in which teams incorporate the organizational structure as they apply an activity-based approach. Teams are encouraged to use the reproducible forms found in the volume appendix (following Chapter 10) to assist in the implementation of the approach and are invited to modify the forms discussed here. The three parts of the organizational structure are described in length in Chapter 4. The following are highlights regarding each form followed by brief explanations of various completed forms.

INTERVENTION GUIDES

The main purpose of an intervention guide is to bridge the gap between the goal development process and the intervention process. Because individualized family service plans (IFSPs)/individualized education programs (IEPs) are not treatment or intervention plans, it is important for teams to insert a step between the development of goals for individual children and intervention. In this appendix, we discuss variations of an intervention guide. One type of intervention guide can be used when IFSP outcomes are written as broad statements and the team needs to develop associated goals. Figure A4.1 provides an example of an intervention guide for Kennedy's IFSP outcome. The goal of walking independently was targeted, and individualized interventions, ongoing monitoring procedures, and decision rules were developed to ensure Kennedy made sufficient progress.

A second type of intervention guide can be used to show the alignment between a child's individual goals and state or agency standards. Increasingly, teams are being asked to document or show how intervention is not only resulting in progress for individual children but also is resulting in progress in the general curriculum. Figure A4.2 is an example of an intervention guide for Nicolas's IEP goal of using a variety of two and three word phrases. Specifically, how the target goal aligns or addresses standards for preschoolers in his state are noted. Finally, as with Kennedy, the intervention guide prompts teams to consider individualized interventions, ongoing monitoring procedures, and decision rules.

Intervention Guide

1. Basic information

Child's name: _Kennedy Bennet_

Team members: _parents, Early Head Start teacher, early intervention specialist,_
and physical therapist

Date intervention initiated: _September 2003_   Date intervention completed: _September 2004_

2. Goal, objectives/benchmarks, program steps

Goal 1.0
   At home, at school, and in the community, Kennedy will walk independently for 15 feet across three different surfaces (e.g., grass, carpet, tile), each day
   for 1 week.

Objectives
   1.1 At home, at school, and in the community, Kennedy will walk with one
       hand support for 15 feet across two different surfaces (e.g., grass, carpet,
       tile), each day for 2 weeks.
   1.2 At home, school, and in the community, Kennedy will move around by
       holding onto furniture or other stationary objects. She will move her
       feet, taking at least two steps in any direction, three times a day for 1
       week.

Program step
   1.3.1 At home, school, and in the community, Kennedy will pull herself up
       from a squatting position to a standing position two times a day for 2
       weeks.

3. State standard(s) or IFSP outcome(s)

Individualized family service plan outcome: We want Kennedy to walk by
herself so we don't have to carry her and so she can get different toys.

Figure A4.1.   Completed intervention guide for Kennedy.

4. Multiple and varied learning opportunities, functional and generative goals, timely and integral feedback or consequences

Antecedents designed to provide learning opportunities	List of possible child responses: targeted (+) and nontargeted (–)	Feedback or consequences
1.3.1. Physical assistance by placing hands on her trunk	Pulls to a stand (+) Remains sitting (–)	Praise and smiles from adult (+) Wait a few seconds and then encourage Kennedy to try again (–)
1.2 Place interesting objects out of reach	Holds onto furniture or stationary objects and takes two or more steps in the direction of the object (+) Points to desired object (–) Crawls toward object (–)	Gets object or toy (+) Prompt/encourage Kennedy to walk to get the toy (–)
1.1 Provide verbal cue (e.g., "Let's go see Dad" or "Let's go outside") and one-hand assistance	Takes steps holding an adult's or peer's hand for support (+) Uses two hands for support (–) Stays where she is and continues playing (–)	Encouragement to take additional steps (+) Praise from Dad (+) Playing outside (+) Takes additional steps, and adult tries to remove hand for support (–) Encourage Kennedy to walk again later (–)

5. Accommodations, modifications, and intervention strategies

Keep pathways clear of barriers.

Show Kennedy which furniture or stationary objects she can use for support.

Integrate therapeutic exercise techniques into daily activities to improve Kennedy's joint range of motion (including continuous passive motion), increase her strength and endurance (isotonic and isometric), and improve her balance and coordination.

continued

Figure A4.1.   *(continued)*

6. Data collection procedures

Who (person responsible for collecting the data)	Where (which activities or locations)	When (how often or on which days)	How (which methods)
Early Head Start teacher	During classroom transactions (e.g., from outside to inside, from carpet area to tile in snack area)	Daily (Monday through Friday)	Probe
Physical therapist	During classroom transitions	Weekly (Mondays and Wednesdays)	Probe
Early intervention specialist and parents	Home and Grandma's house	Weekly home visit and weekends	Probe

7. Decision rules

If adequate progress does not occur in _____1–2 weeks_____ (specify time frame for when the team will review the data), then the team will (check all that apply):

_____ change which goals are targeted

_____ change selected antecedents or feedback/consequences

__X__ change accommodations, modifications, or intervention strategies

_____ change how often learning opportunities are provided

_____ change where learning opportunities occur

_____ other (describe) _____

_____

Intervention Guide

1. Basic information

Child's name: _Nicolas Macy_

Team members: _Early childhood special education teacher, speech-language_

pathologist, and parents

Date intervention initiated: _September 2003_   Date intervention completed: _September 2004_

2. Goal, objectives/benchmarks, program steps

Goal 1.0
> Using a variety of two and three words, Nicolas will **request** objects, people, or materials three times a day, **inform** others three times a day, and **greet** others two times a day, for 2 weeks.

Objectives
> 1.1 Using a variety of two and three words, Nicolas will **request** objects, people, or materials from others (adults or peers) three times a day for 2 weeks.
>
> 1.2 Using a variety of two and three words, Nicolas will **inform** others (adults or peers) about daily activities three times a day for 2 weeks.
>
> 1.3 Using a variety of two and three words, Nicolas will **greet** others (adults or peers) two times a day for 2 weeks.

3. State standard(s) or IFSP outcome(s)

Link to English Language Arts Standards
> Speaks clearly and understandably to express ideas, feelings, and needs. Retells information from informational text.

Link to Math Standards
> Identifies, names, creates, and describes common two-dimensional shapes in the environment and play situations (e.g., circles, triangles, rectangles, squares).
>
> Demonstrates and begins to use the language of the relative position of objects in the environment and play situations (e.g., up, down, over, under, top, bottom, inside, outside, in front, behind, between, next to, right side up, upside down).

continued

Figure A4.2.   Completed intervention guide for Nicolas.

Figure A4.2. *(continued)*

Link to Science Standards

Identifies parts and wholes of familiar objects.

Identifies the intended purpose of familiar tools.

Uses his own words to offer explanations that may be correct or incorrect.

Link to Social Studies Standards

Labels days by function (e.g., school day, stay home day, swim day, field trip day).

Uses time words such as next, before, soon, after, now, and later as related to the classroom daily schedule.

Shares personal family story.

Obtains things he wants (goods and services) in socially acceptable ways.

Approaches familiar adults for assistance when needed.

4. Multiple and varied learning opportunities, functional and generative goals, timely and integral feedback or consequences

Antecedents designed to provide learning opportunities	List of possible child responses: targeted (+) and nontargeted (–)	Feedback or consequences
1.1 Model request (e.g., "More juice please.")	Uses two or three word utterances to inform, greet, or make a request (+)	Comment on what he is doing (+) Other children respond to his greeting (+) Provide or fulfill request (+)
1.2 Ask Nicolas to tell about what he is doing or what he is playing	Uses a single word (–)	Model a two or three word utterance (–) Model saying good morning to other children (–)
1.3 Verbal prompt (e.g., "Tell Serina Good Morning.")		Wait and prompt Nicolas to make a request if he needs or wants something (–)

5. Accommodations, modifications, and intervention strategies

Include in favorite activities peers that can provide two to three word models

Use milieu language strategies including incidental teaching, mand-model, and time delay

Use nondirected strategies such as visible but unreachable and piece by piece

6. Data collection procedures

Who (person responsible for collecting the data)	Where (which activities or locations)	When (how often or on which days)	How (which methods)
Teacher	Snack, outside time, and free play	Mondays, Wednesdays, and Fridays	Probes
Speech-language pathologist	Circle time and small group time	Monthly	Language sample

7. Decision rules

If adequate progress does not occur in _____2 weeks_____ (specify time frame for when the team will review the data), then the team will (check all that apply):

_____ change which goals are targeted

__X__ change selected antecedents or feedback/consequences

_____ change accommodations, modifications, or intervention strategies

__X__ change how often learning opportunities are provided

_____ change where learning opportunities occur

_____ other (describe) _____

_____

EMBEDDING SCHEDULE

The main purpose of embedding schedules is to ensure multiple and varied learning opportunities are provided across daily activities. Embedding schedules allow team members to discover at a glance what they are teaching, how they are teaching, and where they are teaching. Embedding schedules are typically created following the development of the intervention guide. The information placed on an embedding schedule often includes the appropriate antecedents and feedback/consequences derived when developing the intervention guides.

Given the growing popularity of embedding schedules, however, a number of variations to the layout described in Chapter 4 have been created. In all, Figures A4.3–A4.8 illustrate six variations of embedding schedules. Figure A4.3 provides an example of an embedding schedule for a child receiving home-based services and highlights when learning opportunities can be embedded across different daily routines. In other words, the Xs found within the intersect boxes are visual reminders of where learning opportunities can be embedded. Teams are encouraged to discuss with caregivers which routines are optimal for addressing children's target goals (Bricker, 2002). In this example, the family identified the routines of dressing, eating, playing, traveling, and bathing as times when learning opportunities could be provided related to Max's target goals of using two-word utterances and using objects as intended or designed.

Figure A4.4 provides a similar embedding schedule as found in Figure A4.3 but for a group of children. This embedding schedule notes when learning opportunities can be embedded across daily classroom activities for a group of children—Patrice, Serina, Tianna, and Alyson—attending a center-based program. The children have multiple target goals, and this variation of the embedding schedule allows a team to identify which daily classroom activities provide the best opportunities to address each of the target goals. This form also serves as a reminder to team members, allowing them to check the schedule before each activity to see which target goals to focus on for each child.

Three additional embedding schedule variations, Figures A4.5, A4.6, and A4.7, are used for summarizing similarities and differences among children in a group. Specifically, Figure A4.5 is an embedding schedule organizing Samantha's, De'Shawn's, and Paul's target goals around major areas or domains of development, including fine motor, cognitive, social-communication, and social. This type of schedule can help teams understand the range of skills children bring to different activities as well as where overlaps exist between children. Similarly, Figure A4.6 organizes Samantha's, De'Shawn's,

Embedding Schedule

Child's name: _Max_

Team members: _Parents, early intervention specialist, speech-language pathologist_

Dates schedule will be used: _Month of October_

Family routine	Target goal Max will use two word utterances to express possession and negation	Target goal Max will use objects as intended or designed
Dressing	X	
Eating		X
Playing	X	X
Traveling	X	
Bathing		X

Figure A4.3.   Completed embedding schedule for Max.

Group Embedding Schedule

Children's names: _Patrice, Serina, Tianna, and Alyson_

Team members: _Classroom staff, occupational therapist_

Dates schedule will be used: _School year with changes made as needed_

Children and target skills		Daily classroom activities					
	Arrival	Circle activities	Free play	Snack	Art and discovery	Outside time
Child's name: _Patrice_						
1. Greets peers	X			X		
2. Uses toilet	X			X		
3. Follows routine directions		X	X		X	X
4. Plays cooperatively			X			X
Child's name: _Serina_						
1. Manipulates a variety of objects	X		X		X	
2. Says a variety of one and two words			X	X	X	
3. Uses one object to represent another		X	X			X
Child's name: _Tianna_						
1. Expresses likes/dislikes		X		X		
2. Sorts like objects			X		X	
3. Uses spoon to feed self				X		
Child's name: _Alyson_						
1. Walks with walker	X				X	X
2. Uses words to request objects		X	X	X		

Figure A4.4. Completed group embedding schedule for Patrice, Serina, Tianna, and Alyson that shows learning opportunities during classroom activities.

Group Embedding Schedule

Children's names: _Samantha, De'Shawn, and Paul_

Team members: _Classroom staff, speech-language pathologist, parent volunteers_

Dates schedule will be used: _First quarter (September–November)_

Area of development	Target goals for _Samantha_	Target goals for _De'Shawn_	Target goals for _Paul_
Fine motor		Uses two hands to manipulate objects, toys, and materials	Releases hand-held object with each hand
Cognitive	Identifies letters		Categorizes like objects
Social-communication	Uses word phrases and sentences to inform, direct, and greet	Articulates the /l/ sound correctly when describing, informing, or greeting	
Social	Expresses likes/dislikes	Participates in large-group activities	Turns and looks toward person speaking

Figure A4.5.　Completed group embedding schedule for Samantha, De'Shawn, and Paul that shows target goals by areas of development.

Group Embedding Schedule

Children's names: __Samantha, De'Shawn, and Paul__

Team members: __Classroom staff, speech-language pathologist, parent volunteers__

Dates schedule will be used: __First quarter (September–November)__

Content area	Target goals for __Samantha__ Uses word phrases and sentences to inform, direct, and greet	Target goals for __De'Shawn__ Uses two hands to manipulate objects, toys, and materials	Target goals for __Paul__ Releases hand-held object with each hand
Literacy	Understands the meaning of new words from the context of conversation, the use of pictures that accompany text, or the use of concrete objects		
Math		Writes numerical representations (e.g., scribbles, reversals) or numerals in meaningful context	
Science	Develops the science skills of wondering, questioning, investigating, and communicating, to enable her to begin to develop a sense of the world	Learns the characteristics of objects, tools, and materials, and how they move	Learns the characteristics of objects, tools, and materials and how they move

Figure A4.6. Completed group embedding schedule for Samantha, De'Shawn, and Paul that shows how target goals link to content areas.

and Paul's target goals, showing the link or alignment between their IEP goals and content areas. In particular, state standards/indicators are noted in the intersecting boxes to illustrate how addressing a child's individual goals simultaneously allows the child to have access to and make progress in the general curriculum. For example, Samatha's goal of using word phrases and sentences to inform, direct, and greet aligns itself with a state indicator of understanding the meaning of new words from the context of conversation. Figure A4.7 illustrates how the individual goals of multiple children (i.e., Samantha and De'Shawn) can be addressed (i.e., embedded) across the different centers within the classroom (e.g., housekeeping, book corner, art and discovery).

Figure A4.8 contains a final variation of an embedding schedule for Samantha, De'Shawn, and Paul. This embedding schedule serves the dual role of reminding team members of children's target goals and allowing them to monitor children's progress as they interact during a variety of daily activities. In this example, the classroom teacher, speech-language pathologist, and parent volunteer use the embedding schedule to organize which target goals they will monitor and how data will be collected. Additional variations and procedures for creating embedding schedules (also called *activity schedules* or *activity matrixes*) are found throughout the literature (e.g., Grisham-Brown, Pretti-Frontczak, Hemmeter, & Ridgley, 2002; Hemmeter & Grisham-Brown, 1997; Raver, 2003).

ACTIVITY PLANS

The main purpose of activity plans is to create additional learning opportunities during planned activities. Many times teams find that they are able to generate ideas for activities but have difficulty addressing children's target goals during the activities. Using activity plans helps teams to create "reusable" activities that are fun and interesting to children but also provide multiple learning opportunities related to target goals and/or broader curricular outcomes. Activity plans can be created for individual children or for groups of children. Teams providing home-based services where a single child is the focus of intervention efforts should review the floor play/blanket time activity plan in Figure A4.9.

Activity plans are beneficial not only to home-based providers to give their visits focus and purpose but also to caregivers to assist them in providing intervention during their daily routines. Figure A4.10 is an activity plan for children receiving center-based services. When groups of children are served, teams need to consider how the individual needs of children will be accommodated within the same activity. How will children be expected to

Group Embedding Schedule

Children's names: _Samantha and De'Shawn_

Team members: _Speech-language pathologist and occupational therapist_

Dates schedule will be used: _Mondays and Thursdays_

Classroom centers	Target goals for _Samantha_ _Uses word phrases and sentences to inform, direct, and greet_	Target goals for _De'Shawn_ _Uses two hands to manipulate objects, toys, and materials_
Housekeeping	_Samantha can inform others (adults or peers) about her play in the housekeeping area or greet peers as they enter the center._	_De'Shawn can hold pot with one hand and stir with the other or button or zip clothing on self or baby dolls._
Book corner	_Samantha can inform others (adults or peers) about what she is reading and what characters in the book are doing or saying._	_De'Shawn can practice holding books/magazines with one hand and turning the pages with the other hand._
Art and discovery	_Samantha can direct the teacher to look at artwork or to help obtain desired objects._	_De'Shawn can paint at the easel and hold the paint in one hand while using the paintbrush with the other. De'Shawn can pour different substances at the discovery table from one container to another._

Figure A4.7. Completed group embedding schedule for Samantha and De'Shawn that shows how target goals can be addressed at various classroom centers.

Group Embedding Schedule

Children's names: *Samantha, De'Shawn, and Paul*

Team members: *Classroom teacher, speech-language pathologist, parent volunteers*

Dates schedule will be used: *First quarter (September–November)*

Adult responsible for monitoring	Target goal *Uses word phrases and sentences to inform, direct, and greet*	Target goals *Uses two hands to manipulate objects, toys, and materials or Releases hand-held object with each hand*
Classroom teacher	**For Samantha** Record examples of informing. _____ _____ _____ Record examples of directing. _____ _____ _____ Record examples of greeting. _____ _____ _____	**For De'Shawn** List/circle the toys, materials, or objects he manipulated with both hands. books blocks cars zipper spoon and bowl strings small figures buttons playdough Other: _____ _____ **For Paul** List the objects/toys/materials he released with each hand. _____ _____
Speech-language pathologist	**For De'Shawn** How many utterances were intelligible? none some most all **For Paul** Record a sample of utterances during the group activity. _____ _____ _____	
Parent volunteer		**For De'Shawn** Circle the toys, materials, or objects manipulated. books cups playdough blocks writing implements zippers

Figure A4.8. Completed group embedding schedule for Samantha, De'Shawn, and Paul that allows the team to monitor children's progress on target goals.

Activity Plan

1. Activity name

Floor time/Blanket play

2. Materials

Large blanket and an open space (indoors)

Containers of toys that make sounds and light up when activated

Small blanket

Light snack (e.g., Cheerios, crackers) and drink in a sippy cup

3. Environmental arrangement

Place large blanket in an open space and place toys in different locations on the blanket. Place the snacks and the small blanket within your reach, but not where the child can reach.

4. Sequence of steps

Beginning

When the child is alert and engaged with you, have the child select additional toys he or she is interested in playing with, and carry the toy to the blanket while maintaining joint attention with the child. Encourage the child to crawl/walk over to the large blanket by calling the child's name and/or activating one of the toys.

Middle

The child moves around the blanket independently or at your request to activate and manipulate different toys. Hide different toys under the small blanket, and encourage the child to find the hidden toy. You can also sing familiar songs and rhymes such as "Row, Row, Your Boat"; "Head, Shoulder, Knees, and Toes"; and "Pat-a-Cake." Offer the child something to eat or drink as a break from playing with the toys. During the activity, see if the child is hungry or thirsty or respond to his or her initiations for food/drink.

Figure A4.9.　Activity plan for Floor time/Blanket play activity.

End

Give a reminder to the child that it is almost time to clean up and begin placing one toy at a time into a large container. You can ask the child to hand you toys to put away and/or to say "Bye, Bye" to the toys as they go into the container. Encourage the child to crawl/walk away from the blanket so it can be folded.

5. Embedded learning opportunities

Learns/practices fine motor skills
  Transfers object from one hand to the other
  Grasps pea-size object with either hand using fingers in a raking and/or scratching movement
  Releases hand-held object onto and/or into a larger target with either hand
  Turns object over using wrist and arm rotation with each hand
  Uses either hand to activate objects
Learns/practices gross motor skills
  Creeps forward using alternating arm and leg movements
  Assumes balanced sitting position
Learns/practices adaptive skills
  Bites and chews soft and crisp foods
  Drinks from cup and/or glass held by adult
Learns/practices cognitive skills
  Visually follows object and/or person to point of disappearance
  Locates object in latter of two successive hiding places
  Maintains search for object that is not in its usual location
  Correctly activates mechanical toy
  Reproduces part of interactive game and/or action in order to continue game and/or action
  Imitates motor action that is commonly used
  Imitates words that are frequently used
  Retains one object when second object is obtained
  Moves barrier or goes around barrier to obtain object
  Uses simple motor actions on different objects
  Says nursery rhymes along with familiar adult
Learns/practices social-communication skills
  Follows person's gaze to establish joint attention

continued

Figure A4.9. *(continued)*

Responds with a vocalization and gesture to simple questions

Uses consistent consonant–vowel combinations

Carries out one-step direction with contextual cues

Uses descriptive words

Learns/practices social skills

Responds appropriately to familiar adult's affective tone

Initiates simple social game with familiar adult

Meets internal physical needs of hunger, thirst, and rest

6. Planned variations

1. Invite a playmate to join you and the child on the blanket to play with toys and sing songs.
2. Place blanket and toys outside.
3. Include books, and read stories.

7. Vocabulary

Colors (red, blue, green, yellow)

Attributes (big, fat, bright, flash)

Actions (pat, bang, pull)

Words to songs/rhymes (row, boat, bake, cake, man, head, shoulders, knees, toes)

Other single words (on, off, more, me)

8. Peer interaction opportunities

Playmate or sibling hides toys and encourages the child to find them.

Playmate or sibling shows child how to activate different toys.

Playmate or sibling exchanges toys and labels his or her actions (pat, bang, pull).

9. Caregiver involvement

Caregiver can facilitate the activity.

Caregiver can help generate list of vocabulary and/or skills that can be addressed during the activity.

Caregiver can collect data while other adult (e.g., early intervention specialist or therapist) facilitates activity.

Activity Plan

1. Activity name

Beanbag toss

2. Materials

1 large round plastic bucket with rope handles on each side
Approximately 10 hand-sized beanbags (e.g., different colors and/or textures)
1 large tambourine
Duct tape
Wipe-off board and markers
Pictures of materials that are part of the game (i.e., bucket, beanbags)

3. Environmental arrangement

Select a large carpeted area for a group of 6–10 children—children sit in a circle around the bucket.
Cover or close the cabinets displaying or storing toys/materials to eliminate distractions.
Prepare the round bucket with tambourine taped inside.
Prepare wipe-off board with children's names and columns titled "in" and "next to."

4. Sequence of steps

Beginning

Begin activity by asking the children if they want to play a beanbag toss game. Then, ask the children to find a friend and locate the item that matches the labeled picture given to them. For example, give one pair a picture of the bucket to get from the closet. Give another pair a picture of the plastic bags with the beanbags in them. When the children return, place the bucket in the middle of the group and ask the children to pass out the beanbags. The children can specify the color of the one they want.

Middle

Children take turns tossing their beanbag into the bucket. You or a child record on the board if the beanbag was tossed "in" or "next to" the bucket. If a child's beanbag lands "next to" the bucket, adults/peers can encourage the child to try again by chanting, "It's okay, it's all right, try again, and it just might." Children continue playing until they have tossed their beanbags into the bucket three times.

continued

Figure A4.10.   Activity plan for Beanbag toss activity.

Figure A4.10.   *(continued)*

End

Give a warning to those children still participating a few minutes before it is time to stop playing and help put materials away. To close the activity, review the number of tosses by each child on the board, and invite the children to count the number they got "in" or "next to" the bucket. After the review, the children help put materials away and move to the next activity.

5. Embedded learning opportunities

Learns/practices fine motor skills
   Passes out beanbags to peers
Learns/practices cognitive skills
   Counts beanbags
   Counts peers who are playing the game
   Counts the number of times beanbags land "in" and "next to" the bucket
   Sorts like beanbags when cleaning up
   Demonstrates one-to-one correspondence by handing out beanbags
   Recognizes name by making tally mark on board after tossing beanbag
   Demonstrates understanding of spatial concepts (e.g., in and next to)
   Explains directions to peers
Learns/practices gross motor skills
   Tosses beanbags into bucket
   Walks around the room getting materials
Learns/practices social-communication skills
   Says encouraging phrases after peer tosses beanbag
   Greets and invites new peers to join in and play the game
   Requests beanbags
   Uses name of peer to tell peer it is his or her turn
   Asks questions about the game (use listener/speaker roles)

6. Planned variations

1.   *Change name to "Animal Tricks" and have the children use small stuffed animals and try to toss them into the bucket doing one or more of the following: a) closing eyes or being blindfolded, b) standing with their back to the bucket, and/or c) dropping the animal with elbows or other body part.*

2. Place a cardboard face of an animal and its mouth over the top of the bucket and call the game, "Feed the Bear." Children toss plastic fruit or vegetables into the bear's mouth.

3. Hang a Hula-Hoop from a tree and make it a standing beanbag toss that can be played outdoors.

4. Add a tape measure and colored tape so an adult can record the distance a child throws the beanbag through the Hula-Hoop. The adults or children can mark the distance with the tape, and the children can write their names on the tape.

5. Provide cutout plastic milk jugs for children to use to catch the beanbags. Children play this catching game in pairs.

7. Vocabulary

Colors (e.g., red, orange, blue, yellow, green)

Animal names (e.g., frog beanbags)

Spatial words (e.g., in, out, next to, beside, in front of)

Names of other children

Numbers (1–10)

Encouraging phrase ("It's okay, it's all right, try again, and it just might.")

Pronouns (e.g., I, he, she, we, me)

8. Peer interaction opportunities

Pair children to retrieve objects/materials to set up for the game (e.g., bucket, beanbags).

Child passes out beanbags to other children or asks them their preferences.

Children return materials in pairs when game is over.

Children say encouraging phrase to peers during the game.

9. Caregiver involvement

Caregiver contributes fabric for beanbags and/or offers to sew them.

Caregiver volunteers to lead the activity with the children.

Caregiver offers to make cardboard animal faces for variation.

Caregiver suggests new variations.

Caregiver collects data on children's utterances, counting skills, and interactions with peers.

behave and perform differently? How will they be allowed to participate in different ways? The activity plan for the beanbag toss illustrates the wide range of skills that can be addressed in a single activity.

The activity plan examples demonstrate how multiple and varied learning opportunities can be embedded across all steps of an activity. Furthermore, the activity plans note how teams can consistently address children's communication skills, ensure peer interactions, and provide a continuum of options for caregiver involvement.

REFERENCES

Bricker, D. (Series Ed.). (2002). *Assessment, Evaluation, and Programming System for Infants and Children* (2nd ed., Vols. 1–4). Baltimore: Paul H. Brookes Publishing Co.

Grisham-Brown, J., Pretti-Frontczak, K., Hemmeter, M.L., & Ridgley, R. (2002). Teaching IEP goals and objectives in the context of classroom routines and activities. *Young Exceptional Children, 6*(1), 18–27.

Hemmeter, M.L., & Grisham-Brown, J. (1997). Developing children's language skills in inclusive early childhood classrooms. *Dimensions of Early Childhood, 25*, 6–13.

Raver, S. (2003). Keeping track: Using routine-based instruction and monitoring. *Young Exceptional Children, 6*(3), 12–20.

5

Application of Activity-Based Intervention

T he successful application of activity-based intervention requires that interventionists and caregivers engage in the following practices: 1) conduct comprehensive and ongoing assessments; 2) create multiple and varied learning opportunities during child-directed, routine, and planned activities; 3) target functional and generative goals; and 4) systematically monitor children's progress. This chapter describes these practices, using three examples to illustrate the application of an activity-based approach across three broad service delivery models: home based, center based, and itinerant.

CONDUCT COMPREHENSIVE AND ONGOING ASSESSMENTS

As discussed in Chapter 3, administration of a curriculum-based measure is designed to assist teams in gathering comprehensive and ongoing information about young children. Results from curriculum-based measures such as the Assessment, Evaluation, and Programming System for Infants and Children, Second Edition (AEPS; Bricker, 2002), should be used to provide a detailed description of children's strengths, interests, and emerging skills. This summary is often referred to as a *present level of performance* and should serve as a guide for identifying needs as well as a baseline for comparing progress over time. Recommended practice suggests that written summaries of children's present levels of performance

1. Focus on strengths and emerging skills

2. Reveal patterns of behaviors that affect their access to and participation in daily activities

3. Use objective and jargon-free terms

4. Include multiple perspectives

5. Provide specific examples of children's behaviors across settings

One component of conducting comprehensive and ongoing assessments is gathering information about a family's resources, priorities, and concerns. The information provided by family members should be used in selecting goals and making intervention decisions. A number of methods exist for gathering information from families including interviews, observations, and surveys. Measures such as the AEPS Family Report (Bricker, 2002), Choosing Outcomes and Accommodations for Children (COACH; Giangreco, Cloninger, & Iverson, 1998), and the Developmental Observation Checklist System (DOCS; Hresko, Miguel, Sherbenou, & Burton, 1994) can be helpful in gathering and organizing information from the family.

Information gathered may include caregiver concerns or needs related to their child's development, insight regarding the parent–child interaction, historical events that continue to influence the family, or even a family's hopes and dreams regarding their child. Gaining information about a family's resources, priorities, and concerns is critical to developing appropriate services; however, the information can be sensitive and should be gathered respectfully and held in confidence. Furthermore, the professional members of teams need to ensure that they collect information from families for the purpose of improving services. It does not benefit a family to share their insights and concerns if the team is unable to address their concerns or unwilling to accept their observations and interpretations regarding their child.

CREATE MULTIPLE AND VARIED LEARNING OPPORTUNITIES

As noted in Chapter 4, a learning opportunity is created when an antecedent is presented or occurs that encourages the child to practice, perform, or attempt to produce a target skill. For example, if targeting the skill of signing MORE correctly, a variety of antecedents could be provided to elicit the target response, such as asking the child if he or she wants more, modeling how to sign MORE, withholding an object or placing an object out of the child's reach, or providing hand-over-hand assistance to make the sign MORE. In this example, a learning opportunity is created by the occurrence of any of the above-mentioned antecedents as long as the antecedents encourage/allow the child to practice, perform, or attempt to make the sign MORE.

Furthermore, a learning opportunity is only created when an antecedent is presented/occurs that has the potential of allowing the child to continue an action or maintain the child's inferred intent or interest within the activity or with materials that are present. If the antecedent modifies or extends the child's action or attention, it must not shift the child's behavior or focus away from his or her inferred intent or interest and should not require the child to shift attention away from that in which he or she is interested or engaged. Continuing with the example of a child learning to sign MORE, a learning opportunity would not have been created with the presentation of the antecedents listed previously if, for example, the child was not looking or attending when the adult modeled the sign, if the child was uninterested in the withheld object, or if the child did not require full assistance and withdrew from the interaction as a result.

Initially, selecting antecedents to create learning opportunities can appear to be a simple and straightforward process; however, selecting the appropriate or correct antecedent is quite complex. First, teams need to understand the array of existing antecedents. Although beyond the scope of this volume, a number of resources exist that define and describe various antecedents (e.g., Barnett, Bell, & Carey, 1999; McWilliam, 1996; Noonan & McCormick,

1993; Sandall & Schwartz, 2002). Second, teams need to select antecedents that will create a learning opportunity for the child to practice and use target goals and, therefore, must know each child's individual target goals. Third, teams need to deliver multiple and varied antecedents across activities when children are interested and able to take advantage of their interests and motivation.

In addition to selecting antecedents that will provide multiple and varied learning opportunities, teams need to be diligent in their selection of feedback or consequence provided to children. As with antecedents, a continuum of types of feedback or consequences exist (e.g., praise; attention; rewards such as stickers, gaining a desired toy, completing a puzzle, or getting to eat or drink). Feedback/consequences can include adult (e.g., teacher, caregiver, therapist) responses; peer/sibling responses; and/or environmental objects, events, pictures, signs, or words that follow a child's responses. The appropriateness of the feedback/consequence selected can only be determined by its effect on the child. To be effective, feedback/consequences should be timely and integral (i.e., directly related to or contingent on children's behaviors or associated with, connected to, or a logical outcome of the activity, action, or response). Timely feedback is necessary so the child can discern the relationship between the response and subsequent consequences. Integral feedback is necessary so children will learn that responses produce related and meaningful outcomes.

TARGET FUNCTIONAL AND GENERATIVE GOALS

Targeting functional and generative goals is critical to the application of an activity-based approach. Creating and embedding multiple learning opportunities related to target goals is at the heart of this approach. When functional and generative goals are targeted, interventionists and caregivers should have little difficulty addressing them across child-directed, routine, and planned activities. For example, the goals of manipulating objects, walking across different surfaces, taking care of physical needs, playing with objects/toys, expressing wants and needs, and interacting with familiar adults and peers can be addressed during family routines (e.g., meals, dressing, watching television, driving, bath time), in center-based program activities (e.g., center time, free play, outdoor time), and community activities (e.g., visiting grandparents, shopping, going to the park).

Conversely, finding multiple ways to address goals that are *not* functional and generative can force interventionists and caregivers to rely on highly structured and contrived situations. For example, the goals of stacking 1-inch cubes, walking on a balance beam, pushing numbers on a play phone, and labeling pictures on flashcards may limit interventionists and caregivers in terms of the number and types of activities in which they can effectively create and embed learning opportunities. That is, most daily activities do not involve balance beams, play telephones, or flashcards or readily lend themselves to stacking 1-inch cubes. Likewise, targeting a specific skill such as one particular game played with one particular person limits opportunities for the child to practice a more generative skill such as initiating social games with familiar adults. Teams are encouraged to select goals that will address children's needs and that are functional and generative; however, they also need to ensure that the number of goals targeted can be reasonably addressed and monitored.

SYSTEMATICALLY MONITOR CHILDREN'S PROGRESS

A variety of methods exist for systematically monitoring children's progress. No universal data collection system is appropriate for use with all children, all goals, or all programs. Teams will likely function more effectively if they adopt a decision-based model that guides how and when data are collected. Decision-based models may be useful because these models 1) emphasize the cyclic nature of the evaluation process, 2) begin and end with the purpose or reason for collecting data, and 3) require teams to collect ongoing data (i.e., daily or weekly child progress data) and impact data (i.e., quarterly or annual child progress data) (e.g., McAfee & Leong, 1997).

Teams will likely need to use a variety of methods to collect enough data to make accurate decisions. Gathering data on children's performance should inform teams about

1. What progress has been made toward target goals

2. Which antecedents and/or consequences produce change

3. What accommodations, modifications, or intervention strategies are used

4. How often learning opportunities are provided

5. Where learning opportunities occur

Gathering more global data on children's developmental progress and/or their progress in the general curriculum helps teams make program-level decisions and increases the link between intervention efforts and accountability requirements. While beyond the scope of this text, a number of resources exist for helping teams create data collection systems for collecting daily/weekly data, quarterly data, and annual data on children and/or, when appropriate, families or other program aspects. For example, Alberto and Troutman (2003) and McLean, Wolery, and Bailey (2004) provide detailed examples of how to collect ongoing data regarding children's performance on target goals as well as strategies for collecting impact data regarding children's overall developmental progress and progress in the general curriculum. In the following section, some particularly useful data collection methods are discussed.

Data Collection Methods

When implementing an activity-based approach, teams need to gather data related to children's performance on target goals as well as their overall developmental progress and progress in the general curriculum. Data regarding children's performance on target goals can be gathered using three methods: written descriptions (e.g., running records, anecdotal notes, jottings), permanent records (e.g., diagrams, writing samples, pictures), and counts and tallies (e.g., sampling procedures, rating scales, probes). Regardless of the method, teams should ensure the following:

- Data collection procedures are directly linked to the criterion written for a target skill (e.g., if the criterion states that the child will manipulate three different objects with both hands performing different movements, then information regarding the number and type of objects and how a child manipulates them should be collected).

- Data collection procedures are flexible and applicable across settings, events, and people.

- Data collection procedures yield valid and reliable data.

- Data collection responsibilities are shared by team members (e.g., direct service personnel, consultants, caregivers).

- Data collection procedures are compatible with available resources (e.g., time, skills, materials).

Data regarding children's overall developmental progress and their progress in the general curriculum is often gathered through quarterly administrations of curriculum-based measures. These data are useful for gauging the effects of intervention on individual children as well as groups of children. Information from quarterly evaluations, in particular, provides feedback about the child's developmental progress and helps clarify where intervention modifications or revisions may be necessary. In addition, beginning of the year and end of the year administrations of standardized norm-referenced or curriculum-based measures allow programs to evaluate general effects for groups of children and for providing accountability information.

The four practices described thus far in this chapter, 1) conducting comprehensive and ongoing assessment, 2) creating multiple and varied learning opportunities, 3) targeting functional and generative goals, and 4) monitoring children's progress, are thought to be necessary for the successful application of activity-based intervention. In the next section, these practices are operationalized in three examples that demonstrate the application of an activity-based approach across three service delivery models: home based, center based, and itinerant.

APPLYING THE ACTIVITY-BASED INTERVENTION APPROACH

This section illustrates the application of activity-based intervention. The first example describes a toddler who is receiving home-based services focused on enhancing his communication goals. The second example looks at a preschool-age child who is receiving center-based services designed to assist her in developing play skills, intelligible communication, and fine motor manipulation skills. The third example details the application of activity-based intervention in an itinerant service delivery model. In this example, the preschool-age child participates in a Head Start program and is visited weekly by an early childhood interventionist to address the target goal of fine motor object manipulation.

Jae Hyung: Home-Based Services

Jae Hyung is a 21-month-old boy eligible for EI services. Jae Hyung receives weekly home visits from an EI specialist and 30 minutes per week with a speech-language pathologist. Information related to his present level of performance was gathered through a comprehensive assessment conducted by his mother and father (Haejung and Gui-jin), EI specialist (Dara), and speech-language pathologist (Winifred). Assessment observations are based on daily interactions with Jae Hyung and guided by the AEPS (Bricker, 2002). Jae Hyung was observed during daily routines including meals, playtime, and bath time. Information was also gathered from the AEPS Family Report completed by Jae Hyung's mother. Finally, the team reviewed Jae Hyung's current individualized family service plan (IFSP). The following information is a summary of Jae Hyung's interests and abilities related to his participation in daily activities.

Assessment Summary

Jae Hyung wakes up from his afternoon nap, stands up in his crib, and cries until his mother or father comes to get him. When his mother or father enters the room, he holds up his arms indicating he wants to be picked up.

While his parents are changing his diaper, he uses vocalizations such as "i," "i," "i." Jae Hyung walks up and down stairs holding onto the side rails and places two feet on the same stair before he moves to the next.

While Jae Hyung plays with his toys, he uses his forefinger to turn on a music box. He can activate toys, such as See 'n Say, by pulling the crank on the side. Using both hands, he can connect large blocks such as Legos. Jae Hyung can stack blocks on top of one another and place them in a row. He plays with a push toy, which he can push while standing up and maneuver around barriers. He also sits on the toy, moving it by using his feet and steering around barriers. While playing, he vocalizes vowel sounds. He also vocalizes while pointing to a desired object and playing with his toys.

When he needs assistance with an object, he brings it to his mother or another adult. For example, he will bring a box of alphabet disks to his mother to open, and she will ask him what he wants. Jae Hyung points to the box lid to request it be opened. His mother signs the word OPEN, Jae Hyung repeats the sign, and his mother opens the box. Jae Hyung removes the disks and puts them back in the box one by one. When reading books, he is able to turn individual pages in board books and is beginning to correctly orient the book. When given a crayon, he inconsistently scribbles on paper using a three-finger grasp. When Jae Hyung wants to continue an activity, he frequently uses the sign for MORE.

Jae Hyung plays with his 5-year-old brother, Jae-sun, often with plastic and cloth balls. Jae Hyung throws the balls and walks around obstacles, toys, or pillows to retrieve them. He is able to throw the balls back to his brother, using a one-handed grasp on small balls and two-handed grasp on larger balls. When throwing smaller balls, he uses an overhand throw, and for the large balls, he uses an underhand throw. He is able to kick a ball to his brother. Jae Hyung's mother and brother report he can climb up and down inclines and play on a slide. He requires assistance climbing the ladder. His mother and speech-language pathologist report that Jae Hyung interacts with peers by playing near them and accepting toys from them.

His mother reports that he demonstrates an understanding of opposite pairs (i.e., up/down, open/closed, full/empty, big/little) by answering questions with gestures and following directions. For example, when asked, he will correctly point to a large or small ball. He will occasionally use the sign for UP to request his mother to pick him up and use the sign for DOWN to be placed on the floor.

When Jae Hyung eats, he uses a bent spoon to scoop and spear food. When he wants more to eat, he uses the sign MORE. He can drink from a sippy cup independently and a cup without a lid with adult assistance. He vocalizes while eating (e.g., "i," "i," "i" and "ah," "ah," "ah"). He appears to use these expressions to communicate that he likes the food. He also makes simi-

lar vocalizations to request getting down from his high chair. When Jae Hyung wants something to drink, he will go to the refrigerator or get his cup and use the signs for MILK or JUICE.

Jae Hyung's mother and speech-language pathologist report that he uses other vocalizations such as "da," "eh," "hi," and "ay." They report he uses the signs MORE, DONE, GO, STOP, and MOM. Jae Hyung waves bye-bye and says "Hi" as a greeting. He will look toward his mother when asked, "Where's Mommy?" and he will look toward his brother when asked, "Where is your brother?" He can locate items his mother requests such as a ball, book, or cards.

Before bath time, Jae Hyung removes his shoes, socks, and elastic waist-band pants. He is able to remove a pullover shirt, with large head openings. In the bathtub, he vocalizes and uses some gestures. He points to the faucet to indicate he wants the water off or on. His mother reports that Jae Hyung tries to imitate his brother's motor behavior. When he is done in the bath-tub, he signs DONE.

Target Goals

From the assessment information summarized in Jae Hyung's present level of performance, the team identifies a number of family outcomes, including using words or signs so family members and friends can understand what he wants or needs. The team then writes a measurable goal and associated objec-tives to guide them in meeting the stated family outcome. The team uses a revised version of the Goals and Objectives Rating Instrument (GORI; Notari-Syverson & Shuster, 1995) to ensure the goal and associated objectives are meaningful to and understood by all team members. Jae Hyung's target goal is to say or sign 30 single words, including 5 descriptive words, 5 action words,

2 pronouns, 15 object and/or event labels, and 3 proper names, over a 2-week period. The team then takes steps to ensure daily activities promote acquisition and use of this target skill.

Individualized Intervention

The three forms (i.e., intervention guides, embedding schedules, and activity plans) described in Chapter 4 are used to assist the team in creating and embedding multiple and varied learning opportunities. Jae Hyung's team reviews his present level of performance, identifies his needs, and considers how to individualize intervention. They create an intervention guide for each IFSP outcome by selecting a target goal and associated objectives/benchmarks, outlining specific antecedents and consequences, and determining needed accommodations and modifications and possible intervention strategies. Figure 5.1 contains an intervention guide for the target goal of "says or signs 30 single words."

Because Jae Hyung receives home-based services, the team discusses the family's daily routine activities, which are considered the primary context for embedding learning opportunities. Using the AEPS Family Report as a guide, the team collects information from the family regarding: 1) daily routine activities, 2) the time and frequency of each routine activity, 3) the sequence of events occurring in routines, 4) a description of Jae Hyung's participation in routines, and 5) whether the routine can be used to embed a learning opportunity. The team identifies wake-up, breakfast, playtime, lunch, and bath time as possible daily routines to embed learning opportunities. The EI specialist and speech-language pathologist create additional learning opportunities during their weekly visits. They then develop an embedding schedule that prompts adults about which antecedents to provide and when to embed learning opportunities across the selected daily routines. Figure 5.2 contains an embedding schedule for Jae Hyung. The team creates an embedding schedule that allows them to incorporate the antecedents from the intervention guide into prioritized family routines. Finally, the team develops several planned activities to be used by the EI specialist or the speech-language pathologist during their home visits and by the family as desired. Figure 5.3 contains an activity plan for a treasure hunt.

Data Collection

The team reviews the intervention guide to develop a data collection system to monitor Jae Hyung's progress on target goals. After reviewing the intervention guide, the team makes a number of data collection decisions:

- The parents will record in a notebook the number and type of words and signs Jae Hyung uses on a daily basis (i.e., during wake-up, breakfast, playtime, lunch, and bath time).

Intervention Guide

---

1. Basic information

Child's name: <u>Jae Hyung Heo</u>

Team members: <u>Haejung (Mom), Gui-jin (Dad), Dara (EI specialist),</u>

<u>Winifred (speech-language pathologist)</u>

Date intervention initiated: <u>September 2003</u> Date intervention completed: <u>August 2004</u>

---

2. Goal, objectives/benchmarks, program steps

Goal 1.0

   Jae Hyung will say or sign 30 single words including five descriptive words, five action words, two pronouns, 15 object and/or event labels, and three proper names over a 2-week period.

Objectives

   1.1.   Jae Hyung will say or sign five different descriptive words (e.g., big, little, hot, red) over a 2-week period.

   1.2.   Jae Hyung will say or sign five different action words (e.g., open, go, eat, sit) over a 2-week period.

   1.3.   Jae Hyung will say or sign two different pronouns (e.g., me, mine, it, my, I, you, this) over a 2-week period.

   1.4.   Jae Hyung will say or sign 15 different object and/or event labels (e.g., ball, cup, hat, bubbles) over a 2-week period.

   1.5.   Jae Hyung will say or sign three different proper names (e.g., Mom, Dad, Jae Hyung) over a 2-week period.

---

3. State standard(s) or IFSP outcome(s)

   IFSP outcome: We want Jae Hyung to use words or signs so family members and friends can understand what he wants or needs.

---

continued

Figure 5.1.   Completed intervention guide for Jae Hyung.

Figure 5.1.   *(continued)*

4. Multiple and varied learning opportunities, functional and generative goals, timely and integral feedback or consequences		
Antecedents designed to provide learning opportunities	List of possible child responses: targeted (+) and nontargeted (−)	Feedback or consequences
1.1 Ask questions about objects, people, and/or events that require a single descriptive word/ sign response (e.g., "Do you want to big block or little block?") Model single words/ signs to describe objects, people, and/or events (e.g., colors, shapes, sizes, quantity) Encourage Jae Hyung to describe objects, people, and events using a single word/ sign (e.g., "Jae Hyung, say blue.")	Jae Hyung says or signs descriptive words (e.g. big, little, hot, red) (+) Jae Hyung vocalizes vowel sounds (−) Jae Hyung points to objects, people, and/or events (−) Jae Hyung does not respond to questions, models, or encouragement (−)	Verbal confirmation or affirmation (+) Receive object (+) Continue activity (+) Imitate vocalization and model single word/ sign (−) Model single word/ sign (−) Wait several seconds and then ask question again, or model the word/sign again (−)
1.2 Provide objects/ toys or people that perform an action (e.g., balls bounce/ roll, lights flash, brother runs/goes, teddy bear sits) Model single action words/signs or label actions of objects, people, and/or events (e.g., open, go, sit, eat) Encourage Jae Hyung to say or sign an action word (e.g., "Jae Hyung, say/sign up.")	Jae Hyung says or signs action words (e.g. open, up, go, eat, run, kick sit) (+) Jae Hyung vocalizes vowel sounds (−) Jae Hyung points to or looks at objects and/or people, performing an action (−) Jae Hyung does not respond to models or encouragement (−)	Affirmation (+) Receive object (+) Continue activity (+) Imitate vocalization and model single word/ sign (−) Wait several seconds and then move the object/ toy closer, refer to the person performing an action (−) Encourage Jae Hyung to say or sign action word (−)

Antecedents designed to provide learning opportunities	List of possible child responses: targeted (+) and nontargeted (−)	Feedback or consequences
1.3. Ask questions about objects that require saying or signing a single pronoun as a response (e.g., "Whose book is this?") Say/sign single pronouns Encourage Jae Hyung to say/sign pronouns (e.g., "Jae Hyung, say/sign me.")	Jae Hyung says or signs pronouns (e.g., me, mine, it, my, I, you, this) (+) Jae Hyung vocalizes vowel sounds (−) Jae Hyung does not respond to questions, models, or encouragement (−)	Affirmation (+) Receive object (+) Continue activity (+) Imitate vocalization and model single word/ sign (−) Wait several seconds and then ask the question again, or model the word/sign again (−)
1.4 Ask questions that require Jae Hyung to label objects or events (e.g., "What do you have?") Say or sign object/ event labels Encourage Jae Hyung to say or sign object/event labels	Jae Hyung says or signs object/event label (+) Jae Hyung vocalizes vowel sounds (−) Jae Hyung looks at or points to object/event (−) Jae Hyung does not respond to questions, models, or encouragement (−)	Affirmation (+) Receive object (+) Continue activity/event (+) Imitate vocalization and model single word/ sign (−) Model single word/sign to label object or event he points to or looks at (−) Wait several seconds and then ask the question again, or model the word/sign again (−)
1.5 Ask questions about objects, people, and/or events that require saying or signing a proper name (e.g., "Who is playing with you?") Say/sign single proper names Encourage Jae Hyung to say/sign proper names (e.g., Mom, Dad, Jae Hyung, Jae-sun)	Jae Hyung says or signs proper names (e.g., Jae-sun, Mom, Dad, Jae Hyung) (+) Jae Hyung vocalizes vowel sounds (−) Jae Hyung looks at or points to person (−) Jae Hyung does not respond to questions, models, or encouragement (−)	Affirmation (+) Receive object (+) Continue activity (+) Imitate vocalization and model single word/ sign (−) Model single word/sign to label proper name of person he points to or looks at (−) Wait several seconds and then ask the question again, or model the word/sign again (−)

continued

Figure 5.1.   *(continued)*

5. Accommodations, modifications, and intervention strategies

Ensure joint attention and then pair single words/signs with verbalizations.

Wait at least 5 seconds for Jae Hyung to respond before restating or prompting again.

Use milieu language strategies including incidental teaching, mand-model, and time delay.

Use nondirected strategies such as visible but unreachable and piece by piece.

6. Data collection procedures

Who (person responsible for collecting the data)	Where (which activities or locations)	When (how often or on which days)	How (which methods)
Parents	Home (wake-up, breakfast, playtime, lunch, bath time)	Daily (3 activities a day)	Record number and type of words/signs Jae Hyung uses
Dara	Home visit during planned activity	Weekly	Record number and type of words/signs Jae Hyung uses
Winifred	Home during 30 minutes of speech therapy	Monthly	Collect language sample using audiotape

7. Decision rules

If adequate progress does not occur in _____1 month_____ (specify time frame for when the team will review the data), then the team will (check all that apply):

_____ change which goals are targeted

_____ change selected antecedents or feedback/consequences

__X__ change accommodations, modifications, or intervention strategies

_____ change how often learning opportunities are provided

__X__ change where learning opportunities occur

_____ other (describe) _____

_____

Embedding Schedule

Child's name: Jae Hyung Heo   Team members: Mom, Dad, Dara, and Winifred   Date: October and November

Family routine	Says/signs five different descriptive words (e.g., big, little, hot, red)	Says/signs five different action words (e.g., open, go, eat, sit)	**Target skills** Says/signs two different pronouns (e.g., me, mine, it, my, I, you, this)	Says/signs 15 different object and/or event labels (e.g., ball, cup, hat, bubbles)	Says/signs three different proper names (e.g., Mom, Dad, Jae Hyung)
Wake up	Ask questions, "What color shoes, shirt, pants, socks?"	Label actions Jae Hyung completes throughout morning routine.	Sing, "Good morning to you."	Label common objects in bedroom and bathroom.	Greet Jae Hyung with proper name to serve as a model.
Breakfast	Describe breakfast food (e.g., hot, cold, soft, crunchy).	Label actions of placing household items on table.			Greet people with proper name as they enter the room to serve as a model.
Playtime	Describe Jae Hyung's play with objects.	Label action of child and toy (e.g., "Car go up/down.").	Use pronouns to label turn taking (e.g., my turn, your turn).	Label toys or pictures in book.	Label pictures of family members to serve as a model.
Bath time	Describe the texture of items used during bath time (e.g., "The towel is soft.").	Label actions of water (e.g., pour in, out, on, over).		Label common toys from playtime in bath.	
Weekly visit from Dara and/or Winifred		Label actions of Jae Hyung with toys (e.g., in, out, on, over, under).	Use pronouns to label turn taking (e.g., my turn, your turn).		Greet Jae Hyung and family with proper names to serve as a model.

Figure 5.2.   Completed embedding schedule for Jae Hyung.

119

Activity Plan

1. Activity name

Treasure hunt

2. Materials

Large container holding sand
Basket of pictures/cards with familiar objects
Salad tongs
Treasure chest or other container with lid
Corresponding objects (e.g., cup, spoon, car, ball, plastic people, dinosaur,
    blocks, plate)

3. Environmental arrangement

The container with sand needs to be arranged so Jae Hyung can maneuver around its perimeter. The container also needs to be at a height appopriate for Jae Hyung to be able to reach into without straining.

4. Sequence of steps

Beginning

A treasure chest (or any container with a lid) is presented to Jae Hyung. Encourage him to open and close the lid. Have Jae Hyung collect favorite toys/objects and place them in the chest. Label, describe, and ask questions regarding each toy/object placed in the chest. Take the chest of items to the container and bury the toy/object in the sand.

Middle

Jae Hyung pulls a picture card out of a basket and is prompted to hunt for the
    matching object in the sand.
Jae Hyung can use the salad tongs to remove the object from the sand.

Figure 5.3.   Completed activity plan for Jae Hyung.

Jae Hyung places both the card and the object in the treasure chest (or container with the lid).

Jae Hyung continues to match objects to picture cards until all objects are found.

End

Review toys/objects placed and cards not found in the treasure chest. Clean toys/objects and replace them.

5. Embedded learning opportunities

Learns/practices fine motor skills

    Explores sand and finds objects

    Grasps of various objects

    Transfers objects to treaure chest

    Uses tong pinchers to increase grasp strength and eye–hand coordination

Learns/practices cognitive skills

    Repeats word/sign that labels object with descriptor

    Counts objects

    Demonstrates one-to-one correspondence by placing object on correct picture

    Demonstrates understanding of spatial concepts by placing objects in treasure chest

    Matches object to correct picture

Learns/practices social-communication skills

    Repeats targeted words and signs (descriptions, actions, pronouns, labels, proper names)

    Labels pictures of objects to be found in the sand with word/sign

    Uses proper name of family members to tell them it is their turn

    Uses listener/speaker roles

continued

Figure 5.3.   *(continued)*

6. Planned variations

Vary the objects that will be placed in the container.

Vary the substance in which objects are hidden (e.g., change sand to beans or shredded paper).

Objects of specific function or attribute could be placed in the container to focus attention on a specific cognitive concept (e.g., spoon, bowl, cup, pot holder, and spatula are items found in a kitchen; banana, chick, duck, and cheese are all yellow).

7. Vocabulary

Descriptive words (e.g., big, little, tall, red, hot, cold, more, old, new)

Action words (e.g., in, out, on, over, stop, go)

Pronouns (e.g., me, mine, it, my, I, you, this)

Object and/or event labels (e.g., cup, spoon, car, ball, plastic people, dinosaur, blocks, plate)

Proper names (e.g., Mom/Uhm-ma, Dad/Ap-ba, Jae Hyung, Jae-sun, Dara, Winifred)

8. Peer interaction opportunities

Jae-sun could assist Ja-Hyung in collecting the favorite objects, labeling them, and burying them in the sand. A parent could review the words/signs with Jae-sun prior to the activity to ensure use of proper labels.

Neighborhood children could also be invited to participate.

9. Caregiver involvement

Parents can facilitate the activity and/or record the words/signs Jae Hyung uses.

Jae Hyung's family could adapt the treasure hunt and select meaningful family items and hunt for them in the sand.

- Dara (EI specialist) will record the number and type of words and signs Jae Hyung uses during her weekly home visits. Every 2 weeks, she will also review all data and summarize total number and types of words and signs used.

- Winifred (speech-language pathologist) will collect a language sample one time a month using an audiotape during the 30 minutes of weekly speech therapy.

- All team members will review data monthly to make decisions regarding changes to the intervention strategies and where learning opportunities are embedded.

The team also discusses how to create a data collection system that 1) is accessible and usable by everyone on the team, 2) keeps writing to a minimum, and 3) includes situational information and performance information. To create the form, the team brainstorms possible single words/signs Jae Hyung is likely to be exposed to and use on a daily basis. The team alphabetizes the words/signs so they can easily mark when one is demonstrated. Furthermore, because the team needs data on whether Jae Hyung is using words, signs, or signs with words and how he is using them (e.g., description, action, label), the form also includes a means of recording this information. Once data are collected, the team meets regularly to summarize their findings and make intervention decisions. Figure 5.4 contains a completed data collection form used by the team.

Serina: Center-Based Services

As described in the appendix to Chapter 3, Serina Johnson is 4-year-old girl eligible for ECSE services under the category of general developmental delay. Serina attends a neighborhood preschool program 3 days per week, in which she receives ECSE services including occupational and speech-language therapy. Information related to Serina's present level of performance was gathered through a comprehensive assessment conducted by her parents (Marcia and Don), ECSE teacher (Gwen), classroom assistant (Tashana), occupational therapist (Denise), and speech-language pathologist (Debra). Assessment observations are based on daily interactions with Serina and guided by AEPS (Bricker, 2002). The following information is a summary of Serina's interests and abilities related to her participation in daily activities.

Assessment Summary

Most days begin with Serina taking a bath followed by selecting the clothes she will wear for the day. She can pull her pajama bottoms off after her mother gives her some initial assistance by pushing them down. She raises

Data Collection Form

Child's name: _Jae Hyung_   Team members: _Parents, Dara, and Winifred_

Collected the week of: _November 22, 2003_

Alphabetized list	Word	Sign	Word/sign	Summary of utterance				
				Description	Action	Pronoun	Label	Proper name
Ap-ba		Ɫ卄1						5
Ball	Ɫ卄1		I				6	
Big	I		II	3				
Bug		II					2	
Cat	IIII						4	
Cup	Ɫ卄1						5	
Dad	III		II					5
Down	Ɫ卄1				5			
Eat		Ɫ卄1			5			
Go	III		III		6			
Green	I	II		3				
Hat	I	II					3	
He	I					1		
Hot	II		Ɫ卄1	7				
I	I	Ɫ卄1				6		
It	III					3		
Itsy		II		2				
Jae Hyung	I							1
Jae-sun	I	III						4
Me	Ɫ卄1 IIII	II	Ɫ卄1			16		
Mine	I	III				4		
Mom	Ɫ卄1		III					8
More	Ɫ卄1 Ɫ卄1				10			
New				0				
No	Ɫ卄1		Ɫ卄1		10			
Pan	I						1	
Pat	II		II				4	
Red	I	III		4				
Run	Ɫ卄1				5			
Sit	Ɫ卄1 II	III			10			
Stop		Ɫ卄1			5			
Teddy	II			2				
Um-mah	I		III					4
Up	Ɫ卄1				5			
Yell				0				
You		III				3		

Figure 5.4. Completed data collection form for the team to record Jay Hyung's progress.

her arms up, and her mother pulls the pajama top over her head. In the bath-tub, she will point to the toy bag hanging on the shower rack. She likes to reach in and get her containers for filling and pouring. Presently, she uses small hand-sized containers with one hand to scoop water and pour it over her body and hair. After a few minutes of play, she rubs soap over her body parts as her mother names them. Then, she rinses off by scooping and pour-ing water on herself again.

After her mother assists her with drying off, she joins her mother at the dresser and pulls out a matching shirt and short set. Serina will identify her favorite color as pink (e.g., /I/ /wī/ /pin/ for *I like pink*). She is able to match red, yellow, and green colored shirt and short combinations. She consistently follows the routine directions that go with taking a bath and getting dressed. Serina is starting to follow new directions that include location concepts (e.g., in, on, behind, up, down). For example, when her mother or father point to an object on her shirt, she finds it and points or imitates the name of the object, or when asked to hang her pajamas on the hook behind the door, she complies with the request. When asked, Serina is able to inform others of an object's/person's location

Serina can be difficult to understand when she answers questions or makes comments. Specifically, Serina consistently substitutes the initial con-sonant sounds in words that are more difficult to produce (e.g., /ch/ or /j/) with initial consonant sounds that are easier to produce (e.g., /p/ and /d/). For example, she will say /tă/ for *cat*, /dō/ for *go*, /poo/ for *food*, and /dā/ for *grape*. Specifically, Serina substitutes /t/ for /k/, /w/, or /l/; /d/ for /g/ or /j/; /p/ for /f/; /b/ for /v/; and /f/ for /th/. Serina can also be difficult to under-stand because she consistently deletes (i.e., does not produce) the final conso-nants /p/, /b/, /t/, /d/, /k/, or /g/. In other words, she deletes the final con-sonant sounds in words ending with these particular sounds, two-syllable words with these sounds ending a syllable, and words ending with two con-sonants. For example, she will say /tuh/ for *tub* (deleting the final consonant sound), /bah-um/ for *bottom* (deleting the consonant sound in a word with two syllables, or /wan/ for *want* (deleting final consonant sound for a word with two consonants at the end).

After getting dressed, Serina walks independently to the kitchen. She likes to stand on a stool next to her mother and help prepare breakfast. Her mother offers her choices of foods (e.g., different kinds of cereal, fruit, breads, toaster waffle, or pancake). Serina points to food items she desires to make a selection. She sometimes imitates the name of the food offered but, again, has difficulty being understood by adults when the words end in particular consonants or when she makes substitutions for consonants at the beginning of words. For example, Serina will say /poo/ for *fruit*, /mil/ for *milk*, /tōs/ for *toast*, /dā/ /deh wy/ for *grape jelly*, and /pah/ /tah/ for *Pop-Tart*).

Serina also assists with getting her breakfast by shaking the box of cereal into a bowl, stirring batter, or putting waffles/Pop-Tarts in the toaster. Serina is starting to use a plastic knife to cut soft fruits such as bananas, kiwi, and watermelon but requires adult assistance to peel fruit. Serina usually eats the same food for a few days before switching to a new one but eats a variety of foods across the week. She is able to grasp a spoon or fork but needs help from an adult to scoop/spear. She is then able to bring the food to her mouth and remove the food from the utensil with her lips with little spilling. She is also able to drink from a cup without assistance. She is starting to use a large serving spoon to scoop food from a larger bowl to her bowl or plate when she wants more of a particular food. Serina usually moves toward or points to the food if she wants more and will only request food verbally if prompted by an adult (e.g., "What do you want, Serina?").

Once breakfast is finished, Serina throws a small ball or dog toy for her dog, Marley. She is starting to help take care of Marley by assisting with feeding, watering, and taking him for walks. She puts the dog's bowl in the sink and lifts the faucet lever to fill the dish with water. She pushes the button on the electric can opener to start opening the dog food can, and she gets the leash from the closet when it is time to walk the dog. Often, she brings the leash to her father when he gets home from work to indicate that she is ready to take the dog for a walk. If it's raining outside, she will also bring her jacket and wait for her father to assist her with putting it on and zipping it. Her mother and father report that she is most talkative around Marley. She imitates a few two and three word phrases including /Nī/ /Mawy/ for *Nice Marley*, /Dŭ/ /dŏ-ie/ for *Good doggie*, /Weh/ /dō/ for *Let's go*, /tum/ /on/ /Mawy/ for *Come on, Marley*, /Dō/ /deh/ /ĭ/ *Go get it*, and /Mawy/ /poo/ for *Marley's food*.

At school, Serina frequently selects activities in the art and dramatic play areas. She is starting to draw and paint simple shapes (e.g., circles, horizontal and vertical lines that intersect). She can grasp different writing instruments (e.g., crayons, markers, pencils, paint brushes) by grasping with her whole hand (i.e., four fingers wrapped around the instrument). She also makes the letters of her name with hand over hand assistance when asked to put her name on an art project.

She is observant at school and follows the routine directions. She is beginning to sing along to music and can complete movements associated with songs during circle time activities (e.g., act out animal movements, shake hands with friends when prompted). When given a choice, she will choose to shake a tambourine during music time. In the dramatic play area, she wears a puppet on her hand and, along with one or two other children, will move the puppets across a puppet stage and make them dance and talk with the other puppets through gestures and animal sounds. Serina will also exchange her puppet with other children and follow along in the games that they make up with the puppets. Serina often selects the big dog puppet but will trade for the smaller puppy puppet. At home, her mother also reports that Serina shares her toys with her brother.

When changing from inside to outside activities, Serina joins the teacher and other children counting the laminated footprints on the floor. She is starting to count from 1 to 10 in correct sequence with the group. Outside, Serina watches the other children run, jump, and play with a ball. She often requests an adult to put her on the swing (e.g., Me /pin/? for *Me swing?* or /Wan/ /uh/ for *Want up*). She will sit on a tricycle and squeeze the horn. She will also gesture to other children that she wants to sit in the taxi tricycle and have them pedal.

Both at home and at school, Serina demonstrates that she understands concepts related to size, shape, and color when reading books. She responds to questions such as "Where is the circle?" "Where is the blue ball?" and "Where is the big chair?" by pointing or retrieving an object. After pointing or retrieving the object, she will sometimes imitate the target concept word but has difficulty being understood because she will often not produce the final consonant. She can tell others the names of people in family photograph albums or framed pictures of family members in the house. Sometimes, she is also able to recall some information about the person or event (e.g., /My/ /pah-y/ for *My party,* /My/ /hă/ for *My hat,* /Nana/ /tă/ for *Nana's cat,* and /Mawy/ /beh/ for *Marley's bed*). At school, she also has learned the names of a few children. When children's pictures are individually held up by the teacher to dismiss the children from circle to an activity, she listens to the other children call out the child's name.

Target Goals

Based on the comprehensive assessment information and the resulting present level of performance (i.e., assessment summary), the team selects a number of priority goals and associated objectives/benchmarks to target for intervention. Serina's goals include *Manipulates a variety of objects, Says a variety of one and two words,* and *Uses one object to represent another object* (refer to the Chapter 3 appendix for a description of how prioritized goals were selected). The team uses the revised version of the GORI (Notari-Syverson & Shuster, 1995) to ensure that the goals and associated objectives/benchmarks are functional and generative. The team then takes steps to ensure that daily activities promote learning and use of target goals.

Individualized Intervention

The three forms (i.e., intervention guides, embedding schedules, and activity plans) described in Chapter 4 are used to assist the team in creating and embedding multiple and varied learning opportunities. Serina's team reviews her present level of performance and target goals, then considers how to individualize intervention. They create an intervention guide for each prioritized individualized education program (IEP) goal outlining specific antecedents and consequences as well as needed accommodations and modifications and possible intervention strategies. Figure 5.5 contains an intervention guide for the target goal of *Says a variety of one and two words and is understood by others*.

Because Serina receives services at a community preschool, the team considers the daily classroom activities in which she is likely to participate (e.g., arrival, free play, snack). They then develop an embedding schedule that prompts adults as to which antecedents to provide and when to embed learning opportunities across daily classroom activities. Figure 5.6 contains an embedding schedule for Serina and two other children in the class. The team creates an embedding schedule for multiple children (i.e., Serina, Tianna, and Patrice) to help streamline efforts when serving groups of children. Finally, the team develops several weekly planned activities that address Serina's and other children's target goals. Figure 5.7 contains an activity plan that can be incorporated into the classroom activities.

Data Collection

The team reviews the intervention guide to develop a data collection system to monitor Serina's performance on target goals. After reviewing the intervention guide, the team makes a number of decisions:

- The parents will record the number of times Serina uses one and two word phrases several times each month (e.g., during various family routines, at relatives' homes, at the park, during dance class) and whether they could understand words with the target final consonants.

- Gwen (ECSE teacher), Denise (occupational therapist), and Tashana (classroom assistant) will record the number of one and two words Serina uses, the type of utterances (request, inform, greet), and whether they can understand those with the target consonants. Each person will collect data during three different classroom activities. Gwen will also collect data on her monthly home visits. Every month, Gwen and Tashana will collect and summarize the total number of words used and the percentage of words that were understood by others.

- Debra (speech-language pathologist) will collect a monthly language sample during visits to the classroom.

- All team members will review data monthly to make decisions regarding changes to how often learning opportunities are provided and where learning opportunities are embedded.

Intervention Guide

1. Basic information

Child's name: _Serina Johnson_

Team members: _parents, early childhood special education teacher, classroom_

assistant, speech-language pathologist, occupational therapist

Date intervention initiated: _September 2003_   Date intervention completed: _September 2004_

2. Goal, objectives/benchmarks, program steps

Goal 1.0

Using a variety of one and two words, Serina will **request** objects, people, or materials, **inform** others, and **greet** others during daily activities. Two different adults will understand what she says three times a day for 2 weeks.

Across Goal 1.0 and associated objectives, to be understood by other adults means that when Serina says words to request, inform, and/or greet adults will hear Serina produce target final consonant sounds and/or produce target first consonant sounds without making substitutions. The final consonant target sounds are /p, b, t, d, k/, and the first consonant target sounds are /k, l, g, f, v, ch, j, th/.

Objectives

1.1. Using a variety of one and two words, Serina will request objects, people, or materials from others (adults or peers) during daily activities. Two different adults will understand what she says three times a day for 2 weeks. For example, Serina will say words/phrases such as "Up," "Give toy," or "More food."

1.2. Using a variety of one and two words, Serina will inform others (adults or peers) about daily activities. Two different adults will understand what she says three times a day for 2 weeks. For example, Serina will say words/phrases such as "cat," "milk," and "big book."

1.3. Using a variety of one and two words, Serina will greet others (adults or peers). Two different adults will understand what she says three times a day for 2 weeks. For example, Serina will say "Hey," "Hi Marley," "Hi Beth," "Hi Kate," or "Good morning."

Figure 5.5.   Completed intervention guide for Serina.

Figure 5.5.   *(continued)*

3. State standard(s) or IFSP outcome(s)

Link to English Language Arts Standards

    Speaks clearly and understandably to express ideas, feelings, and needs

    Retells information from informational text

    Asks questions about experiences, areas of interest, pictures, letters, words, Legos, or icons

Link to Math Standards

    Identifies, names, creates, and describes common two-dimensional shapes in the environment and play situations (e.g., circles, triangles, rectangles, squares)

    Demonstrates and begins to use the language of the relative position of objects in the environment and play situations (e.g., up, down, over, under, top, bottom, inside, outside, in front, behind, between, next to, right side up, upside down)

Link to Science Standards

    Predicts what will happen next based on previous experience

    Communicates observations and findings with others through a variety of methods (such as pictures, discussion, or dramatization)

    Uses her own words to offer explanations that may be correct or incorrect

Link to Social Studies Standards

    Labels days by function (e.g., school day, stay home day, swim day, field trip day)

    Begins to use the language of time units (e.g., day, night)

    Uses time words such as next, before, soon, after, now, and later as related to the classroom daily schedule

    Shares personal family story

    Recognizes and labels with assistance man-made structures such as home, bridges, roads, and skyscrapers

    Obtains things she wants (goods and services) in socially acceptable ways

4. Multiple and varied learning opportunities, functional and generative goals, timely and integral feedback or consequences		
Antecedents designed to provide learning opportunities	List of possible child responses: targeted (+) and nontargeted (–)	Feedback or consequences
1.1 Place/hold desired object/person/ material with the first consonant sounds of /k, l, g, f, v, ch, j, th/ or the final consonant sounds of /p, b, t, d, k/ within view but out of Serina's reach. Ask Serina questions that require a one or two word response/ request with the first consonant sounds of /k, l, g, f, v, ch, j, th/ or the final consonant sounds of /p, b, t, d, k/ (e.g., Ask "Do you have any pets?" or when playing outside, ask "What do you want to do?")	Uses one and two words to request objects, people, or materials by producing/ saying the first consonant sounds of /k, l, g, f, v, ch, j, th/ or producing/saying the final consonant sounds of /p, b, t, d, k/, in words (+) Uses one and two words to request objects, people, or materials but substitutes the first target consonant sound or does not produce final target consonant sounds (–) Points or looks at the desired object/person/ material (–) Answers question non verbally (e.g., shakes her head, goes to get an object) (–)	Give requested item or comply with request (+) Affirm and repeat what Serina says (+) Model one or two word response with final target consonant sounds (–) Wait and look expectantly for a response or wait and repeat the question (–)
1.2 Ask Serina to inform others (e.g., "Who do you like to sit with?" "What do you have for lunch?") Model one and two words with target first or the final consonant sounds (e.g., "Food," "Dog," "Come on," "Let's go")	Uses one and two words to inform others by producing/ saying the first consonant sounds of /k, l, g, f, v, ch, j, th/ or producing/saying the final consonant sounds of /p, b, t, d, k/ in words (+) Uses one and two words to inform others but substitutes the first target consonant sound or does not produce final target consonant sounds (–) Answers question nonverbally (e.g., by pointing) (–)	Ask a follow-up question (+) Comment on what Serina says (+) Correctly model the one or two words Serina says (–) Tell Serina to answer your question and provide a model of a response (–)

continued

Figure 5.5.   *(continued)*

Antecedents designed to provide learning opportunities	List of possible child responses: targeted (+) and nontargeted (−)	Feedback or consequences
1.3 Peer or adult says, "Hi." Peer or adult says, "Great day." Peer or adult waves. Adult asks Serina, "What do you say to your friend?" Sing the Good Morning song at circle time or other greeting song.	Uses one and two words to greet others by producing/saying the first consonant sounds of /k, l, g, f, v, ch, j, th/ or producing/saying the final consonant sounds of /p, b, t, d, k/ in words (+) Uses one or two words to greet others but substitutes the first target consonant sound or does not produce final target consonant sounds (−) Looks at person but does not respond (−) Waves or smiles at person (−) Remains with the group, but does not say the words to the song (−)	Peer or adult smiles (+) Affirm and repeat what Serina says (e.g., "Yes it is good to see Tom this morning.") (+) Correctly model the one or two word greeting (−) Ask Serina to say one or two word greeting (−) Sing another greeting song and encourage Serina to sing along (−)

5. Accommodations, modifications, and intervention strategies

Ensure joint attention and then provide several massed trials for Serina to produce targeted final consonant sounds.

Use milieu strategies including incidental teaching, mand-models, and time delay.

Use nondirective strategies including novelty (present new and interesting objects with target first or final consonants) and forgetfulness (forget how to say words with target first or final consonants).

6. Data collection procedures

Who (person responsible for collecting the data)	Where (which activities or locations)	When (how often or on which days)	How (which methods)
Early childhood special education teacher (Gwen), occupational therapist (Denise), and classroom assistant (Tashana)	Daily classroom activities and monthly home visit	Three times on Mondays and Wednesdays	Record what Serina says (written descriptions) and the function of her utterances, and note which target consonant sounds were understandable (counts/tallies)
Speech-language pathologist (Debra)	Circle time	Monthly	Record a language sample (written descriptions) to document utterances, length of utterances, function, and intelligibility
Parents (Marcia and Don)	Home, relatives' homes, the park, and dance class	3 or 4 times per month	Record what Serina says (written descriptions) and note whether she was understandable (counts/tallies)

7. Decision rules

If adequate progress does not occur in _____1 month_____ (specify time frame for when the team will review the data), then the team will (check all that apply):

——— change which goals are targeted

——— change selected antecedents or feedback/consequences

——— change accommodations, modifications, or intervention strategies

__X__ change how often learning opportunities are provided

__X__ change where learning opportunities occur

——— other (describe) _____

_____

Group Embedding Schedule

Children's names: _Serina, Tianna, and Patrice_   Date schedule will be used: _First quarter (Sept. to Nov.)_

Team members: _Classroom staff and therapists_

Children and target goals	Daily classroom activities				
	Arrival	Free play	Circle activities	Snack	Centers
Child's name: Serina 1. Manipulates objects	Ask Serina to unzip her coat.	Encourage Serina to play with blocks, puzzles, and art materials.		Provide a spoon or a fork to eat with, foods to prepare, and a knife for spreading or cutting.	Place objects to manipulate in writing center (pencils, scissors) and science center (tweezers, microscope with slides).
2. Uses one and two words to request, inform, and greet	Model saying "Good morning." Ask Serina to greet peers.		Sing the Good Morning song. Ask Serina to request a song. Ask Serina to tell the class what color shoes she has on (including black, pink, gray as targets).	Ask Serina what she is having for lunch. Label words related to snack/eating that end with target consonants (milk, nut, fruit, last).	Model greeting peers as they enter the different centers. Ask Serina what she is doing. Ask Serina where she wants to play or what toys she wants.
3. Uses one object to represent another		Model how to use different size blocks as food or a shoe for a doll's car.			Use a small dust pan or a ladle as a shovel in the discovery table. Use sticks as paintbrushes in the art area.
Child's name: Tianna 1. Expresses likes and dislikes			Present song options for Tianna to choose.		Ask Tianna which activities she likes and does not like.
2. Sorts like objects		Ask Tianna to put all of the books together and all of the puppets together.		Encourage Tianna to put all cups on one table and all snack food on another.	
3. Uses spoon to feed self				Provide food requiring spoon use.	
Child's name: Patrice 1. Uses toilet	Ask Patrice if she has to use the bathroom.			Ask Patrice if she has to use the bathroom.	
2. Follows routine directions	Remind Patrice to hang up her coat and put away her lunch.	Ask Patrice to put the blocks away.		Prompt Patrice to take one and pass to her friends.	

Figure 5.6.   Completed embedding schedule for Serina and two other children in her class.

Activity Plan

1. Activity name

Action Books

2. Materials

8½" x 11" construction paper
Scissors, hole punch, brads, markers, glue sticks, cotton swabs, and plastic lids
Precut action figures from magazines or coloring books
Smocks, sponges, and towels
Several examples of completed action books

3. Environmental arrangement

A flat surface is needed for children to sit or stand on to reach associated
materials. Set activity up near a sink if possible and near other art materials
that can be incorporated into the activity as it progresses. Materials in labeled
containers make it easy for children to identify them, use them, and clean
them up. Hang smocks on coat hooks low enough for children to get and
return smocks independently.

4. Sequence of steps

Beginning

Ask children about their favorite book, movie, or television characters. After
they respond with a variety of characters, tell them your favorite character, and
show them a completed action book you created about that character. Other
completed action books made by children should be available to serve as
examples and encourage creativity. Read one or two of the action book stories
and, when finished, ask children if they can guess how the book was made. As
children guess, write down the materials they will need to create their own
action book on a wipe-off board. Once the list is complete, instruct children to
help find the needed items, get a smock, and come to the table to make their
own action book.

Middle

Have children select the colors of the paper for their books. Then, they cut the
paper to the size book they desire. Next, children select several character
pictures from magazines or old coloring books and glue the pictures on their

continued

Figure 5.7.   Completed activity plan for Serina.

Figure 5.7.   *(continued)*

pages. Children can select and glue other objects onto the pages with their character. Ask children to tell what their character is doing, and write phrases or sentences on the page. Then, children punch three holes on the side of the front page to insert brads.

End

Children return materials to their labeled containers and wipe tables with sponges. Then, they remove their smocks. Children transition to the circle area with their books. Invite children to read their book to another child or adult.

5. Embedded learning opportunities

Learns/practices fine motor skills
   Uses hands to manipulate objects
   Uses scissors to cut
   Holds and uses writing instruments
   Copies/prints letters

Learns/practices cognitive skills
   Demonstrates understanding of color, shape, size, quantity, and
      quality concepts
   Follows directions
   Evaluates solutions to problems
   Plans and acts out recognizable event, theme, or storyline
   Counts objects

Learns/practices social skills
   Initiates preferred activities
   Participates in small group activities (remains, watches, follows
      directions)
   Initiates and completes activities

Learns/practices social-communication skills
   Requests materials to make action book
   Informs others about action book and who the characters are and
      what they are doing
   Greets peers who join the activity

6. Planned variations

1.   Children make family books with pictures of family members.
2.   Children use stamps and ink pads for pictures.

3. Children use stickers.

4. Children make favorite animal action books.

7. Vocabulary

Pronouns (e.g., he, she, mine, my, they, him)

Present progressive verbs with "ing" (e.g., flying, climbing, driving, fixing, running, jumping)

Names (e.g., character names)

Nouns (e.g., hole punch, marker, paper, book, glue stick, Q-tip, lid, chalk)

Adjectives (e.g., colors: pink, black, gray; sizes: tiny, big, long, short, fat; quantity: many, any; quality: hot, soft, light, heavy, dry, wet, quiet, fast, dirty)

Position words (e.g., back, front, last, bottom, first)

8. Peer interaction opportunities

Children work in pairs to gather necessary materials.

Children help find pictures/objects for one another's action books.

Children share materials (e.g., magazines, glue sticks).

Children read finished action books to one another.

Children work in pairs to clean up area and return materials.

9. Caregiver involvement

Caregivers contribute magazines and objects with their child's favorite characters.

Caregivers volunteer to lead the activity with the children or a group of the children.

Caregivers suggest new variations.

Caregivers observe and collect data on targeted skills (e.g., the words they use).

Data Collection Form

Child's name: _Serina_   Family routine: _Going to the park_

Collected the week of: _November 3, 2003_

One or two words Serina uses (write how it sounds)	Does she correctly produce target sounds?	
Nï Mawy (Nice Marley)	Yes	(No)
Du doie (Good doggie)	Yes	(No)
Tum on Mawy (Come on, Marley)	Yes	(No)
Dõ! (Go!)	Yes	(No)
Wan (Want)	Yes	(No)
Want uh (Want up) Note: Dad modeled "want."	Yes	(No)

Child's name: _Serina_   Family routine: _Dance class_

Collected the week of: _November 10, 2003_

One or two words Serina uses (write how it sounds)	Does she correctly produce target sounds?	
Want pin (Want pink)	Yes	(No)
Pin (Pink)	Yes	(No)
I want pink Note: Dad modeled "pink."	(Yes)	No
Wan turn (Want turn)	Yes	(No)
My turn	(Yes)	No

Figure 5.8. Completed data collection form for Serina's parents to record her progress.

Data Collection Form

Child's name: _Serina_   Date: _October 24, 2003_

Person collecting data: _Gwen_

Activity	Utterances	Request	Inform	Greet	Intelligible
Activity name: _Circle_ Start time: _10:00_ Stop time: _10:05_	Up, please.	X			No
	Good morning.			X	Yes
	Hi, Beth.			X	Yes
	Wheels on the bus		X		No
	Monday, Tuesday...		X		No
	My turn.		X		No
	I help.		X		Yes
	Today?	X			Yes
Activity name: _Snack_ Start time: _11:15_ Stop time: _11:25_	More juice, please.	X			No
	Grape jelly		X		No
	Cats like milk.		X		No
	More, please.	X			Yes
	Mine?	X			No
	Hungry		X		No
Activity name: _Centers_ Start time: _11:30_ Stop time: _11:40_	Give me toy.	X			No
	Hi, Kate.			X	Yes
	Big book		X		Yes
	Let's go.		X		Yes
	Want help?		X		Yes
	Mine		X		Yes
	My hat		X		No

Figure 5.9. Completed data collection form for Serina's teacher to record her progress.

The team also discusses how to create a data collection system that 1) is accessible and usable by everyone on the team, 2) keeps writing to a minimum, and 3) includes situational information and performance information. Figure 5.8 contains a data collection form parents use, and Figure 5.9 contains a data collection form for classroom personnel. Both forms allow all team members to indicate what they hear Serina say, either by writing it phonetically or by writing what they know she was saying and then determining whether her utterances were intelligible based on criterion stated in her target goal and associated objectives. As the team collects data they meet regularly to discuss Serina's progress and make decisions regarding their intervention efforts.

De'Shawn: Itinerant Services

De'Shawn is a 5-year-old boy eligible for Head Start services. As a preschooler with a disability, he also qualifies for ECSE services. De'Shawn attends a local Head Start program 4 days per week and is visited by the ECSE itinerant teacher weekly. Information related to his present level of performance was gathered through a comprehensive assessment conducted by his mother (Shawna) and grandmother (Teresa), Head Start teacher (Marlene), occupational therapist (Amy), and ECSE itinerant teacher (Nicole). Assessment observations were based on De'Shawn's interactions with others in the Head Start program and guided by AEPS (Bricker, 2002). The following information is a summary of De'Shawn's interests and abilities related to his participation in the general curriculum throughout daily activities.

Assessment Summary

In the morning, De'Shawn tells his mother what he wants to eat using three to four word phrases, such as "I want cereal, please." His mother repeats the words he has difficulty pronouncing correctly, specifically the /l/ sound within words. For example, if he says, "More /mik/, please," his mother will repeat, "Would you like more *milk?*" He feeds himself with an adaptive fork, spoon, and a suctioned bowl and plate. He spears or scoops the food and brings it to his mouth with minimal spilling. He drinks from a cup by bringing it to his mouth and returning it to the table without spilling. After eating, he places his utensils in the sink and pushes in his chair.

To prepare for school, De'Shawn selects his own clothing that matches the day's weather (e.g., long pants when it is cold, shorts when it is hot) and is able to dress himself. For example, he can pull long pants over both feet and pull them up to his waist. He can put on a pullover garment and a front opening garment. He requires adult assistance when zipping or buttoning clothing and tying his shoes. He completes a toileting routine: pulls down pants, uses toilet paper after using the toilet, pulls up pants, flushes toilet, and washes hands. De'Shawn uses a tissue to clean his nose and brushes his teeth with minimal assistance from his mother or grandmother.

When De'Shawn arrives at Head Start, he gets off the bus with the other students but needs adult reminders to stay with the group. He places his coat and bookbag in his area but requires assistance to unzip his clothing. During free play, De'Shawn will initiate context-relevant topics and respond to the topic initiations of other children in one-to-one situations and small groups (i.e., less than four other children). He engages in conversational turn-taking and topical discussions using three to four word phrases. De'Shawn asks peers if he can join them in play (e.g., Can I /pay/? for *Can I play?*), will answer their questions usually with one word responses (e.g., Yes), make requests to peers (e.g., I want the red car), and respond to their requests (e.g., No, I am /paying/ for *No, I am playing*).

During circle time when most of the children in the class join the adults to sing songs, read stories, and talk about the day's events, De'Shawn is able to remain with the large group for a limited amount of time (usually less than 5 minutes). He is able to remain with the group (i.e., walks around the perimeter of the group or sits near one or two other children) with visual and verbal prompts (e.g., Mayer-Johnson Picture Communication Symbol of "sit" paired with the word *sit*). He is beginning to look at objects and people that are the focus of the activity (e.g., books being read, person singing a song). De'Shawn sings songs he has heard many times and that contain repeating phrases (e.g., "Five Little Monkeys," "Old MacDonald").

De'Shawn greets, informs, and requests objects/materials from adults and peers in one-to-one situations and small-group activities. He initiates and completes age-appropriate activities, such as getting puzzles out, putting them together, and then putting them away. He is able to assemble toys by putting the pieces together (e.g., puts Lego pieces together). De'Shawn plans and acts out recognizable events and themes, such as restaurant and grocery store.

During adult-created and led one-to-one activities, De'Shawn consistently demonstrates the understanding of colors, shapes, and sizes during block play, during book reading, and at the art center by matching like colors, following directions related to colors, and naming objects' colors. At snack, he demonstrates one-to-one correspondence by passing out utensils to other classmates. He is able to categorize like toys/objects in the housekeeping area (e.g., puts utensils, food together).

On the playground, De'Shawn is able to jump forward with two feet together from surface to surface (e.g., from grass to cement). He plays games with balls (e.g., bounces it to another peer, catches the ball when it is thrown, kicks and throws overhand).

Target Goals

Based on the comprehensive assessment information and the resulting present level of performance (i.e., assessment summary), the team selects a number of priority goals and associated objectives/benchmarks to target for intervention. De'Shawns goals include *Manipulates variety of small objects; Uses the /l/ sound correctly when greeting, informing, and requesting;* and *participates in group activities by remaining with the group, looking at people talking, and following group directions.* The team uses the revised version of the GORI (Notari-Syverson & Shuster, 1995) to ensure that the goals and associated objectives/benchmarks were functional and generative. The team then takes steps to ensure daily activities promote learning and use of target goals.

Individualized Intervention

The three forms (i.e., individualized guides, embedding schedules, and activity plans) described in Chapter 4 are used to assist the team in creating and embedding multiple and varied learning opportunities. De'Shawn's team reviews his present level of performance and target child service plan goals, then considers how to individualize intervention. They create an intervention guide for each target goal and associated objectives/benchmarks outlining specific antecedents and consequences as well as needed accommodations and modifications and possible intervention strategies. Figure 5.10 contains an intervention guide for the target goal of *Manipulates objects with both hands.*

Because De'Shawn receives services at the Head Start preschool and from the itinerant teacher, the team considers the daily classroom activities in which he is likely to participate (e.g., arrival, free play, small group, snack). The itinerant teacher then assists the Head Start teacher to identify times in the day to embed learning opportunities. The occupational therapist offers suggestions for appropriate antecedents and necessary accommodations and modifications that need to be made throughout classroom activities as well as possible intervention strategies. Figure 5.11 contains an embedding schedule for De'Shawn in which reminders of his target behaviors are noted across six classroom activities. Finally, the team develops several planned activities for each week that address De'Shawn's target goals. Figure 5.12 contains an activity plan that can be incorporated by the itinerant teacher into the classroom routine during her weekly visits.

Intervention Guide

1. Basic information

Child's name: _De'Shawn Reynolds_

Team members: _mom (Shawna), grandmother (Teresa), Head Start teacher (Marlene),_
early childhood special education teacher (Nicole), occupational therapist (Amy)

Date intervention initiated: _Sept. 2003_   Date intervention completed: _Sept. 2004_

2. Goal, objectives/benchmarks, program steps

Goal 1.0
During daily activities, De'Shawn will manipulate a variety of objects, toys, or materials that require use of both hands at the same time, while performing different movements. He will manipulate three different objects, toys, or materials once a day for 2 weeks. For example, De'Shawn will tie shoes, button clothing, thread and zip a zipper, and/or cut out shapes with curved lines.

Benchmark
1.1.   During daily activities, De'Shawn will perform any two-handed task using one hand to hold or steady an object, toy, or material while using the other hand to manipulate the object, toy, or material or perform a movement. He will perform three different two-handed tasks per day for 2 weeks. For example, De'Shawn will hold a piece of paper and draw with a crayon, hold paper and cut paper in half, hold a bowl and spoon up food or liquid, spread food with a knife, zip a zipper, or turn the pages of a book.

3. State standard(s) or IFSP outcome(s)

Link to English Language Arts Standards
Prints letters of own name and other meaningful words with assistance using mock letters and/or conventional print
Begins to demonstrate letter formation in "writing"
Scribble-writes familiar words with mock letters and some actual letters
Plays at writing from top to bottom, horizontal rows as format
Link to Math Standards
Writes numerical representations (e.g., scribbles, reversals) or numerals in meaningful context
Constructs two sets of objects each containing the same number of objects
Joins two sets of objects to make one large set in context of daily routines and play (e.g., combining two bags of raisins, each containing three pieces; combining two groups of blocks, each containing three blocks)

continued

Figure 5.10.   Completed intervention guide for De'Shawn.

Figure 5.10. *(continued)*

Matches identical two- and three-dimensional objects found in the environ-
    ment in play situations (e.g., two squares of same size, two stop signs)
Link to Science Standards
    Learns chracteristics of objects, tools, and materials and how they move
    Manipulates materials that provide many different sensory experiences (e.g.,
        sand, water, soft foam)
    Sets objects in motion many different ways (e.g., pushing, pulling, kicking,
        rolling)
    Manipulates familiar objects to accomplish a purpose or complete a task or
        solve a problem (e.g., using scissors to create paper tickets for a puppet show)
    Explores by manipulating materials using simple equipment (e.g., magnets,
        magnifiers)
    Participates in simple scientific explorations with others (e.g., digging to the
        bottom of the sandbox, testing materials that sink or float)
Link to Social Studies Standards
    Arranges sequences of personal and shared events through pictures, growth
    charts, and so forth

4. Multiple and varied learning opportunities, functional and generative goals, timely and integral feedback or consequences

Antecedents designed to provide learning opportunities	List of possible child responses: targeted (+) and nontargeted (–)	Feedback or consequences
1.0 Present De'Shawn with an object that requires the use of both hands while performing different movements (e.g., pictures with curved lines and a pair of scissors).	De'Shawn manipulates objects that require use of both hands at the same time while performing different movements (+)	Comment on what he is doing (+) Smiles from an adult (+)
Model how to manipulate objects with both hands performing different movements (e.g., thread and zip zipper, cut out shapes).	De'Shawn manipulates object using one hand to hold and steady and the other to manipulate (–)	Wait for a few seconds and then encourage De'Shawn to try again (–)
Ask De'Shawn to complete a task that requires use of both hands performing different movements (e.g., "De'Shawn, tie your shoes, please.").	De'Shawn does not respond to the object, model, or request (–)	Redirect De'Shawn back to the object, model, or request (–)

Antecedents designed to provide learning opportunities	List of possible child responses: targeted (+) and nontargeted (−)	Feedback or consequences
1.1 Present De'Shawn with an object that requires one hand to hold and steady and the other to manipulate (e.g., bowl and spoon, books, pasta shells, shoelace strings). Adult models how to manipulate objects that require one hand to hold and steady and the other to manipulate (e.g., pouring juice into a cup, holding a paper and drawing a line). Ask De'Shawn to complete a task that requires one hand to hold and steady and the other to manipulate (e.g., "De'Shawn, zip up your coat.").	De'Shawn manipulates objects that require one hand to hold and steady and the other to manipulate (+) De'Shawn does not repond to the object, model, or request (−)	Comment on what he is doing (+) Smiles from an adult (+) Wait for a few seconds and then encourage De'Shawn to try again (−) Redirect De'Shawn back to the object, model, or request (−)

5. Accommodations, modifications, and intervention strategies

Provide toys or materials that will help De'Shawn strengthen and control his fine motor movements (e.g., jacks and marbles, spring-type clothespins, hole punch, clay/playdough, garlic press, rolling pin, cookie cutters, rolling pizza slicer (plastic).

Place spray bottles in the housekeeping area and near the sink for use when washing.

Create snacks with foods that are difficult to spread and take strength (e.g., peanut butter sandwiches).

Use the directive strategy of assistance only with novel toys, materials, or objects.

Use the nondirective strategies of piece-by-piece and delay.

continued

Figure 5.10. *(continued)*

6. Data collection procedures

Who (person responsible for collecting the data)	Where (which activities or locations)	When (how often or on which days)	How (which methods)
Head Start teacher (Marlene)	Arrival, free play, outdoor play	Twice a week (Monday and Wednesday)	Probes—prior to, during, or at the end of an activity to see which toys, materials, or objects De'Shawn can manipulate
Occupational therapist (Amy)	Snack	Weekly (Tuesdays)	Probes
Early childhood special education intinerant teacher (Nicole)	Center time or free play	Weekly (Wednesdays)	Probes
Parent volunteers	Center time	Weekly (Thursdays)	Probes

7. Decision rules

If adequate progress does not occur in _____1 month_____ (specify time frame for when the team will review the data), then the team will (check all that apply):

__X__ change which goals are targeted

_____ change selected antecedents or feedback/consequences

__X__ change accommodations, modifications, or intervention strategies

_____ change how often learning opportunities are provided

_____ change where learning opportunities occur

_____ other (describe) _____

_____

Embedding Schedule

Child's name: __De'Shawn__   Date: __First quarter__

Team members: __Shawna, Teresa, Marlene, Nicole, and Amy__

Daily classroom activity	Target skills		
	Manipulates objects/toys/ materials	Uses the /l/ sound correctly when greeting, informing, and requesting	Participates in large group activities (remains, looks, responds to directions)
Arrival	De'Shawn will unzip and remove his coat. De'Shawn will unzip his bookbag and remove his notebook and other materials.	De'Shawn will greet students and adults (e.g., Lynn, Larry, Lisa). He will identify the visual icons for the classroom schedule (e.g., library, lunchroom).	De'Shawn will remain with the group on arrival and follow context-specific rules for arrival (e.g., hold hands with peer and walk from bus to room).
Free play	De'Shawn will manipulate books, blocks, Legos, toy cars, and small figures.	De'Shawn will label clothing while playing laundry in the housekeeping area.	De'Shawn will engage in cooperative game playing with classroom peers with adult intervention (e.g., Candyland, Chutes and Ladders).
Circle time	De'Shawn will use two hands to manipulate objects, toys, and materials that correspond to the story.	De'Shawn will repeat appropriate model of words containing /l/ sound from story or song (e.g., Lizards on a Log).	De'Shawn will respond to questions, recalling information from recent events or stories.
Snack	De'Shawn will pass out eating utensils from a container to the class. De'Shawn will print name cards to use for seating arrangements. De'Shawn will hold a bowl and spoon up food and liquid.	De'Shawn will say, "I would like____, please" when receiving his snack. De'Shawn will tell peers his likes and dislikes at snack.	De'Shawn will remain with the group during snack. De'Shawn will place eating utensils in appropriate area when done with snack.
Center time	De'Shawn will paint at easel and hold paint in one hand while using paintbrush with other hand. De'Shawn will pour different substances in the discovery table from one container to another.	De'Shawn will count lemons at the math center and place them in a twist top container. He should count, "One lemon, two lemons, three lemons..."	De'Shawn will participate in an adult-planned activity from start to finish.

Figure 5.11.   Completed embedding schedule for De'Shawn.

Activity Plan

---

1. Activity name

Blocks, Ramps, and Small Vehicles

2. Materials

Variety of sizes and shapes of soft foam blocks
Picture labels of small vehicles
Long soft foam boards for ramps
Variety of small vehicles (e.g., cars, trucks, buses, vans, motorcycles)
One rectangular child-size table
Variety of road sign displays

3. Environmental arrangement

Place rectangular, child-size table on carpet in block area. Encourage children to build roads/garages with soft foam blocks on top of the table. Children can prop long, sanded boards against the table to create ramps.

4. Sequence of steps

Beginning

Introduce the activity by showing children the baskets that contain a variety of vehicles. Prompt children to label the vehicles they would like and have them hold the basket with one hand and remove the vehicles with the other hand. Show children the blocks and road signs and ask them how they could use these materials to make roads and garages for the cars.

Middle

Have children use blocks and boards on the table in the block area. Children create roads, ramps, and garages. They place vehicles on the roads and move the vehicles. They also place road signs at various locations on the roads.

End

Give a 5-minute warning to signal cleanup and the end of the activity. Ask children to return their vehicles to the basket with matching picture labels. Instruct children to place blocks on the shelves and carry long boards to the storage area. Ask children to recall one thing they did during the activity, and record the statements.

Figure 5.12.   Completed activity plan for De'Shawn.

5. Embedded learning opportunities

Learns/practices fine motor skills
  Manipulates a variety of vehicles to provide different sensory experiences
  Stacks blocks to create garages or buildings
  Places vehicles in a row on long boards
  Opens bucket with lid using two hands

Learns/practices cognitive skills
  Groups vehicles by categories (colors, size, transportation mode)
  Counts vehicles
  Counts peers who are playing the game
  Sorts like vehicles when cleaning up
  Demonstrates one-to-one correspondence by handing out vehicles
  Demonstrates understanding of spatial concepts (e.g., in, next to)
  Explains directions to peers (recalls information)

Learns/practices social-communication skills
  Labels the vehicles using descriptors
  Uses conversational turn-taking (ask questions about the vehicles)
  Asks peers their color preference of vehicle
  Uses names of peers to tell them it is their turn

Learns/practices social skills
  Passes out vehicles to peers
  Takes turns with a desired vehicle
  Greets and invites new peers to join in and play the game
  Assists with cleanup

6. Planned variations

1. Add large vehicles.

2. Add props such as a Fisher-Price gas station with people.

3. Tape a large sheet of paper on the table, and let children draw roads.

4. Place materials in the sandbox outside.

5. Provide hats for children to wear that correspond with vehicles
   (e.g., firefighter hat, police officer hat, chauffeur hat).

continued

Figure 5.10.   *(continued)*

7. Vocabulary

Colors (e.g., blue, yellow, red, black, green, orange, lavender, lime, gold, purple)
Sizes (e.g., big, small, long, short, wide, narrow, tall, large, little)
Names of vehicles (e.g., plane, bulldozer, balloon, tricycle, bicycle, car, sailboat, helicopter, mail truck, police car, motorcycle, fire truck, jet plane)
Speed (e.g., fast, slow)
Location (e.g., up, down, around, in, out, beside, next to, on, under, below)
Names of signs (e.g., stop, yield, curve, railroad crossing, school bus stop, one way, no U-turn)

8. Peer interaction opportunities

Use long boards that require two children to pick up and move them.
Direct children's attention to peers' actions in activity.
Prompt children to imitate a particular action of peer.
Encourage children to plan together roads they will lay out on the floor with boards and blocks.

9. Caregiver involvement

Parents can provide different types of blocks.
Visit worksites of parents who use particular vehicles for their jobs (e.g., mail trucks, fire trucks, police cars, dump trucks, school bus).

Data Collection

The team reviews the intervention guide to develop a data collection system to monitor De'Shawn's performance on target goals. After reviewing the intervention guide, the team makes a number of decisions:

- Marlene (Head Start teacher) will record the objects/toys/materials De'Shawn manipulates prior to, during, or at the end of three different activities (i.e., arrival, free play, and outdoor play) two times a week. Marlene will also contact his mother and grandmother each month to see how De'Shawn is doing at home, then summarize the total number of different objects/toys/materials manipulated each month.

- Amy (occupational therapist) will record the objects/materials De'Shawn manipulates prior to, during, or at the end of snack one time a week.

- Nicole (itinerant teacher) will record the objects/toys/materials De'Shawn manipulates prior to, during, or at the end of either center time or free play one time a week.

- Parent volunteers will record the objects/toys/materials De'Shawn manipulates prior to, during, or at the end of center time one time a week.

- All team members will review data monthly to make decisions regarding changes to how goals are targeted and the accommodations, modifications, and intervention strategies provided.

The team also discusses how to create a data collection system that 1) is accessible and usable by everyone on the team, 2) keeps writing to a minimum, and 3) includes situational information and performance information. To create such a form, the team brainstorms the different objects that can be manipulated as De'Shawn participates across classroom activities. They consider objects and materials present within the different planned and routine activities (e.g., during snack time). The occupational therapist helps the team order the list from materials that are more difficult to manipulate (examples of the target goal) to materials that are easier to manipulate (examples of target benchmarks). The form is completed by merely noting or checking which objects he manipulates independently, with assistance, or does not yet manipulate. Figure 5.13 contains a data collection form the team uses to collect data on De'Shawn's target goal of manipulating objects. The team then meets regularly to discuss De'Shawn's progress and make intervention decisions.

SUMMARY

Four practices for applying an activity-based approach to intervention are discussed in this chapter: 1) conducting comprehensive and ongoing assessments; 2) targeting functional and generative goals; 3) selecting appropriate

Data Collection Form

Child's name: _De'Shawn_   Collected the week of: _September 8, 2003_

Person recording the data: _Shawna, Teresa, Marlene, Nicole, and Amy_

Examples of target behavior	Activity	De'Shawn's performance
Tie shoes	Arrival	–
Button clothing	Housekeeping	–
Thread and zip a zipper	Housekeeping	–
Cut out shapes with curved lines	Art	–
Hold a piece of paper and draw with a crayon, paintbrush, pencil, or marker	Free play	A
Hold a bowl and spoon up food or liquid	Snack/lunch	X
Hold container and pour substance (e.g., hold glass and pour juice, hold beaker and pour water, hold bucket and pour beans)	Discovery	X
Hold a container and dispense items (e.g., hold container and pass out napkins or utensils)	Snack/science	A
Hold a marker in one hand and push cap on with other, or hold onto Lego and connect another Lego	Art	X
Spread food with a knife (e.g., put peanut butter on bread)	Snack/lunch	A
Zip a zipper	Bathroom	A
Stack blocks	Free play	X
Turn pages of a book	Centers	X

Preformance scoring key:

X = manipulated the object without assistance
A = manipulated the object with physical assistance
– = made no attempt to manipulate the object even after prompts by an adult

Figure 5.13. Completed data collection form for De'Shawn's team to record his progress.

antecedents and consequences to deliver during child-directed, routine, and planned activities; and 4) monitoring the effects of intervention. Three examples illustrating the application of an activity-based approach across three broad service delivery models—home based, center based, and itinerant—are also provided.

REFERENCES

Alberto, P.A., & Troutman, A.C. (2003). *Applied behavior analysis for teachers* (6th ed.). Upper Saddle River, NJ: Merrill/Prentice-Hall.

Barnett, D., Bell, S., & Carey, K. (1999). *Designing preschool interventions: A practitioner's guide.* New York: The Guilford Press.

Bricker, D. (Series Ed.). (2002). *Assessment, Evaluation, and Programming System for Infants and Children* (2nd ed., Vols. 1–4). Baltimore: Paul H. Brookes Publishing Co.

Bricker, D. (Series Ed.). (2002). *Assessment, Evaluation, and Programming System for Infants and Children: Family Report* (2nd ed.) Baltimore: Paul H. Brookes Publishing Co.

Giangreco, M.F., Cloninger, C.J., & Iverson, V.S. (1998). *Choosing outcomes and accommodations for children: A guide to educational planning for students with disabilities.* Baltimore: Paul H. Brookes Publishing Co.

Hresko, W.P., Miguel, S.A., Sherbenou, R.J., & Burton, S.D. (1994). *Developmental observation checklist system: A systems approach to assessing very young children.* Austin, TX: PRO-ED.

McAfee, R., & Leong, D. (1997). *Assessing and guiding young children's development and learning.* Boston: Allyn & Bacon.

McLean, M., Wolery, M., & Bailey, D. (2004). *Assessing infants and preschoolers with special needs* (2nd ed.). Columbus, OH: Charles E. Merrill.

McWilliam, R.A. (1996). *Rethinking pull-out services in early intervention: A professional resource.* Baltimore: Paul H. Brookes Publishing Co.

Notari-Syverson, A., & Shuster, S. (1995). Putting real life skills into IEP/IFSPs for infants and young children. *Teaching Exceptional Children, 27*(2), 29–32.

Noonan, M., & McCormick, L. (1993). *Early intervention in natural environments: Methods and procedures.* Pacific Grove, CA: Brookes/Cole.

Sandall, S.R., & Schwartz, I.S. (with Joseph, G.E., Chou, H.-Y., Horn, E.M., Lieber, J., Odom S.L. & Wolery, R.). (2002). *Building blocks for teaching preschoolers with special needs.* Baltimore: Paul H. Brookes Publishing Co.

6

Activity-Based Intervention and the Team

As has been indicated throughout this volume, acceptable developmental progress for most children who have or are at risk for disabilities requires the contribution and involvement of a range of professionals, paraprofessionals, and caregivers. This range of individuals has been referred to as the child's *team*. This chapter describes how the successful implementation of activity-based intervention requires teams to work together across assessment, goal development, intervention, and evaluation processes.

THE TEAM

The composition of early intervention/early childhood special education and early childhood education teams varies across states, programs, agencies, and children. That is, one program may have a team composed of a special educator, caregiver, occupational therapist, and speech-language pathologist, whereas another agency may have a team composed of a Head Start teacher, itinerant teacher, and caregiver. The variability in team composition occurs for several reasons: local/state requirements, availability of personnel, agency resources, location of programs, program/agency philosophy, and children's individual needs. Although we recognize the variability in team composition, teams should ideally be composed of three populations: direct service delivery personnel, consultants, and caregivers.

Direct service delivery personnel are those people who provide the daily/weekly "hands on" interventions to the child and/or the family. Direct service delivery personnel can be early childhood teachers (e.g., Head Start/ Early Head Start, public/private school), child care workers, home visitors, paraprofessionals/assistants, or early interventionists/early childhood interventionists. Direct service delivery personnel tend to have their primary training in child development, child and family studies, general education, or special education. Increasingly, these personnel are being required to have additional training and hold licensure specific to working with young children with disabilities and their families (Bricker & Widerstrom, 1996; Malone, Straka, & Logan, 2000; Stayton & Bruder, 1999).

The second constituency group that should be represented on a team is consultants. These individuals have special disciplinary training that culminates with a professional licensure and can include occupational therapists, physical therapists, physicians, nurses, communication specialists, school psychologists, social workers, mental health specialists, nutritionists, vision specialists, hearing specialists, autism specialists, mobility specialists, itinerant teachers, and family therapists. As made clear in the IDEA Amendments of 1997 (PL 105-17), teams should include the expertise and perspectives from the range of disciplines necessary to address child and family needs (Huef-ner, 2000; Yell, Drasgow, & Ford, 2000). It is well documented that many children and families who participate in early intervention/early childhood special education and early childhood education programs have multiple challenges requiring assistance from a range of specialists (Bauer, Joseph, & Zwicker, 1998; Bricker & Veltman, 1990; Guralnick, 1997; Olson, Murphy, & Olson, 1998). Complex human needs require thoughtful solutions that can be derived only by examining the numerous facets of the problem and by developing procedures that are effective and able to be implemented. This process can best be ensured through the active cooperation and collaboration of a range of consultants.

The third constituency group that should be represented on teams is caregivers, including parents, grandparents, other relatives, foster parents, and, in some cases, friends. The inclusion of caregivers on the team is criti-cal to the successful application of activity-based intervention. The funda-mental tenets of the approach such as selecting meaningful skills, embedding learning opportunities in daily activities, and promoting learning through the daily transactions that occur between young children and their physical and social environment require that caregivers be involved throughout the processes of assessment, goal development, intervention, and evaluation. Without the integral participation of caregivers, professionals will find it dif-ficult to identify family values and priorities, address the needs of young chil-dren, or transform daily activities and transactions into meaningful learning opportunities (Jung, 2003).

Ideally, teams should be formed with representatives from these three constituency groups; however, this is only the first step to ensure a balanced and effective team. Unfortunately, little empirical information is available concerning the functioning of teams in general, and within an activity-based approach in particular. Therefore, the majority of our knowledge about teams and the application of activity-based intervention has been derived from experience.

Having the necessary skills to fill critical roles is of fundamental impor-tance; however, we also believe that it is equally important for team mem-bers to share an attitude about how children learn and how to best facilitate that learning. Going through the motions of an approach in a mechanical, nonenthusiastic manner is likely to lead to little change in children. The re-verse is also true; that is, any approach may be effective if delivered with commitment and enthusiasm (Friend & Cook, 2003; Walther-Thomas, Ko-rinek, & McLaughlin, 1999). To maximize children's progress, it seems best to adopt the approach with the greatest likelihood of success and then to employ this approach with genuine enthusiasm and the belief that it will be effective.

Teams wishing to adopt an activity-based approach in particular must be committed to a transactional perspective; that is, they need to recognize that learning occurs as a function of the child's interactions with, and feedback from, the environment (Sameroff & Fiese, 2000; Warren, Yoder, & Leew, 2002). Fundamental to change and growth are the daily interactions that occur between children and their social and physical environments. These exchanges or transactions should serve as the focus of team efforts. Team members should recognize that it is not the behavior of the child or adult in isolation but the cumulative effect of their exchanges that creates change.

Not only is it important to be enthusiastic about the chosen approach, it is also important that team members bring with them an attitude that fosters collaboration with and respect for other team members. The field has acknowledged for some time that no single person, discipline, and, in many cases, agency/program can meet the needs of diverse families and their children who have or are at risk for disabilities (Johnson, Ruiz, LaMontagne, & George, 1998; Park & Turnbull, 2003). Children may show an array of disabilities or needs that require the expertise of motor, communication, psychological, medical, or nutritional specialists. Their families may need an equally comprehensive range of services, including legal, educational, and therapeutic, or they may need assistance in day-to-day survival. Teams are necessary to address the many needs of children and families who are eligible for services. To maximize the services rendered to children and families, team members should convey to each other their mutual interdependence. Holding attitudes that foster respect and collaboration is an essential underpinning of effective team functioning.

In addition to displaying respect for professional expertise, similar attitudes toward caregivers should be nurtured. The inclusion of caregivers as team members should not be pro forma but instead be a genuine extension of equal partnership rights. The information and perspectives that caregivers bring to a team are essential in creating an accurate picture of the child's strengths, interests, and emerging skills demonstrated across settings. In addition, without caregiver participation, the determination of family values and priorities is an educated guess at best.

Teams implementing an activity-based approach will need to follow a number of specific guidelines related to practices in assessment, goal development, intervention, and evaluation. As described in Chapter 3, activity-based intervention is a comprehensive approach that is most successful when conceptualized and implemented within a linked system. The roles of direct service delivery personnel, consultants, and caregivers that appear necessary for the successful application of activity-based intervention within a linked system are described in the following section.

Table 6.1. Team guidelines for enhancing linked system processes

Linked system process	Guideline
Assessment	Use a comprehensive curriculum-based measure that addresses all of the important areas of development and encourages participation from all team members.
	Ensure all team members participate in gathering, summarizing, and interpreting information from the assessment process.
	Select assessment procedures that identify family resources, priorities, and concerns.
Goal development	Allow and encourage all team members to participate in selecting and prioritizing target goals.
	Select priority goals that address multiple areas of development and can be addressed by all team members. For example, selecting *Manipulates objects with both hands* as a target goal can be addressed by direct service providers, consultants, and caregivers alike to promote a child's ability to play with toys and gain independence with dressing and feeding.
	Use the revised version of the Goals and Objectives Rating Instrument (Notari-Syverson & Shuster, 1995) or other measures to ensure that target goals are understandable to all team members and functional for the child.
Intervention	Use the three forms (i.e., intervention guides, embedding schedules, and activity plans) discussed in Chapter 4 as a means of organizing intervention efforts among team members.
	Include caregivers in the planning and implementation of intervention efforts (e.g., designing or selecting activities, preparing materials, providing learning opportunities), and ensure that caregivers' priorities are incorporated in the design of daily activities.
	Encourage team members to demonstrate effective meeting skills so that the limited time they do have is spent on planning individualized instruction.
	Impress on administrators the need for adequate planning time with other team members.
Evaluation	Distribute the responsibilities for data collection among team members.
	Select data collection methods and procedures that are able to be understood and used by all team members. Avoid complicated procedures that require extensive training or time.
	Use planning time to review and interpret data to make joint decisions.

LINKING PROCESSES: A TEAM EFFORT

The successful application of activity-based intervention within a linked system requires that all team members work together across assessment, goal development, intervention, and evaluation processes. Table 6.1 provides a number of guidelines or suggestions for enhancing the team's work across the four processes of a linked system.

Principles to Guide Teams

Attention to developing models of team collaboration is growing by necessity, and an underlying theme of these models is that professionals and caregivers must coordinate their efforts (Bricker & Widerstrom, 1996; Briggs,

1997; Friend & Cook, 2003; Snell & Janney, 2000). Once such models are adopted, the next stage is to prepare individuals to use them. The following section presents a discussion of six principles that should guide teams in their application of activity-based intervention.

Principle 1

Team members need to understand and be committed to the approach. Previous sections of this chapter noted the importance of appropriate attitude and enthusiasm for the approach of choice. Team members should be willing to fulfill the roles necessary for the implementation of activity-based intervention. Individuals who are skeptical about the approach (as well as team collaboration) will likely not gain the skills necessary for successful application of activity-based intervention.

Principle 2

Team members need to engage in comprehensive and ongoing observations of young children across situations. Observing children's behavioral repertoires and determining under which conditions responses occur are fundamental to the successful use of activity-based intervention. Team members should be comfortable with the process of observing and not feel compelled to constantly respond or direct children's actions. For example, teams should observe children during play, during interactions with friends and siblings, and during the completion of daily routines rather than pulling them aside or creating contrived testing situations. To be efficient and useful, observation needs to be focused and yield objective findings. In other words, teams should be aware of the behaviors they intend to document and encourage the child to demonstrate these behaviors during authentic activities. Finally, team members should be able to discriminate between observable behavior (e.g., "Luis cried for 10 minutes following his mother's departure from the classroom") and inferences (e.g., "Because Luis was sad, he cried when his mother left the classroom"). Decisions need to be based on children's observable actions not on adult inferences of their actions.

Principle 3

Team members need to follow or respond to children's leads (Warren, 2000; Warren et al., 2002). Team members may see their roles as organizers of children's days by planning a series of activities or sets of therapy sessions. Although such planning is required to ensure the necessary infrastructure for activity-based intervention, the structure should not be used to direct activities but to ensure that opportunities are provided for children to practice target goals and objectives and that applicable interventions are incorporated into daily activities.

Principle 4

Team members need to shape child-directed, routine, or planned activities in directions that will yield desired outcomes. Through the careful use of antecedents and consequences, team members can become adept at designing and selecting activities that retain children's interest and involvement. For example, a caregiver can place specific items within a child's reach (e.g., crayons) to encourage practicing target fine motor skills or use attention and comments to encourage the continuation of an activity that promotes interaction with a peer. Team members should discuss the antecedents and consequences deemed appropriate and then ensure intervention efforts are consistent. This level of collaboration and consistency often requires joint planning time and the development of intervention guides such as the ones discussed and illustrated in Chapters 4 and 5.

Principle 5

Teams need to provide adequate numbers of opportunities for children to practice target goals and objectives. Our observations of center- and home-visiting programs suggest that caregivers, direct service delivery personnel, and consultants do not consistently recognize or make use of the many learning opportunities that could be vehicles for acquiring and practicing target goals and objectives. Often, one type of activity or most obvious activity is selected to address a child's particular needs, and other potential opportunities are disregarded. Again, careful observation may lead to appreciating children's interests and the environmental opportunities that may capture those interests, which, in turn, may significantly increase the number of available learning opportunities that occur across a child's day. Furthermore, a team approach is necessary to ensure adequate numbers of opportunities are provided across daily activities (Jung, 2003).

Principle 6

Teams need to create a balance among the types of activities employed through systematic monitoring of child progress. Given that intervention is integrated into functional daily events and activities, team members need to devise and use monitoring strategies that provide accurate feedback on children's progress toward target goals and objectives (Raver, 2003). Devising nonintrusive strategies that yield reliable findings at low cost is a challenge. The appropriate use of activity-based intervention, however, is not complete without attention to evaluation of child and family outcomes. Team members should work together to devise a system for monitoring children's performance and to share in data collection responsibilities. Teams need to consider the most efficient and effective methods for documenting children's behaviors. As discussed in Chapter 5, three main methods exist for documentation: written descriptions, permanent records, and counts and tallies. Advantages and disadvantages exist for each method. The three data collection methods are discussed in length by McLean and her colleagues (2004).

ADOPTING AND USING AN ACTIVITY-BASED APPROACH

Assisting team members in adopting and using activity-based intervention has been a goal since its inception as an approach to working with young children who have or are at risk for disabilities. We have provided information, in-service and preservice training, and support to thousands of professionals and caregivers. From this extensive experience, we have distilled three general levels of support and training that new users of the approach may wish to consider: 1) understanding the basics of the approach, 2) initiating application of the approach, and 3) refining the delivery of the approach. In addition, a range of support materials has been developed to assist team members in using and understanding the effects of an activity-based intervention. Table 6.2 highlights many of these materials, including printed materials, web sites, videotapes, and expert contact information. Pretti-Frontczak, Barr, Macy, and Carter (2003) provided a more comprehensive review of materials/resources related to an activity-based approach to intervention. Teams considering the use of activity-based intervention should review these materials/resources as well as examine the training levels described next to determine what type of assistance might be most useful to them.

Support and Training Levels

Consideration of adopting activity-based intervention should begin with team members developing an understanding and appreciation of the processes that underlie the approach. Acquiring a basic understanding of activity-based intervention can be accomplished by reading the material contained in this volume or other sources related to the approach, viewing videotapes illustrating the approach, visiting other programs implementing the approach, attending an introductory workshop that covers the basics of the approach, or getting information from a consultant who is an expert in the approach. Again, refer to Table 6.2 for a summary of available resources and Pretti-Frontczak and colleagues (2003) for a more extensive review. Teams should decide which strategy or strategies would likely be most useful to them. Teams also need to consider what resources are affordable. Many programs will be unable to pay for an individual consultant but they may have the resources to attend a regional workshop.

After acquiring a basic understanding of activity-based intervention, the second level is for team members to consider how to implement the approach given their environment and families served. It may be wise to begin small. For example, each teacher or interventionist might target one or two children and focus on embedding learning opportunities for these children's target goals across daily activities. Other program staff may find it more useful to begin with changing their approach to assessment. For example, if a program does not use curriculum-based measures to select goals and objectives, it will be necessary to adopt and use a measure that will yield the type of developmental information necessary to write functional and generative goals and objectives. Staff from such programs may want to begin by selecting a curriculum-based measure and become fluent in its use as a first step (see Bagnato, Neisworth, & Munson, 1997, for a review of curriculum-based measures).

The third level of refining the team's skills in using the approach could also be thought of as going to scale. That is, the team can move from focusing on one or two processes or children to implementing the entire system with all participating children and families. We believe that this level, as well

Table 6.2. Overview of support materials available for teams using an activity-based approach

Type	Examples
Printed materials	Bricker, D. (Series Ed.). (2002). *Assessment, Evaluation, and Programming System for Infants and Children* (2nd ed.). Baltimore: Paul H. Brookes Publishing Co.
	Sandall, S., & Schwartz, I. (2002). *Building blocks for teaching preschoolers with special needs.* Baltimore: Paul H. Brookes Publishing Co.
Web sites	Early Literacy Project (http://www.ced.appstate.edu/projects/earlyliteracyproject/index.htm)
	Individualizing Inclusion in Child Care (http://www.fpg.unc.edu/~inclusion/)
	Project PLAY—Promoting Positive Outcomes Through an Activity-Based Approach with Young Children with Severe Disabilities (http://fpsrv.dl.kent.edu/play)
	Project TaCTICS—Therapists as Collaborative Team Members for Infant/Toddler Community Services (http://tactics.fsu.edu/)
Videos	Bricker, D., Veltman, M., & Munkres, A. (1995). *Activity-based intervention* [videotape]. Baltimore: Paul H. Brookes Publishing Co.
	Mandell, C. (2000). *Project ENHANCE: Using an activity-based approach to intervention with young children with low incidence disabilities and their families* [videotape]. Bowling Green, OH: Bowling Green State University.
	Woods Cripe, J.J., & Crabtree, J. (1995). *Family-guided activity-based intervention for infants and toddlers* [videotape]. Baltimore: Paul H. Brookes Publishing Co.
Expert contact information	Inquiries regarding scheduled workshops and/or available consultants should be directed to the following contacts or web sites:
	Misti Waddell, University of Oregon (waddemis@darkwing.uoregon.edu) (http://www.uoregon.edu/~eip/AEPS/aeps.html)
	Paul H. Brookes Publishing Company, Brookes On Location (http://www.brookespublishing.com/onlocation/)
	Model demonstration sites implementing an activity-based approach can be found in the following states:
	Kentucky—Contact Jennifer Grisham-Brown (jgleat00@pop.uky.edu) regarding Project PLAY model demonstration sites in Kentucky.
	Ohio—Contact Kristie Pretti-Frontczak (kprettif@kent.edu) regarding Project PLAY model demonstration sites in Ohio.
	Texas—Contact Lynn Sullivan (lsullivan@esc11.net) regarding Region XI activity-based intervention teams.

as level two, is the best approach when possible in the context of the program rather than in artificial situations (e.g., workshops). Superimposing training on activities that occur in the home or center permits addressing real concerns and challenges team members to confront and solve real problems in order for the application of the approach to be successful. Professional development in the home and center should also help to maximize generalizability of what team members learn. Again the most effective strategy is likely having a consultant who can work with the team. Programs with limited resources may have to look for creative alternatives. For example, there may be a local expert who would not require travel expenses, the team might be able to videotape sessions that could be mailed to a consultant for review and feedback, or team members might learn to assist each other in improving their use of the approach.

Learning to follow children's initiations and embedding learning opportunities into daily activities appear to be two of the more challenging aspects of applying activity-based intervention for many caregivers and professional team members. Some caregivers and interventionists appear to follow children's initiations naturally while others, particularly those with a long history of orchestrating children's activities, may find it difficult to wait for children to initiate actions. Videotaping adult–child interactions can be illuminating for interventionists who tend to overdirect children's activities. Videotaping interventionists or collecting frequency data on number of learning opportunities embedded may also provide valuable feedback to interventionists who miss significant numbers of teachable moments.

SUMMARY

The successful application of activity-based intervention requires the collaboration of teams consisting of direct service delivery personnel, consultants, and caregivers. Teams need to find strategies that permit collaboration across the four major processes of assessment, goal development, intervention, and evaluation. This chapter presents six principles that can be used to guide teams in the application of activity-based intervention. Three levels of training and resources teams may find useful as they move to implement the activity-based approach are also described.

REFERENCES

Bagnato, S.J., Neisworth, J.T., & Munson, S.M. (1997). *LINKing assessment and early intervention: An authentic curriculum-based approach.* Baltimore: Paul H. Brookes Publishing Co.

Bauer, A., Joseph, S., & Zwicker, S. (1998). Supporting collaborative partnerships. In L.J. Johonson, M.J. LaMontagne, P.M. Elgas, & A.M. Bauer (Eds.), *Early childhood education: Blending theory, blending practice* (pp. 63–80). Baltimore: Paul H. Brookes Publishing Co.

Bricker, D., & Veltman, M. (1990). Early intervention programs: Child-focused approaches. In S.J. Meisels & J.P. Shonkoff (Eds.), *Handbook of early childhood intervention* (pp. 373–399). New York: Cambridge University Press.

Bricker, D., & Widerstrom, A. (Eds.). (1996). *Preparing personnel to work with infants and young children and their families: A team approach.* Baltimore: Paul H. Brookes Publishing Co.

Briggs, M. (Vol. Ed.). (1997). A systems model for early intervention teams. In K.G. Butler (Series Ed.), *Building early intervention teams: Working together for children and families* (pp. 87–122). Gaithersburg, MD: Aspen Publishers.

Friend, M., & Cook, L. (2003). *Interactions: Collaboration skills for school professionals* (4th ed.). Boston: Allyn & Bacon.

Guralnick, M.J. (1997). Second-generation research in the field of early intervention. In M.J. Guralnick (Ed.), *The effectiveness of early intervention* (pp. 3–20). Baltimore: Paul H. Brookes Publishing Co.

Huefner, D. (2000). The risks and opportunities of the IEP requirements under IDEA '97. *Journal of Special Education, 33,* 195–204.

Individuals with Disabilities Education Act Amendments of 1997, PL 105-17, 20 U.S.C. §§ 1400 *et seq.*

Johnson, L., Ruiz, D., LaMontagne, M., & George, E. (1998). The history of collaboration: Its importance to blending early childhood education and early childhood special education practices. In L.J. Johnson, M.J. LaMontagne, P.M. Elgas, & A.M. Bauer (Eds.), *Early childhood education: Blending theory, blending practice* (pp. 1–17). Baltimore: Paul H. Brookes Publishing Co.

Jung, L. (2003). More is better: Maximizing natural learning opportunities. *Young Exceptional Children, 6,* 21–26.

Malone, D., Straka, E., & Logan, K. (2000). Professional development in early intervention: Creating effective inservice training opportunities. *Infants and Young Children, 12,* 53–62.

McLean, M., Wolery, M., & Bailey, D. (2004). *Assessing infants and preschoolers with special needs* (2nd ed.). Columbus, OH: Charles E. Merrill.

Notari-Syverson, A., & Shuster, S. (1995). Putting real life skills into IEP/IFSPs for infants and young children. *Teaching Exceptional Children, 27*(2), 29–32.

Olson, J., Murphy, C., & Olson, P. (1998). Building effective successful teams: An interactive teaming model for inservice education. *Journal of Early Intervention, 21,* 339–349.

Park, J., & Turnbull, A. (2003). Service integration in early intervention: Determining interpersonal and structural factors for its success. *Infants and Young Children, 16,* 48–58.

Pretti-Frontczak, K., Barr, D., Macy, M., & Carter, A. (2003). An annotated bibliography of research and resources related to activity-based intervention, embedded learning opportunities, and routines-based instruction. *Topics in Early Childhood Special Education, 23,* 29–39.

Raver, S. (2003). Keeping track: Using routine-based instruction and monitoring. *Young Exceptional Children, 6,* 12–20.

Sameroff, A., & Fiese, B. (2000). Transactional regulation: The developmental ecology of early intervention. In J. Skonkoff & S. Meisels (Eds.), *Handbook of early childhood intervention* (pp. 135–159). New York: Cambridge University Press.

Snell, M.E., & Janney, R. (2000). *Teachers' guides to inclusive practices: Collaborative teaming.* Baltimore: Paul H. Brookes Publishing Co.

Stayton, V., & Bruder, M. (1999). Early intervention personnel preparation for the new millennium: Early childhood special education. *Infants and Young Children 12,* 59–69.

Walther-Thomas, C., Korinek, L., & McLaughlin, V. (1999). Collaboration to support students' success. *Focus on Exceptional Children, 30*(3), 1–18.

Warren, S. (2000). The future of early communication and language intervention. *Topics in Early Childhood Special Education, 20,* 33–37.

Warren, S., Yoder, P., & Leew, S. (2002). Promoting social-communicative development in infants and toddlers. In S.F. Warren & J. Reichle (Series Eds.) & H. Goldstein, L.A. Kaczmarek, & K.M. English (Vol. Eds.), *Communication and language intervention series: Vol 10. Promoting social communication: Children with developmental disabilities from birth to adolescence* (pp. 121–149). Baltimore: Paul H. Brookes Publishing Co.

Yell, M., Drasgow, E., & Ford, L. (2000). The individuals with disabilities education act amendments of 1997: Implications for school-based teams. In C.F. Telzrow, & M. Tankersley (Eds.), *IDEA Amendments of 1997: Practice guidelines for school-based teams* (pp. 1–28). Bethedsa, MD: National Association of School Psychologists.

7

Issues Associated with the Use of an Activity-Based Approach

Activity-based intervention is built on straightforward principles that are grounded in theory and research. The application of the approach, however, as with any comprehensive approach, offers a number of challenges. These challenges surface because of the complexities associated with human learning and the intervention process. This edition of *An Activity-Based Approach to Early Intervention* makes a number of changes from previous editions that are intended to make activity-based intervention more effective and more easily understood, but it is likely that the reader will still confront important issues associated with the implementation of the approach. To anticipate the reader's questions and concerns, this chapter discusses the salient issues that have been identified by professionals and caregivers using or thinking of using activity-based intervention.

During the more than 20 years that activity-based intervention has been employed to assist young children in reaching their developmental and learning goals, a number of implementation issues have been identified. These issues include 1) following children's lead, 2) feeling a loss of control, 3) creating opportunities to practice target skills, 4) applying the approach to children with severe disabilities, 5) using the approach in community-based programs, and 6) needing collaboration among team members.

FOLLOWING CHILDREN'S LEAD

Capitalizing on activities that are of interest to children is an important element of activity-based intervention. Following children's lead and initiations or using activities that children find inherently motivating keeps interest high and usually alleviates the need for artificial feedback and consequences. Furthermore, following children's lead and interests allows many child–environment transactions to focus on learning from the adult's perspective while remaining fun from the child's perspective. For example, if an interventionist wants a child to practice articulation skills (e.g., s-blend sounds) and knows the child likes Scooby Doo, the interventionist can create multiple learning opportunities just by introducing several large cardboard Scooby Doo books. As a result of the child's interest in Scooby Doo, he is likely to respond to questions and cues that prompt him to make s-blend sounds (e.g., *Scooby, snack, Shaggy, stone, stick, start, scary*) while looking at the books. The child is also able to share information with peers about the characters and actions in the book, providing additional opportunities to practice s-blend sounds during authentic child–environment transactions.

Following children's lead and interests raises an issue of whether children will direct their initiations or interests to activities that will necessarily address their particular cognitive, social, communicative, adaptive, or motor delays. It may be unrealistic to expect children, especially those with challenging physical, mental, or emotional needs, or a combination of needs, to consistently select activities that would enhance or expand their current repertoires. For example, a child with a serious articulation problem may find it both unproductive and unrewarding to ask for desired objects. The child who walks with difficulty may not be inclined to engage in actions that require walking. Furthermore, a child who has difficulty interacting with others is unlikely to seek out peers and engage in cooperative play activities. These examples make it evident that team members cannot always wait for children to initiate activities that will necessarily lead to practicing target skills in areas of need.

Successful application of activity-based intervention requires that child-directed activities be balanced with embedding multiple and varied learning opportunities and providing timely and integral feedback/consequences that addresses individual priority goals and objectives during routine and planned activities. The balancing of these elements is essential. Children are encouraged to initiate and direct activities; however, the activities should incorporate their individual needs. For example, children may indicate the desire to sing the same songs at group time. The interventionist may be able to adapt the children's requests by adding new target words or actions to the songs, by introducing new songs containing similar components of desired songs, or by interspersing other activities between songs into which practice opportunities for target skills can be embedded.

Successful application of activity-based intervention also requires the careful scrutiny of child initiations to ensure that practice on target skills occurs and, if it does not occur, to shape child-directed activities so that they do incorporate target goals. For example, Keith has a motor impairment that requires the use of a wheelchair. A priority goal for Keith is to move to avoid obstacles (e.g., toys, furniture, people), go up and down inclines, and travel across different surfaces (e.g., cement, carpet) when operating his wheelchair. Not surprising, this 5-year-old would rather play computer games with his friends than practice maneuvering his wheelchair. Thus, when implementing an activity-based approach, the teacher arranges multiple situations for Keith to maneuver his wheelchair during daily activities (e.g., moving around other peers to get to the computer, moving around play equipment to get to where his friends wait). These examples of authentic opportunities capitalize on Keith's interest (i.e., playing computer games and being with his friends) to practice the target skill of using and maneuvering his wheelchair. With thought and planning, embedding learning opportunities that may appear incompatible with high-interest activities can be accomplished while still respecting children's choices and reinforcing their initiations.

Efficient child change will not occur unless children's needs are frequently and systematically addressed. Furthermore, within an activity-based approach, interventionists are responsible for including caregivers in intervention activities to ensure multiple and varied opportunities are provided for children during daily routines and other preferred activities. Children's needs should be reflected in their individualized family service plan (IFSP) outcomes or individualized education program (IEP) goals and objectives/benchmarks, which, in turn, should guide and direct intervention efforts. If caregivers and interventionists are aware of the children's educational and therapeutic goals and objectives, then activities that are child-directed, routine, and planned can be used to address the acquisition, strengthening, and/or generalization of target skills. Using IFSPs/IEPs to guide intervention efforts ensures that activity-based intervention is directed by the developmental needs of children while attending to their unique interests and developmental readiness.

To reiterate, activity-based intervention is not a laissez-faire approach that is directed totally by children and their interests. The approach is designed, when possible, to use the activities initiated and enjoyed by children. The use of child initiations, however, does not preclude the introduction of planned activities or the use of routine activities, nor does it preclude the redirection of child-directed activities. The balance among child-directed, routine, and planned activities ensures children's needs are systematically addressed.

FEELING A LOSS OF CONTROL

Direct service delivery personnel, consultants, and caregivers who have typically scripted and directed children's activities have reported feeling a significant loss of control when first employing child-directed approaches such as activity-based intervention. Team members who have traditionally chosen the intervention activities may be uncomfortable using an approach that responds to and encourages child initiations. Furthermore, the training that many professionals have experienced—particularly those working with individuals who have disabilities—has taught them the importance of structure and the need to occupy children with productive tasks.

Interventionists may sense the loss of some control when children are permitted to reshape an activity or introduce an unanticipated action; however, if that activity is directed toward the children's goals and objectives, then the lack of predictability for the interventionist is likely not important. Furthermore, the role of the interventionist is actually more critical within this approach given the need to ensure frequent and meaningful practice opportunities to address target skills and child-directed, routine, and planned activities are provided. In other words, rather than losing control, activity-based intervention offers team members additional ways of encouraging children's learning of important target skills.

Some professionals have also voiced concern that following children's leads or initiations may result in children's engagement in nonproductive activities or in moving from activity to activity without sustained interest or involvement. Most professionals have encountered children whose attention span is short and who, if permitted, cycle quickly through many activities, apparently without learning new skills. Is activity-based intervention appropriate for such children? Does this approach encourage and intensify their inability to focus and sustain attention? If team members are following children's leads and encouraging self-initiated activities, will children learn they can control the situation and shift activities at the expense of learning new skills or expanding their behavioral repertoires? We believe use of activity-based intervention and in particular following children's leads or responding to their interests does not necessarily result in loss of control. In fact, the appropriate application of activity-based intervention does not permit children to engage in nonproductive or inappropriate actions. Rather, the approach provides an underlying structure that we believe enhances children's learning and use of functional and generative skills. The following example illustrates how interventionists might shape a child's nonproductive initiations into productive outcomes.

Bailey

Bailey is a 2-year-old with a moderate developmental delay. She frequently initiates action but rarely spends more than a few minutes involved in any single activity. Bailey might look at a book for a few seconds, then discard the book to pick up a toy which, in turn, is quickly dropped in order to snatch another toy from her brother. Although her activities are child directed, to permit Bailey to continue such behavior does not represent an appropriate application of activity-based intervention. Activity-based intervention does not require that interventionists and caregivers relinquish total control over children and their activities.

When employing activity-based intervention with a child like Bailey, an initial step would be for the team to document patterns in Bailey's behavior through ongoing observations. Such observations are critical for 1) understanding what motivates and interests Bailey, 2) determining Bailey's present level of performance to ensure adult expectations are consistent with her current skill level, and 3) creating daily activities and interactions that provide sufficient structure and guidance to support Bailey's acquisition of target skills. Such observations and systematic exploration by varying activities and feedback should culminate in the team learning how to use Bailey's initiated actions in ways that are appropriate and sustained. Effective use of activity-based intervention should permit Bailey to initiate a variety of actions while simultaneously permitting the interventionists/caregivers to shape and guide these initiations into productive behavior.

To repeat, use of activity-based intervention does not require that interventionists or caregivers follow child initiations when they do not lead to productive outcomes. *Productive outcome* refers to improvement in children's IFSP/IEP goals and objectives as long as those goals and objectives are functional. The development of functional and generative goals is fundamental to the appropriate use of activity-based intervention. The selection of meaningful intervention targets provides the necessary guidance for selecting meaningful antecedents and activities and for monitoring change over time. Child-directed, routine, or planned activities should always address the acquisition of children's goals and objectives. If goals for Bailey include those that address her interactions with toys and others in her environment, then the interventionist would instigate activities or support child-directed activities that provide opportunities to work on these goals. Caregivers could use a variety of strategies to encourage sustained interactions with Bailey's favorite materials or toys. For example, if Bailey gets a book from her bedroom, adults may encourage her to select books that allow her to perform an action (e.g., *Pat the Bunny,* or Peek and Lift Tab books), thereby increasing the likelihood that she will remain with the activity for a longer period of time but still building on her interest or initiations.

Underlying this discussion of control is the need for advanced planning by interventionists, preferably with other team members (Grisham-Brown & Pretti-Frontczak, 2003). Without advanced planning, interventionists may struggle in terms of selecting appropriate intervention targets or strategies and interpreting outcomes correctly. Furthermore, without advanced planning, interventionists may not capitalize on or blend learning opportunities found in child-directed, routine, or planned activities. The framework underlying activity-based intervention and organizational strategies that require advanced and ongoing planning are discussed in Chapters 3 and 4, respectively.

CREATING OPPORTUNITIES TO PRACTICE TARGET SKILLS

How many and what type of learning opportunities should be presented to children is an important issue for those using activity-based intervention as well as any other intervention approach. Providing multiple opportunities to learn target goals and objectives seems particularly important for young children with disabilities, and it is likely that the magnitude or severity of the disability is correlated with the amount of practice necessary for children to learn target skills. Unfortunately, there is little empirical work to permit drawing firm conclusions about how frequently opportunities should be presented, how much contextual conditions should vary, and what type of opportunities should be presented. Finding empirical answers to these important questions should become part of the research agenda; however, until there are objective findings, practitioners must rely on guidelines derived from their collective experience.

How frequently should learning opportunities be presented? The answer is likely tied to such factors as child characteristics, nature of the target skills, and available resources. Nonetheless, offering multiple opportunities to practice important skills appears necessary to promote the acquisition of new skills and the strengthening and generalization of existing skills. In general, interventionists and caregivers are encouraged to provide or create many authentic learning opportunities as illustrated in the following example.

Cameron

Cameron is a 5-year-old boy with developmental delays. His team is planning intervention activities to address his IEP goal. During the process, team members consider each of Cameron's target goals, his interests, and the possible authentic activities that occur during the school day into which opportunities to address specific goals could be embedded. In this case, the team addresses Cameron's goal to print his name. They use Cameron's interest in computers to arrange authentic opportunities to practice printing his name. The interventionist places a sign-up sheet next to the computer and makes it clear to all children the need to print their names on the list if they wish to use the computer. In addition, the interventionist can use the same sign-up strategy for children, and in particular Cameron, to gain access to other desired activities (e.g., the sand table).

The team also targets creating nametags that can be hung on various objects that belong to Cameron (e.g., his lunch bag), or places (e.g., his bedroom door), or children (e.g., his friends) as another activity that offers opportunities for Cameron to print his name. A planned post office activity may also offer a number of opportunities for Cameron to print his name (e.g., signing letters). Finally, Cameron's goal could be addressed by making sure pencils, pens, or crayons are available to write his name on any art project. The choice of these activities to embed learning opportunities for Cameron to address his goal is largely directed by his interests.

When offering children opportunities to practice target goals, how much should conditions and settings vary? For skills to be maximally useful, chil-

dren need to be able to execute them across a variety of settings and conditions rather than being tied to specific antecedents or activities. For example,
if a child is learning the names of common objects, then she can work on
labeling objects many times throughout the day. The caregiver or interventionist should examine the child's daily schedule and note the different settings and conditions where the child could potentially practice target object
names. For example, opportunities might be available to practice object-
naming skills during reading time, snack time, and bath time. Such activities
may provide numerous authentic opportunities where labeling an object is
meaningful and useful to the child. The example provided next illustrates
how Karlee's intervention team systematically varied settings and conditions
to reach a skill targeted on her IFSP.

Karlee

Karlee is a 2-year-old who is not yet walking; consequently, an important
IFSP outcome is to walk independently across a variety of surfaces using alternating steps so her family will not have to carry her. Because Karlee has

low muscle tone in her legs and is hypersensitive to touch, the team decides the initial opportunities to address her walking goal should occur with her mother in the living room. In this setting, Karlee's mother provides Karlee with hip support, and the carpeted floor is less offensive to touch. Over time, Karlee's mother reduces the amount of physical assistance she provides her daughter. Once Karlee is able to take a few independent steps on the rug, her mother encourages her to walk on the kitchen's tile floor and across the hallway to look out the window. In addition, opportunities to walk to her father, the neighbor, and her siblings are offered across settings. Eventually, Karlee's mother takes her to the park to provide her with opportunities to use her walking skills in a new setting that offers different conditions.

Within an activity-based approach, interventionists are encouraged to use variety when creating learning opportunities. Specifically, activity-based intervention does "not attempt to teach children to respond to specific cues under specific conditions, rather, [it] attempts to teach generative and functional skills across development domains" (Losardo & Bricker, 1994, p. 745). The important aspect to consider is the need to vary the opportunities (i.e., vary the setting, people, materials, and strategies) not only to ensure the initial acquisition of critical skills, but also to ensure the eventual generalization of skills. As shown in the example with Karlee, conditions, settings, and people gradually changed to ensure that the child is able to successfully walk in more challenging environments.

What type of learning opportunities should be presented? We believe that learning opportunities should be meaningful and relevant to children to the extent possible. Our underlying belief is that when antecedents and feedback are matched to children's interests and developmental level and integrated into authentic activities, positive outcomes are likely to occur.

The skills targeted for intervention should be taken from children's IFSP/IEPs; therefore, it is essential that program staff develop high-quality IFSPs/IEPs. To serve as the primary source for targeting intervention efforts, target skills should be developmentally appropriate, address important behaviors, and produce genuine functional outcomes for children and families (Hemmeter & Grisham-Brown, 1998).

Interventionists and caregivers should ensure that children acquire and generalize important response classes that include problem solving, communication, physical manipulation of environmental objects, mobility, and adaptive and social interaction skills. Targeting the response class of mobility, for example, does not mean that all children will learn to walk, but it does mean that independent mobility should be a goal for most children, whether mobility is accomplished by foot, walker, wheelchair, or other adapted system. The comprehensive and pervasive nature of response classes provides numerous opportunities for thoughtful and innovative caregivers and interventionists to use child initiations or to embed practice opportunities into routine and planned activities as is illustrated in the following example.

Andre

Andre is a 4-year-old who meets his needs by pointing and vocalizing. After a comprehensive assessment, his intervention team targets two important social communication goals: Andre will use consistent word approximations, and Andre will locate objects, people, and/or events without contextual cues. These goals were taken from the Assessment, Evaluation, and Programming System for Infants and Children, Second Edition (Bricker, 2002), and meet the criteria specified previously for meaningful goals. That is, these two goals are developmentally appropriate, address important developmental skills, and should produce functional outcomes for Andre and his family. In addition, the type of social communication goals selected for Andre permits the team to identify numerous activities in which learning opportunities targeting these goals can be embedded. These goals also permit the use of a wide range of authentic activities. For example, Andre's access to desired objects or events can be made contingent on his use of consistent word approximations. A range of events and games can be structured around having Andre locate named objects or people. Adults can even provide Andre with choices between different objects to give additional opportunities to practice the target skill of using word approximations. The selection of appropriate and useful goals will do much to ensure intervention efforts with children are effective and produce desired outcomes.

APPLYING THE APPROACH TO CHILDREN WITH SEVERE DISABILITIES

Another important issue is the applicability of activity-based intervention to infants, toddlers, and young children with moderate to severe disabilities. Children considered to be typically developing and those who have or who are at risk for mild disabilities tend to engage in many more diverse activities than do children with more severe disabilities. In addition, children with less severe disabilities are often more easily engaged, and their attention may be maintained longer. Children with less severe disabilities tend to initiate action and respond more frequently than do children with more severe disabilities. In fact, a major characteristic of many people with severe disabilities is the lack of appropriate self-initiated activity (e.g., Koegel, Koegel, Frea, & Smith, 1995).

An important question is whether the lack of initiation—or at least appropriate initiation—in individuals with severe disabilities is physiologically based or is systematically fostered by their being ignored or punished by the social environment (Guess & Siegel-Causey, 1985). We believe that the low frequency of useful initiations by children with severe disabilities stems from a combination of biological problems and previous experience. As Drasgow, Halle, Ostrosky, and Harbers (1996) pointed out, many young children with severe disabilities have a number of subtle or idiosyncratic behaviors that could be used or shaped into useful responses. Our experience suggests, however, that often these responses are ignored, and instruction is directed toward adult imposition of the response to be performed by the child.

For children without disabilities, play and self-initiated activities provide essential vehicles for learning increasingly more complex social, communicative, cognitive, and motor skills. We believe that play and child initiations are equally important ways for children with severe disabilities to learn new skills. Activity-based intervention supports this form of learning by emphasizing the importance of child-directed interactions within daily caregiving routines, play, and planned activities. Caregivers and interventionists need to carefully observe and respond to the occurrence of children's signals and actions, however minimal and idiosyncratic, and to build on these responses or redirect them into more useful and meaningful response forms. For example, Denzel is a preschool child with a severe cognitive disability who has an IEP goal of initiating and responding to communicative interactions. He spends much of his day sitting and gazing around his environment without initiating interactions with others; however, the staff have noticed that he often responds to music and singing by turning to the source of the sound, smiling, and initiating small body movements. The intervention team decides to introduce the song, "Row, Row, Row Your Boat" in an interactive manner. An interventionist sits on the floor across from Denzel and holds both his hands. While singing, she moves Denzel's body gently back and forth. Denzel responds to the action/song by rocking back and forth with the interventionist. The interventionist ceases singing and rocking and waits for Denzel to initiate some communicative action (e.g., pulling on her hands) that results in continued singing and rocking. In addition, the interventionist prompts the use of the sign for MORE.

We believe that increased attention to enhancing appropriate child-directed activity (not self-destructive or stereotypical behavior) may enhance the ability of children with severe disabilities to show caregivers and interventionists what they like and what interests them. In fact, some treatment by level of development analyses (i.e., aptitude) find that younger children with fewer skills benefit more from child-driven interventions than from adult-driven approaches (e.g., Cole, Dale, & Mills, 1991; Yoder, Kaiser, & Alpert, 1991; Yoder et al., 1995). These findings, however, do not negate the need for structure and careful programming for children with severe disabilities.

The adequacy of instruction across areas of need requires coordination and joint planning by team members involved in a child's intervention program. This coordination and planning is especially important for children with severe disabilities if they are to develop functional and generalizable skills that, as indicated previously, have consistently been identified as serious problems for this population (e.g., Drasgow et al., 1996; Horner, Dunlap, & Koegel, 1988). Furthermore, a primary challenge of working with young children with severe disabilities stems from medical issues and conditions that affect learning and may interrupt team members' plans. Such interruptions (e.g., hospitalization) may result in significant regression that may require retargeting previously learned skills. Teams should remain flexible in order to adapt to changes in the children's environments or conditions.

Activity-based intervention uses the behavior analytic techniques known to be successful in helping individuals with severe disabilities acquire useful and meaningful skills. The approach incorporates the people and places important to children by intervening in daily routines, and it emphasizes skills with immediate utility by providing something helpful or desirable for children as needs arise (e.g., getting the child a cup of juice when he vocalizes and points to the juice pitcher). Intervention targets are addressed across activities to ensure that learning opportunities occur under different conditions to increase the generalizability of skills.

Activity-based intervention does not preclude, nor is it incompatible with, the use of adult-directed strategies or a massed-trial format (i.e., asking the child to repeat the same response across several sequential trials). The magnitude and number of problems presented by children with severe disabilities will likely require team members to employ a variety of teaching strategies if they are to ensure systematic child progress. The successful use of activity-based intervention requires the thoughtful balancing of planned activities with child initiations and the balancing of learning opportunities across activities.

USING THE APPROACH IN COMMUNITY-BASED PROGRAMS

Increasing numbers of children with disabilities are being placed in community-based child care, educational, and recreational programs (Janko, Schwartz, Sandall, Anderson, & Cottam, 1997; Odom, Favazza, Brown, & Horn, 2000; Wolery et al., 1993). Most of these programs were designed to accommodate typically developing children and their families. Furthermore, these staff members generally have training and experience focused on typically developing children and their families. Thus, the placement of children with disabilities into community-based programs presents a number of challenges

(Bricker, 2001; Grisham-Brown, Pretti-Frontczak, Hemmeter, & Ridgley, 2002). Community staff need to be prepared to offer children with disabilities specialized instruction or to manage the children's behavior successfully. Community staff members often operate with limited budgets, which may not permit individualized attention to participating children. The use of activity-based intervention cannot solve all of these problems; however, the approach's reliance on routine activities and child initiations makes it compatible with how most community-based programs function and, therefore, applicable for use in these programs.

The significant compatibility between activity-based intervention and the philosophy and operation of many community-based programs is present because activity-based intervention's foundation evolved, in part, from the child development and early education literature and practice rather than exclusively from special education. Encouraging child initiations and child-directed actions within the context of routine and play activities is familiar to most child care workers and early childhood teachers.

In addition, activity-based intervention is compatible with developmentally appropriate practice (DAP) that guides quality child care and early education programs. Both activity-based intervention and DAP encourage child exploration and initiation, embed consequences into child activity, target tasks that are developmentally appropriate for children, and view adults as supporters of children's actions and interests.

Activity-based intervention encourages the physical, social, and instructional inclusion of children with disabilities in all activities rather than relocating children into isolated settings for specific instruction. The activity-based approach emphasizes the use of antecedents and consequences that can be provided in child-directed as well as teacher-directed activities. These emphases blend well with most approaches used in community-based programs; however, the application of activity-based intervention in community-based settings will likely require modifications in the approach.

The successful use of activity-based intervention in community-based programs depends on whether mechanisms are in place to ensure that children with disabilities are assessed, appropriate IFSP/IEP goals are developed, ample opportunities to practice target skills are provided, and progress is monitored. Most child care workers and early education personnel are not prepared or trained to conduct these activities. Consequently, the use of activity-based intervention will likely require that training and support be provided to the staff of community-based programs. The philosophical congruence between activity-based intervention and DAP, however, as well as the compatibility between activity-based intervention and the previous experiences of early childhood workers should enhance the understanding and openness to this training.

NEEDING COLLABORATION AMONG TEAM MEMBERS

Implementation of an activity-based approach depends on linking key processes including assessment, goal development, intervention, and evaluation.
Procedures and rationale for linking processes are described in Chapter 3.
Due to the interrelatedness of processes and many of the issues described
previously, we have found that when adults work collaboratively, implementation of activity-based intervention is more likely to be successful. That
said, we also understand the reality in which interventionists are expected
to deliver services, and we recognize the challenges collaboration presents.
For information on team collaboration, refer to Bricker and Widerstrom
(1996), Dinnebeil, Haleand, and Rule (1999), Snell and Janney (2000), and
Swan and Morgan (1993). This section addresses the reasons team collaboration is important to the implementation of activity-based intervention. Chapter 6 also provides a number of suggestions for implementing an activity-based
approach as a team.

Activity-based intervention lends itself well to an integrated and collaborative team approach, primarily because participating children and families
need support from professionals with different expertise. Thus, a primary
reason for promoting collaboration among team members (e.g., caregivers,
teachers, therapists) is to address the complex needs of young children who
experience problems, young children with severe disabilities, and young children who are at risk, all of whom often require a cadre of personnel to meet
their needs (e.g., educational, therapeutic, social, and medical professionals). It is vital that these personnel work together in addressing the needs of
the child within the context of the child's family and larger community.

A second, though no less important, reason for team collaboration within an activity-based approach is to ensure the targeting of functional and
generative skills across environments. Recommended practice suggests that
prioritized skills targeted for intervention address children's needs for participation in daily activities (e.g., feeding, playing) and participation in family
routines (e.g., eating at restaurants, going to the grocery store) (Sandall, Mc-
Lean, & Smith, 2000). Thus, team members often need to cross traditional discipline boundaries to address target skills, rather than relocating children into
isolated settings for specific instruction. For example, a speech-language
pathologist or another team member assigned to a preschool classroom does
not need to request separate space away from classmates to practice a child's
target language skills. The specialist can join the child in the classroom and
observe and embed opportunities to practice language skills in usual classroom activities. Specialists can also observe ongoing activities, then give the
preschool teacher feedback regarding the opportunities he or she could cre-

ate for the child and how to build on these opportunities. Intervention is likely to be more effective if used across settings and conditions more available to the preschool teacher than to a specialist who visits infrequently.

Finally, as noted throughout this text, a key aspect of an activity-based approach is the provision of multiple and varied learning opportunities. In order to provide these necessary learning opportunities, all members of the child's team need to understand and participate in the intentional and individualized instruction deemed necessary to meet target skills. Thus, caregivers, therapists, and other interventionists need to work together in designing, implementing, and evaluating the effects of intervention.

SUMMARY

In this chapter, we discuss the most critical concerns raised about the application of activity-based intervention. We also try to offer solutions or strategies found to be effective in addressing these issues. Nonetheless, some readers may still feel uneasy about adopting the approach for at least two reasons. First, the issues raised in this chapter are important and represent some of the more serious challenges facing the field. For example, finding effective strategies to be used with groups of children with severe disabilities has and will continue to be a significant problem. We believe the activity-based intervention approach can be successfully employed with children with severe disabilities, but that does not mean that these children will be able to function without substantial assistance from their caregivers. At this time, there are no techniques that will completely eliminate or compensate for the limitations experienced by individuals with severe disabilities. Second, maintaining a familiar approach is less difficult and threatening than instituting change. Professionals who resist exploring alternatives should, we believe, weigh the challenges of change, which are real, against the potential for improved outcomes for young children and their families.

REFERENCES

Bricker, D. (2001). The natural environment: A useful construct? *Infants and Young Children, 13*(4), 21–31

Bricker, D. (Series Ed.). (2002). *The Assessment, Evaluation and Programming System for Infants and Children* (2nd ed., Vols. 1–4). Baltimore: Paul H. Brookes Publishing Co.

Bricker, D., & Widerstrom, A. (Eds.). (1996). *Preparing personnel to work with infants and young children and their families: A team approach.* Baltimore: Paul H. Brookes Publishing Co.

Cole, K., Dale, P., & Mills, P. (1991). Individual differences in language delayed children's responses to direct and interactive preschool instruction. *Topics in Early Childhood Special Education, 11*(1), 99–124.

Dinnebeil, L., Hale, L., & Rule, S. (1999). Early intervention program practices that support collaboration. *Topics in Early Childhood Special Education, 19*(4), 225–235.

Drasgow, E., Halle, J., Ostrosky, M., & Harbers, H. (1996). Using behavioral indication and functional communication training to establish an initial sign repertoire with a young child with severe disabilities. *Topics in Early Childhood Special Education, 16*(4), 500–521.

Grisham-Brown, J.L, & Pretti-Frontczak, K. (2003). Using planning time to individualize instruction for preschoolers with special needs. *Journal of Early Intervention, 26,* 31–46.

Grisham-Brown, J., Pretti-Frontczak, K., Hemmeter, M., & Ridgley, R. (2002). Teaching IEP goals and objectives in the context of classroom routines and activities. *Young Exceptional Children, 6*(1), 18–27.

Guess, D., & Siegel-Causey, E. (1985). Behavioral control and education of severely handicapped students: Who's doing what to whom? And why? In D. Bricker & J. Filler (Eds.), *Severe mental retardation: From theory to practice* (pp. 230–244). Reston, VA: Council for Exceptional Children.

Hemmeter, M., & Grisham-Brown, J. (1998). Developing children's language skills in inclusive early childhood classroom. *Dimensions in Early Childhood Classrooms, 25*(3), 6–13.

Horner, R.H., Dunlap, G., & Koegel, R.L. (Eds.). (1988). *Generalization and maintenance: Life-style changes in applied settings.* Baltimore: Paul H. Brookes Publishing Co.

Janko, S., Schwartz, I., Sandall, S., Anderson, K., & Cottam, C. (1997). Beyond microsystems: Unanticipated lessons about the meaning of inclusion. *Topics in Early Childhood Special Education, 17*(3), 286–306.

Koegel, R., Koegel, L.K., Frea, W.D., & Smith, A.E. (1995). Emerging interventions for children with autism: Longitudinal and lifestyle implications. In R.L. Koegel & L.K. Koegel (Eds.), *Teaching children with autism: Strategies for initiating positive interactions and improving learning opportunities* (pp. 1–15). Baltimore: Paul H. Brookes Publishing Co.

Losardo, A., & Bricker, D. (1994). Activity-based intervention and direct instruction: A comparison study. *American Journal on Mental Retardation, 98*(6), 744–765.

Odom, S.L., Favazza, P.C., Brown, W.H., & Horn, E.M. (2000). Approaches to understanding the ecology of early childhood environments for children with disabilities. In T. Thompson, D. Felce, & F.J. Symons (Eds.), *Behavioral observation: Technology and applications in developmental disabilities.* (pp. 193–214). Baltimore: Paul H. Brookes Publishing Co.

Sandall, S., McLean, M., & Smith, B. (2000). *DEC recommended practices.* Longmont, CO: Sopris West.

Snell, M., & Janney, R. (2000). *Teachers' guides to inclusive practices: Collaborative teaming.* Baltimore: Paul H. Brookes Publishing Co.

Swan, W., & Morgan, J. (1993). *Collaborating for comprehensive services for young children and their families.* Baltimore: Paul H. Brookes Publishing Co.

Wolery, M., Holcombe-Ligon, A., Brookfield, J., Huffman, K., Schroeder, C., Martin, C., Venn, M., Werts, M., & Fleming, L. (1993). The extent and nature of preschool mainstreaming: A survey of general early educators. *Journal of Special Education, 27*(2), 222–234.

Yoder, P., Kaiser, A., & Alpert, C. (1991). An exploratory study of the interaction between language teaching methods and child characteristics. *Journal of Speech and Hearing Research, 34,* 155–167.

Yoder, P., Kaiser, A., Goldstein, H., Alpert, C., Mousetis, L., Kaczmarek, L., & Fisher, R. (1995). An exploratory comparison of milieu teaching and responsive interaction in classroom applications. *Journal of Early Intervention, 19*(3), 218–242.

8

Conceptual Foundations for an Activity-Based Approach

People working in the first community-based programs for children with disabilities recognized that alternative intervention approaches were needed. Their search for alternatives led to an exploration of theories and findings from developmental research that suggested more effective approaches to working with young children and their families were possible. The ideas garnered from this extensive search led to the development of the conceptual foundation for activity-based intervention.

This chapter offers the reader a framework for understanding and appreciating the theoretical underpinnings of activity-based intervention. The chapter begins with a brief discussion of the initial shift of services for young children with disabilities from institutionalized settings to the first community-based programs. This discussion is offered as background for understanding the need to develop alternative intervention approaches such as activity-based intervention.

The chapter also addresses the shifting perceptions about early experience held by researchers and practitioners. The shifting views on early experience are traced over time to provide the reader with a contextual background for developing intervention alternatives that account for the immediate and long-term impact of early experience on children and their caregivers.

Next, the chapter describes our conceptual framework—an approach that builds on the interests of children and is effective in producing desired growth and learning. In designing this approach, we found that no single theory or perspective was adequate or suitably broad to generate a satisfactory, comprehensive intervention alternative. Rather, we found it necessary to adopt a number of theories or theoretical tenets. Our search for a conceptual foundation became paired with the need to synthesize a number of theoretical positions and assumptions in order to build a comprehensive and cohesive intervention approach. The adoption of a range of theoretical perspectives set the stage for changing, broadening, and making more appropriate intervention efforts with young children experiencing developmental and learning problems.

The changes and expansions of theoretical perspectives in concert with a growing body of knowledge focused on child development and learning served as the major catalysts for the creation of activity-based intervention. The chapter concludes by establishing the indirect and direct links between the adopted perspectives and features of activity-based intervention.

WORKING WITH YOUNG CHILDREN WITH DISABILITIES

As outlined in Chapter 1, the beginning work with young children with moderate to severe learning and developmental disabilities was undertaken in residential settings (Bricker & Bricker, 1975). Prior to the 1970s, the majority of children with significant disabilities were institutionalized, often at very young ages. Because these children lived in environments that rarely reflected typical home settings (e.g., large hospital wards with little appropriate physical or social stimulation), they often learned to engage in an array of atypical, nonproductive, and often self-destructive behaviors. The only intervention that appeared to be effective was the experimental analysis of behavior that used carefully defined and controlled antecedents, responses, and consequences. With few exceptions, intervention efforts for young children with disabilities were highly structured and completely adult directed. In addition, these approaches took little account of children's developmental levels and often had children engage in nonrelevant and nonmeaningful activities (see Bricker & Bricker, 1975; Guess, Sailor, & Baer, 1974). To maintain children's interest and modify their behavior, children were offered tangible rewards. Although these highly structured approaches did not produce typical repertoires, they did produce significant changes in children's behavior. More important, these approaches reinvigorated the idea that young children with moderate to severe disabilities could learn and, therefore, should not be shut away in custodial facilities—a monumental accomplishment for the disability community (Wolfensberger, 1972).

In the early 1970s, the first community-based intervention programs for young children with learning and developmental disabilities and their families appeared (Tjossem, 1976). Initially, these programs were operated using the techniques found effective with children housed in residential settings; however, children living at home with their parents turned out to be resistive to highly structured, nonrelevant training activities, were uninterested in having teachers direct the majority of their daily activities, and generally did not change their behavior when offered food rewards (Bricker & Bricker, 1976). This negative feedback from children living in nurturing and interesting environments forced a reevaluation of what intervention approaches might prove to be engaging as well as produce desired change in young children with disabilities.

One of the first community-based early intervention programs initiated at Peabody College in the early 1970s included both children with and without disabilities (perhaps the first inclusive program for toddlers and preschoolers). The program provided staff the opportunity to observe the daily interactions of typically developing young children, as well as children with disabilities, with their peers, parents, and the physical environment (Bricker & Bricker, 1976). These observations made clear that the behavior of young children with disabilities being raised by their parents was more similar to typically developing young children than their institutionalized counterparts. Consequently, attention was turned to the array of new information on early development and learning as well as theories that attempted to explain how children typically learn and develop. This exploration, eventually encompassing years of work, led to significant changes in the conceptualization and implementation of intervention efforts with young children with disabilities (Bricker, 1986; 1989; Bricker & Bricker, 1976).

As interventionists for young children and their families continued to evolve, it became clear that a single theory or conceptual framework was not able to offer an adequate explanation for the complex undertaking called early intervention. Some theories addressed cognitive learning, some addressed the integration of developmental processes, and others focused on the learning mechanisms of environmental feedback. Still others highlighted the impact of historical as well as contemporary contexts. Each of these perspectives addressed, at least in part, what appeared to be essential features of designing a comprehensive intervention approach. Consequently, the development of activity-based intervention came to be based on a range of diverse but complementary theoretical underpinnings.

THEORETICAL FOUNDATIONS

As Miller (1989) noted, no single developmental theory is up to the task of generating a comprehensive set of definitions, constructs, intervening variables, and hypotheses that adequately account for all learning and development across children. Nor has any one theory been able to explain or accommodate the array of existing empirical data that have been generated around children's development and learning. Nonetheless, even given the current shortcomings of existing theory, theoretical frameworks to organize and give meaning to facts and to guide future research are of fundamental importance (Emde & Robinson, 2000; Miller, 1989). In addition to understanding and explaining development and learning, a theoretical foundation is necessary to the development of a coherent, cohesive, and effective intervention approach for young children with disabilities.

Most young children without genetic or biological complications appear to develop predictably. Expected behavioral patterns emerge when these children are exposed to "reasonable" environments, whereas children born with or who develop problems or who are raised in nonnurturing environments do not fare well without intervention (Farran, 2001; Guralnick, 1997; Shonkoff & Phillips, 2000). Crafting intervention approaches that assist children with disabilities and those who are at risk is essential to maximize their development, learning, and adjustment. The crafting of intervention approaches is likely to be more successful if based on solid theoretical foundations, rather than operating with a divergent set of guidelines and strategies that may not address the important facets of development and may not be consistent and complementary with each other.

As noted previously, the lack of a single comprehensive theory of development or intervention has required the creation of a conceptual foundation that has tapped a range of theoretical writings. Exploring and adopting a variety of theoretical tenets has been necessary in order to address the many facets associated with the enhancement of development and learning in young children with disabilities and those who are at risk.

The remainder of this chapter addresses the theoretical positions that have been used to fashion a set of conceptual tenets that underlie activity-based intervention. The discussion 1) begins by examining changing perceptions based on early experience, 2) identifies major theoretical perspectives, 3) reviews theories of particular relevance, and 4) links directly and indirectly these theoretical perspectives to the features of activity-based intervention.

CHANGING PERCEPTIONS BASED ON EARLY EXPERIENCE

To most professionals working with young children, the importance of early experience seems obvious; however, this has not always been true, and delving into the early experience literature suggests that the interpretation of the concept has shifted significantly over time. Before the 1950s, early experience was not seriously entertained as a potentially important factor in determining developmental outcomes in children. Ramey and Baker-Ward (1982) noted that prior to World War II the predominant belief was that developmental outcomes were largely determined by genetics and the rate of development was controlled by maturation. Environmental influences, and therefore early experiences, were seen as unimportant.

A dramatic shift occurred in the 1960s. The prevailing point of view changed from genetic predetermination to the primacy of environmental influences. This shifting position placed great importance on early experience (Hunt, 1961). Inherent in the initiation of early intervention programs in the 1960s for children from low-income families—and in the 1970s for children with disabilities—was the conviction by many researchers and interventionists that miracles could be accomplished. By providing stimulating and carefully orchestrated environmental input arranged to compensate for a genetic or biological deficit or a nonnurturing home, children could be made "normal." In addition, intervening early would inoculate children from future environmental failures. Early intervention could "fix" children, and they would stay "fixed" even when confronted with subsequent poor environments (Bricker, 1989).

Since those early optimistic days, information has been accumulating that has required yet another reinterpretation of the primacy of early experience and critical periods (Bailey, Bruer, Symons, & Lichtman, 2001). This new information and the reinterpretation of previous findings have led to two important conclusions. First, early experience should be seen as but one link in the chain of growth and development. Although a good start is important and clearly desired, protective, supportive, stimulating, and appropriate early experiences do not necessarily protect children against future adversity (e.g., the development of a disability, subsequent neglectful or abusive environments, poor instruction). Early experiences are important but so are subsequent experiences for children.

Second, early experience is composed of an array of important, but often difficult to define and measure, internal and external variables that interact in complex ways. A simplistic view of early experience must be replaced by a complex view of the ongoing interaction between children's genetics, neurophysiological intactness, and their environmental contexts and interactions. For example, a growing body of research has made clear the significant and complex relationship between the brain and early experience (Bruer & Greenough, 2001; Schore, 1997). This complex relationship between the brain and behavior is well summarized by McCall and Plemons:

> Essentially all human behavior—looking, listening, speaking, thinking, loving, worshiping, imagining, and socializing—is governed by the brain. Therefore, it should not be surprising that any experience that changes the behavior of an infant, child or adult also produces a change in the brain of that individual. (2001, p. 268)

Thus, it seems fair to conclude that initial concepts about early experience were simplistic and often inaccurate. The synergistic effects of genetics, biology, and environment are now better understood; however, future research will likely bring an even more complete and accurate understanding of how the characteristics of individual children affect their behavior and how, in turn, neural functioning affects behavior.

Our understanding of early experience and its effect on children has changed since the 1950s. We have come to understand the need to place early experience in the larger context of lifelong development and learning. We have also come to understand, in all its surrounding complexity, that the types of early experiences offered to young children not only affect their current repertoires but also may be highly instrumental in shaping their futures. These findings provide significant impetus for the development of early intervention approaches that can offer the necessary supports for children whose early experience is insufficient to produce typical outcomes because of disability, environmental shortcomings, or both.

MAJOR THEORETICAL PERSPECTIVES

As indicated previously in this chapter, the formation of a comprehensive intervention approach for young children who have or are at risk for disabilities is a complex and challenging undertaking. Learning and development are more complex than many initial theories of human development proposed (Miller, 1989). Before describing the particular theories that are foundational to activity-based intervention, it is useful to present six important perspectives that can be extracted from prominent theories of learning and development. These tenets identify variables or dimensions that underlie directly or indirectly the activity-based intervention approach.

1. Child characteristics (e.g., temperament, biological intactness, reactivity) and the integration of developmental processes affect development and learning.

2. The immediate environment and the larger historical and contemporary sociocultural context have a significant influence on development and learning.

3. Active, child-directed transactions across environmental settings promote development and learning.

4. Authentic environmental transactions promote learning and generalization.

5. The nature of environmental antecedents and learning opportunities affects development and learning.

6. The delivery of meaningful feedback is necessary for development and learning.

Over the years, we have explored various theories and conceptual frameworks but have not found one theory that addresses the many facets of effective intervention efforts. We have, therefore, found it necessary to create a conceptual framework for activity-based intervention by adopting perspectives from the written works of Vygotsky, Piaget, Dewey, Cicchetti and his colleagues; social learning theorists such as Bandura; and situated cognitive theorists such as Brown. In addition, we have been heavily influenced by the work of behavior analysts who have repeatedly demonstrated that behavioral learning principals remain the most effective intervention strategies available. This conceptual framework underlies the activity-based intervention framework presented in Chapter 2.

Sociohistorical Theory

Sociohistorical theory and particularly the writings of Vygotsky have greatly influenced other theorists as well as helped draw the attention of practitioners and interventionists to the effects that the immediate and historical socio-ocultural surroundings have on the developing child (John-Steiner & Souberman, 1978; Moll, 1990). The dialectical approach, although admitting the influence of past cultural events and current society on the individual, asserts that the individual, in turn, influences his or her culture and society. These changes create new conditions that in turn continue to affect society and culture (Vygotsky, 1978). As Vygotsky noted, learning is a profoundly social process that is affected by the history of the child and the child's culture (Moll, 1990).

Vygotsky acknowledged the biological basis of development; however, he also argued that the interactions between a child and the social environment affect the development of the child as well as the larger social context. Hart and Risley (1995) noted this phenomenon while conducting their longitudinal study of language acquisition in young children. These investigators observed that parental responses became more sophisticated as their children acquired more sophisticated language; this in turn led to the children's production of yet more complex language. Vygotsky's interactional perspective recognized the bidirectionality of effects between children and their immediate social environment. His position also addressed sociocultural change that results from the individual's action on and reaction to the sociocultural times, which may modify the sociocultural context for future generations. For example, the introduction of new words (e.g., *cyberspace*) or changes in word meaning (e.g., *cool*) reflect and may produce more cultural shifts.

Vygotsky's writings preceded ecological models (Bronfenbrenner, 1977) and interactional positions such as those described by Sameroff and Chandler (1975; Sameroff & Fiese, 2000). Transactional or interactional positions focus, in part, on child–environment exchanges as foundational to development and learning. The appreciation of cultural history and how it has shaped contemporary events and children's past and present environmental transactions underlies activity-based intervention. The activity-based approach is built on the premise that the daily transactions between children and their social and physical environments provide the most useful, appropriate, and likely effective opportunities for producing desired change. Following on this premise is the importance placed on an appreciation for the child's, family's, and community's history and current values as critical to effective intervention efforts.

Developmental Theory

Theories of emerging development provide a rich resource for understanding and predicting the evolution of change in individual children and groups of children over time. A number of developmental theories offer perspectives and insights that, if not directly applicable to the design of effective intervention approaches, provide an important context from which to view children's growth and learning. The organizational perspective on developmental psychopathology proposed by Cicchetti and Cohen (1995) has particular relevance for activity-based intervention.

Cicchetti and Cohen's organizational perspective on development "focuses on the quality of integration both within and among the behavioral and biological systems of the individual . . . and specifies how development proceeds" (1995, p. 6). This theory postulates development as a series of "qualitative reorganizations" within and among biological and behavioral systems (e.g., cognitive, social, linguistic, emotional). Change occurs as earlier structures are incorporated into new levels of organization both within and across systems. For example, children acquire more advanced language skills by expanding, rearranging, or changing the syntactic rules that govern sentence production. These changes in language will likely also affect other major systems—that is, because of the interaction between developmental domains and their reciprocal impact, enhanced communications skills may also change the child's cognitive, social, and emotional behavior.

Aspects of the organizational perspective particularly relevant to intervention efforts include attention to the potential interactive effects between systems and the systematic reorganization of behavior into more complex behavioral skills. The belief that early developmental processes are interactional and synergistic has important implications for intervention approaches. Intervention efforts should be comprehensive (e.g., children with language delays are also likely to experience cognitive and social problems), taking into account all major systems or areas of development. A second implication for intervention is the need for accurate, ongoing, and in-depth assessment of a child's full repertoire across important behavioral systems. Activity-based intervention is designed as a comprehensive approach that emphasizes the targeting of important skills across developmental areas. The approach requires that developmental targets be determined through in-depth comprehensive and functional assessment to ensure that all systems (i.e., behaviors) are addressed and that the behaviors are used appropriately and meaningfully.

Cognitive Theory

The influence of cognitive theory, specifically Piaget's writings, on the formulation of an intervention approach for young children has been profound. Piagetian theory postulates that children act on their environment to construct an understanding of how the world operates (Piaget, 1952, 1967). Various interpretations of Piagetian theory have provided an important tenet underlying the activity-based intervention approach. His theory emphasizes the need for children to be actively involved in constructing knowledge of their physical environment. Children need to explore, experience, manipulate, and receive feedback from their actions on objects in order to move from the sensorimotor stage to representational and formal operations—that is, to manipulate symbols internally.

A critical aspect of children's active exploration of their environment is the relevant and direct feedback they receive. As young children examine objects within their reach, they find that a ball being thrown is different from a ball being squeezed. Children discover through systematic feedback from their actions that, for example, books are to look at, whereas hammers are better for pounding. Many professionals understand and respect the need to act on their environment in meaningful ways.

Piaget's writings and his many interpreters have greatly enhanced appreciation for the development of higher mental functions in children. Piaget pointed out the importance of children's actions on their environment and the importance of subsequent feedback to the development of increasingly more sophisticated problem-solving behavior. His notion of acting on the environment and learning from these actions underlies activity-based intervention.

Piaget's theory of how children acquire knowledge was instrumental in shaping activity-based intervention, moving it from a singular focus on external behavior to thinking about internal constructions. His theory made clear the importance of the sensorimotor period as a foundation for the development of concrete and formal operations that are the hallmark of thinking beings. Furthermore, Piaget's focus on the importance of young children's constructing their understanding of the world serves as a major impetus for the adoption of children's daily interactions with the physical environment as a basis for activity-based intervention.

Learning Theory

Most intervention approaches have been influenced, at least in part, by learning theory. The basic assumptions underlying activity-based intervention have been particularly affected by John Dewey's writings. Dewey's perspective, like those of Piaget and Vygotsky, rests in part on the idea that the interaction between children and their environments is fundamental to development and learning. For Dewey, genuine education comes about through experience. "Every experience is a moving force. Its value can be judged only on the grounds of what it moves toward and into" (1976, p. 38). According to Dewey, it is necessary for experiences to be interactive and have continuity to move children toward meaningful change.

As Dewey (1959) noted, children by nature are active, and the challenge is how to capture and direct their activity. Through thoughtful organization and planning, experiences (i.e., activities) can be arranged to meet children's interests and to address sound intervention goals. Activities should be meaningful and functional for children and not without focus or direction. "A succession of unrelated activities does not provide, of course, the opportunity or content of building up an organized subject-matter. But neither do they provide for the development of a coherent and integrated self" (Dewey, 1959, p. 122). Dewey's concept of continuity implied that the effective interventionist determines children's present levels of understanding and then arranges experiences in such a way as to move children efficiently toward a higher level of functioning.

Another aspect of Dewey's theory that is of particular relevance to the activity-based intervention approach is that children should be allowed to participate fully in activities. Full participation may include the selection of what to do and how to do it. The interventionist's role is to guide the selection of experiences so that they become interactive and continuous. The interventionist's job, in effect, is to map relevant intervention goals onto the experiences that occur in children's lives—a hallmark of activity-based intervention.

In addition, as Dewey emphasized, learning occurs as a result of all experiences, not just of those designated for formal training. Effective intervention approaches use the array of activities that occur in children's lives on a daily basis. The variety of activities available to young children can often be used to facilitate the acquisition of important knowledge and skills. The child's desire for an object, person, or event can be used to develop and expand communication skills. Playing in a sandbox can be arranged to develop motor and social skills. Rather than routinely having children wash their hands before snack time, adults can turn this task into an activity that demands problem solving (e.g., locate the soap, reach the sink, find the towel) and that is relevant and meaningful to children. The effective use of child-directed, routine, and unanticipated activities is a fundamental part of activity-based intervention.

Social Learning Theory

Social learning theory is considered a version of learning theory and could, as well, be placed under the umbrella of developmental theories (Miller, 1989). Social learning theory offers important perspectives that have been essential to the development of activity-based intervention, in particular the tenet that learning results from the interaction between child and environmental factors. In Bandura's words, "behavior, cognitive and other personal factors, and environmental influences all operate interactively as determinants of each other" (1986, p. 23). Social learning theory emphasizes the importance of the social context, imitation, and observational learning (Miller, 1989). Activity-based intervention has incorporated these important elements of social learning theory by emphasizing the social context for learning (e.g., using meaningful routines to embed learning opportunities), incorporating the insight that learning can occur indirectly through observation, and finally, encouraging imitation of functional and generative behaviors that will enhance children's problem solving and independence.

The behavioral learning principles that have been distilled from operant learning theory with the addition of the more complex cognitive and personal features added by social learning theory continue to offer the most effective set of intervention principles available to interventionists (Meichenbaum, Bream, & Cohen, 1983). The primary principles can be conceptualized as a three-part sequence of antecedent, response, and consequence, or ARC unit.

Although the concept of antecedents, responses, and consequences can be presented in a simplistic fashion, in reality, as Bandura (1986) and others pointed out, the multiple conditions under which children and adults learn are more accurately viewed as a complex set of interactions and effects. That is, antecedents may be (and likely are) multifaceted and are influenced by the social context. For example, a mother might say, "Sit there," as she points to a chair. The antecedent "Sit there" may affect a child differently if it is said matter of fact or with great volume and force. The antecedent "Sit there" may be perceived differently if the child is alone or surrounded by several other children. The response, sitting, is also affected by numerous factors, for example, whether the child understands the words or if the child is able to move to the location. Understanding the effect of consequences on behavior is often difficult and complex because consequences are affected by a range of historical and contemporary factors that may be hard to detect or appreciate.

Activity-based intervention focuses on ARC units. That is, interventionists are encouraged to select antecedents that will ensure learning opportunities are embedded during child-directed, routine, and planned activities. Responses are operationalized as functional and generative skills targeted for children to acquire and use. Feedback or a consequence, to the extent possible, is the inherent or logical result of a child's response. How an activity-based approach elaborates on or utilizes basic ARC units to enhance learning and development is shown in Figure 8.1.

Situated Cognitive Learning Theory

The variation of learning and/or cognitive theory, often called *situated learning* or *situated cognition,* encompasses a broad range of perspectives (e.g., Greeno, Collins, & Resnick, 1996; Putnam & Borko, 2000) of relevance to activity-

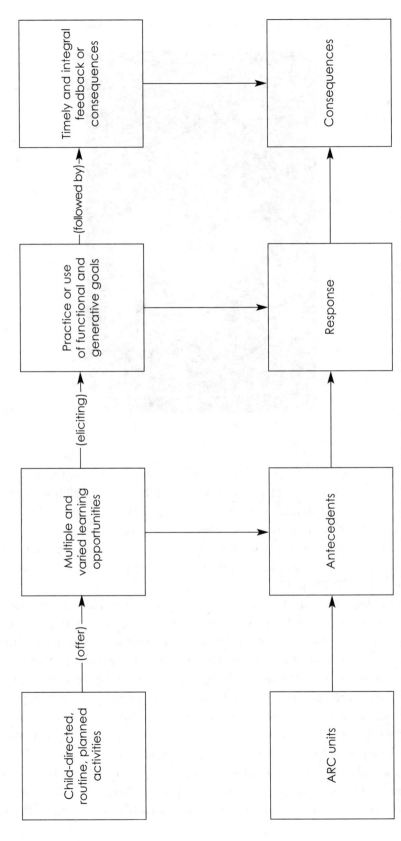

Figure 8.1. The relationship of activities, learning opportunities, goals and objectives, and feedback to antecedent, response, and consequence (ARC) units.

195

based intervention. In particular, activity-based intervention has adopted the situated cognitive perspective of Brown, Collins, and Duguid who argued that "activity and situations are integral to cognition and learning" and "different ideas of what is an appropriate learning activity produce very different results" (1989, p. 32). They also suggested, "by ignoring the situated nature of cognition, education defeats its own goal of providing useable, robust knowledge" (1989, p. 32).

By *situated nature,* Brown and his colleagues mean that learning is an integral part of the activity and situation in which it occurs. "Activity, concept, and culture are interdependent. No one can be totally understood without the other two. Learning must involve all three" (Brown et al., 1989, p. 33). These authors have blended logic and data into a case for what they call *authentic activity* and have argued that the acquisition of knowledge and learning of skills should occur under conditions that are authentic (i.e., the knowledge or skill is necessary, relevant, or useful to cope with real tasks or problems). This belief opposes training or education that employs abstract, fragmented strategies that do not reflect conditions found in nontraining environments. For example, attempting to enhance children's communication skills by conducting 10-minute drill sessions is likely less meaningful than assisting children to expand their communication skills as they need them to negotiate their daily environment.

The applicability of the situated perspective (Brown et al., 1989) is apparent for young children and provides additional conceptual support for activity-based intervention. If Brown and his colleagues are correct, then developing generative, functional, and adaptable response repertoires can be made efficient and effective by embedding learning opportunities and objectives in authentic situations. Authentic situations for young children should include activities that reflect the reality and demands of their daily living as well as play. Authentic activities have, from children's perspective, a logical beginning, a sequence of events, and an ending. They are fundamental to young children's existence (e.g., requesting help), mirror conditions and demands the children face on a routine basis (e.g., dressing), or constitute play activities. Authentic activities permit children to learn and practice skills that will improve their abilities to cope with the many demands offered by their physical and social environments. Children view authentic activities as relevant, as evidenced by their interest and motivation to become involved. Such activities lead children to better understand and respond to their immediate sociocultural context. Furthermore, an authentic activity meets Dewey's criteria of sound educational practice because it "supplies the child with a genuine motive; it gives him experience at first hand; it brings him into contact with reality" (1959, p. 44).

LINKING THEORETICAL PERSPECTIVES TO ACTIVITY-BASED INTERVENTION

The diverse, complex but complementary theories and perspectives briefly reviewed in this chapter provide the conceptual framework for activity-based intervention. Figure 8.2 was developed to offer a concrete illustration of the relationship between these important perspectives and activity-based intervention elements. The figure is divided into two segments. The top segment depicts the relationship between two broad theoretical positions that provide the general foundation of activity-based intervention, and the lower segments list the guidelines that underlie the four elements of an activity-based approach. Two foundational principles are at the top of Figure 8.2:

- Child characteristics and the integration of developmental processes affect development and learning (Ciccheti & Cohen, 1995).

- The immediate environment and the larger historical and contemporary sociocultural context have a significant influence on development and learning (Vygotsky, 1978).

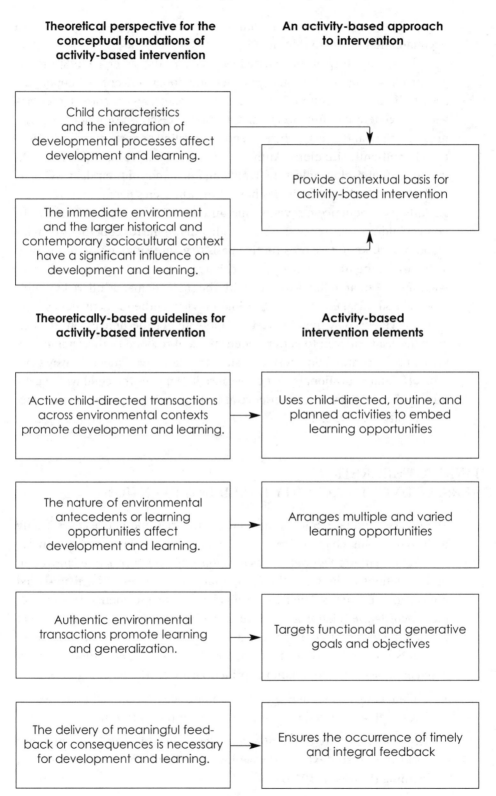

Figure 8.2. The relationship between selected theoretical perspectives and the conceptual foundation for activity-based intervention and the theoretical guidelines for activity-based intervention elements.

These two principles provide the broad conceptual framework for activity-based intervention as indicated by the connecting arrows. The lower segment of Figure 8.2 lists four theoretically based guidelines:

- Active child-directed transactions across environmental contexts promote development and learning (Piaget, 1967; Sameroff & Chandler, 1975).

- The nature of environmental antecedents or learning opportunities affects development and learning (Bandura, 1986; Dewey, 1959).

- Authentic environmental transactions promote learning and generalization (Brown et al., 1989; Dewey, 1959).

- The delivery of meaningful feedback or consequences is necessary for development and learning (Bandura, 1986).

These guidelines underlie the four elements of activity-based intervention. The connecting arrows depict the relationship between the guidelines and activity-based elements.

SUMMARY

The purpose of this chapter is to provide the reader with a conceptual framework for understanding the formulation and application of activity-based intervention. The tenets distilled from the work of a variety of theorists and perspectives give strength to the positions that children are greatly influenced by their social and physical environments and their cultural context, that children need to be actively involved in the construction of higher mental processes, and that the nature of the environmental activities (i.e., experiences) children encounter are fundamental to their development and learning. Given these positions, an intervention approach that uses authentic activities has great appeal.

As Dewey wrote, "There is no such thing as educational value in the abstract" (1976, p. 46). "I believe that the only true education comes through the stimulation of the child's powers by the demands of the social situation in which he finds himself" (Dewey, 1959, p. 20). The purpose of an activity-based approach is to create and use authentic activities in order to enhance children's development and learning.

REFERENCES

Bailey, D.B., Bruer, J., Jr., Symons, F.T., & Lichtman, J.W. (Eds.), (2001). *Critical thinking about critical periods*. Baltimore: Paul H. Brookes Publishing Co.

Bandura, A. (1986). *Social foundations of thought and action: A social cognitive theory.* Upper Saddle River, NJ: Prentice-Hall.

Bricker, D. (1986). *Early education of at-risk and handicapped infants, toddlers and preschool children.* Glenview, IL: Scott, Foresman.

Bricker, D. (1989). *Early intervention for at-risk and handicapped infants, toddlers and preschool children.* Palo Alto, CA: VORT Corp.

Bricker, W., & Bricker, D. (1975). Mental retardation and complex human behavior. In J. Kaufman & J. Payne (Eds.), *Mental retardation: Introduction and personal perspectives.* Columbus, OH: Charles E. Merrill.

Bricker, W., & Bricker, D. (1976). The infant, toddler, and preschool research and intervention project. In T. Tjossem (Ed.), *Intervention strategies for high risk infants and young children.* Baltimore: University Park Press.

Bronfenbrenner, U. (1977). Toward an experimental ecology of human development. *American Psychologist, 32,* 513–531

Brown, J., Collins, A., & Duguid, P. (1989). Situated cognition and the culture of learning. *Educational Researcher, 18*(1), 32–42.

Bruer, J.T., & Greenough, W. (2001). The subtle science of how experience affects the brain. In D.B. Bailey, Jr., J.T. Bruer, F.J. Symons, & J.W. Lichtman (Eds.), *Critical thinking about critical periods* (pp. 209–232). Baltimore: Paul H. Brookes Publishing Co.

Cicchetti, D., & Cohen, D. (1995). Perspectives on developmental psychopathology. In D. Cicchetti & D. Cohen (Eds.), *Developmental psychopathology: Theory and methods* (pp. 3–20). New York: John Wiley & Sons.

Dewey, J. (1959). *Dewey on education.* New York: Columbia University, Bureau of Publications, Teachers College.

Dewey, J. (1976). *Experience and education.* New York: Colliers.

Emde, R., & Robinson, J. (2000). Guiding principles for a theory of early intervention: A developmental-psychoanalytic perspective. In J.P. Shonkoff & S.J. Meisels (Eds.), *Handbook of early childhood intervention* (pp. 160–178). New York: Cambridge University Press.

Farran, D.C. (2001). Critical periods and early intervention. In D.B. Bailey, Jr., J.T. Bruer, F.J. Symons, & J.W. Lichtman (Eds.), *Critical thinking about critical periods* (pp. 233– 266). Baltimore: Paul H. Brookes Publishing Co.

Greeno, J., Collins, A., & Resnick, L. (1996). Cognition and learning. In D. Berlinger & R. Calfre (Eds.), *Handbook of educational psychology* (pp. 15–46). New York: MacMillan.

Guess, D., Sailor, W., & Baer, D. (1974). To teach language to retarded children. In R. Schiefelbusch & L. Lloyd (Eds.), *Language perspectives—acquisition, retardation, and intervention.* Baltimore: University Park Press.

Guralnick, M.J. (Ed.). (1997). *The effectiveness of early intervention.* Baltimore: Paul H. Brookes Publishing Co.

Hart, B., & Risley, T.R. (1995). *Meaningful differences in the everyday experience of young American children.* Baltimore: Paul H. Brookes Publishing Co.

Hunt, J. (1961). *Intelligence and experience.* New York: Ronald Press.

John-Steiner, V., & Souberman, E. (1978). Afterword. In M. Cole, V. John-Steiner, S., Scribner, & E. Souberman (Eds.), *L.S. Vygotsky—Mind in society* (pp. 121–133). Cambridge, MA: Harvard University Press.

McCall, R.B., & Plemons, B.W. (2001). The concept of critical periods and their implications for early childhood service. In D.B. Bailey, Jr., J.T. Bruer, F.J. Symons, & J.W. Lichtman (Eds.), *Critical thinking about critical periods* (pp. 267–288). Baltimore: Paul H. Brookes Publishing Co.

Meichenbaum, D., Bream, L., & Cohen, J. (1983). A cognitive behavioral perspective of child psychopathology: Implications for assessment and training. In R. McMahon & R. DeV. Peters (Eds.), *Childhood disorders: Behavioral-development approaches.* New York: Brunner/Mazel.

Miller, P. (1989). *Theories of developmental psychology.* New York: W.H. Freeman.

Moll, L. (1990). *Vygotsky and education*. New York: Cambridge University Press.

Piaget, J. (1952). *The origins of intelligence in children*. New York: W. W. Norton.

Piaget, J. (1967). *Six psychological studies*. New York: Random House.

Putnam, R., & Borko, H. (2000). What do new views of knowledge and thinking have to say about research on teacher learning? *Educational Researcher, 29*(1), 4–15.

Ramey, C., & Baker-Ward, L. (1982). Psychosocial retardation and the early experience paradigm. In D. Bricker (Ed.), *Intervention with at risk and handicapped infants*. Baltimore: University Park Press.

Sameroff, A., & Chandler, M. (1975). Reproductive risk and the continuum of caretaking casualty. In F. Horowitz, E. Hetherington, S. Scarr-Salapatek, & G. Siegel (Eds.), *Review of child development research* (Vol. 4, pp. 187–244). Chicago: University of Chicago Press.

Sameroff, A., & Fiese, B. (2000). Transactional regulation: The developmental ecology of early intervention. In J.P. Shonkoff & S.J. Meisels (Eds.), *Handbook of early childhood intervention* (pp.135–159). New York: Cambridge University Press.

Schore, A. (1997). Early organization of the nonlinear right brain and development of a predisposition of psychiatric disorders. *Development and Psychopathology, 9,* 595–631.

Shonkoff, J.P., & Phillips, D.A. (Eds.). (2000). *From neurons to neighborhoods: The science of early childhood development*. Washington, DC: National Academy Press.

Tjossem, T. (Ed.). (1976). *Intervention strategies for high risk infants and young children*. Baltimore: University Park Press.

Vygotsky, L. (1978). *Mind in society*. Cambridge, MA: Harvard University Press.

Wolfensberger, W. (1972). *The principle of normalization in human service*. Toronto: National Institute on Mental Retardation.

9

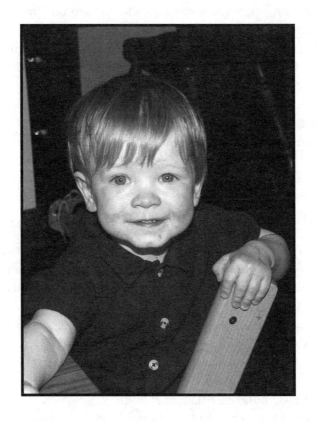

The Empirical Bases for an Activity-Based Approach

Overall, approaches to intervention and specific strategies and procedures have gradually shifted from highly structured, adult-directed procedures (Bricker & Bricker, 1976) to those that are child initiated and directed and make use of play and daily activities (Bricker, 1989). The early programs employed teacher-directed one-to-one instruction that was focused on assisting children to develop specific relationships and dispensed tangible rewards. Later intervention efforts mapped instruction onto routines and child initiations and used social feedback or consequences associated with the action or activity. When possible, these important shifts in intervention procedures were based on empirical findings (e.g., Bricker & Sheehan, 1981; Pretti-Frontczak & Bricker, 2001); however, as noted by Baer (1981), the collection of objective data verifying the effects of intervention efforts is a complex undertaking.

THE CHALLENGE OF INTERVENTION RESEARCH

Indeed, a review of the intervention literature focused on children with disabilities finds few methodologically sound studies of intervention effects, or comparisons of approaches, and virtually no treatment validity studies (Casto & White, 1993; Pretti-Frontczak & Bricker, 2001). Studies focused on risk groups generally have larger samples and have better controls in place than studies using disabilities groups (e.g., see Farran, 2000; Raver, 2002); however, even in methodologically sophisticated studies, careful delineation between the treatment and reliability or fidelity of treatment is often not addressed (Gersten, Baker, & Lloyd, 2000).

The complex process of intervention that must account for multiple effects, or more likely interactional effects of multiple variables on children and families, often is not addressed in intervention studies for at least three important reasons: 1) methodological constraints (e.g., the phenomenon of intervention or children's learning cannot be easily studied in isolation under a microscope); 2) target population (e.g., children with disabilities or those deemed to be at risk and whose behavioral repertoires may be by definition atypical); and 3) prohibitive costs.

Methodological Constraints

A number of methodological constraints confront investigators who are interested in conducting intervention research (Shonkoff & Phillips, 2000). Children, unlike genes, germs, or chemical reactions, cannot be usefully examined in isolation (Lerner, Hauser-Cram, & Miller, 1998). The phenomena of children's learning cannot be placed in a petri dish and watched as it unfolds. Many confounds make it difficult to investigate and measure intervention effects. It is also difficult to parse the intervention efforts into manageable pieces to determine what constellation of factors accounts for change in children. For example, it would be difficult, if not impossible, to tease out the effects of a child's parents or his or her health on learning or performance apart from the effects of intervention content and procedures (Sameroff, 1994).

Equally frustrating from a "scientific" viewpoint is the inability to exercise laboratory control when conducting intervention research. When in the laboratory, investigators may carefully regulate, for example, the presentation of materials, the number of trials, and the consequences following a child's response whereas research conducted in children's homes or classrooms makes controlling such variables much more complicated (Scruggs & Mastropieri, 1994). Intervention research must contend with a multitude of variables that likely affect the manner in which children learn and respond (Baer, 1981; Gersten et al., 2000).

When researchers conduct carefully controlled laboratory experiments with children, a major question arises as to how well conditions reflect circumstances that children are likely to encounter outside the laboratory. In other words, how relevant are the findings or what is the external validity of the outcomes? The relevance of results is an important question for interventionists/ teachers and parents (Kennedy, 1997). Findings that have little or no relevance to a child's daily interactions may be of questionable use (or validity) when trying to formulate effective interventions that should take into account an array of conditions and variables. For example, will an experimental procedure (e.g., one teacher following specific guidelines) found to expand vocabulary hold up, or replicate, when this procedure is used under less well-controlled conditions (e.g., multiple children, more than one teacher)?

Target Population

Children with disabilities and children exposed to unhealthy or even toxic environments pose a second set of constraints to determining the effectiveness of intervention approaches. Children at risk and children with disabilities are by definition atypical in at least one respect and often are atypical in many other respects. The variability within children who have or are at risk for disabilities may exceed that which is found in groups of typically developing children (Lewis & Wehren, 1982). An intervention approach or strategy found to be successful with a child with a visual and motor impairment might not be successful with a child with a language or behavioral disorder. An approach found effective with a group of children with general developmental delays may be less effective with children with behavior problems. Children who come to a center hungry, tired, or in emotional turmoil may benefit little from any intervention approach until their basic needs are addressed (Raver, 2002).

Economic, cultural, and/or linguistic differences of the target population may also introduce significant challenges. An intervention found to be effective with a group of children with middle-income, well-educated parents may not be appropriate or effective with children whose backgrounds or learning styles differ (Gersten et al., 2000; Vincent, Salisbury, Strain, McCormick, & Tessier, 1990).

Prohibitive Costs

The third constraint that faces intervention researchers is cost. Delivering comprehensive interventions to children under experimental conditions can be an extraordinarily expensive undertaking if investigators are to control even the major relevant variables thought to affect intervention outcomes (e.g., size and constitution of sample, effect of parents/caregivers, teacher comparability, comparison of intervention features). As Baer pointed out,

> The sociological incredibility of analytic research to untangle the separate effects of the components of [curricular] packages is identical to the sociological incredibility of the research necessary to compare one package from a certain theoretical orientation to another package from a different theoretical orientation . . . getting to that point is incredibly expensive. (1981, p. 572)

And, we might add, highly unlikely. The cost of collecting an array of critical information on intervention effects is magnified by other costs. For example, most intervention research requires a sizeable investment in order to prepare the intervention staff, parents, and other caregivers who may be involved in delivering the intervention content (Escobar, Barnett, & Geotze, 1994; Tarr & Barnett, 2001). Once prepared to deliver the intervention content, interventionists should ensure the continued fidelity of treatment or intervention so unacceptable drift does not occur. Another important cost may be in the potential disruption that the delivery of the content and the data collection may impose on a program. For example, administering child performance measures, accommodating observers, or videotaping teaching sessions may produce conditions that interfere with program operation.

The costs of examining the various features or components of an intervention approach, the cost of preparing personnel, and the cost of ensuring fidelity of treatment might be acceptable if there were adequate resources available. The cost, however, of evaluating the effectiveness of an intervention approach, not to mention evaluations of comparisons between approaches, is greater than state or federal government agencies appear willing to support on a sustained basis except in rare cases such as the Infant Health and Development Program (1990) and the National Early Intervention Longitudinal Study (Bailey, Scarborough, & Hebbeler, 2003).

Single-subject research is probably the least expensive intervention research methodology; however, the requirement for systematic replication to examine generalization of effects to other subjects can drive up costs of this approach as well. Studies of discrete or focused intervention procedures (e.g., Sewell, Collins, Hemmeter, & Schuster, 1998) are much less costly than attempting to examine broad approaches such as activity-based intervention (Bricker & Gumerlock, 1988). Comprehensive intervention approaches are composed of multiple components or features. Attempting to measure the intensity and frequency of each intervention feature as well as examining child and family effects can be, to use Baer's word, *incredibly* expensive (Baer, 1981; Barnett & Escobar, 1990; Casto & White, 1993) and methodologically challenging (Gersten et al., 2000; Losardo & Bricker, 1994). The time and resources necessary for investigators to conduct comprehensive intervention research and for intervention staff to accommodate this research is generally unavailable to most intervention programs on a sustained basis.

The previous discussion is offered to set the stage for an appreciation of the material contained in the remainder of this chapter, to remind readers of the challenges inherent in intervention research, and to temper criticism of the methodological weaknesses that pervade much of the work to date. The purpose of this chapter is not to conduct in-depth literature reviews or analyses of intervention research. Rather, the goal is to summarize findings that illuminate directly or indirectly the effectiveness of early intervention, in general, and activity-based intervention, in particular.

In this literature review, two types of intervention research are examined. First, the findings from some of the extensive reviews available in the literature on general program effects with populations of young children with disabilities and children who are at risk for disabilities are highlighted. Second, the studies that have focused directly on evaluating the effects of activity-based intervention are reviewed.

EFFECTS OF EARLY INTERVENTION

The Effectiveness of Early Intervention (Guralnick, 1997) contains a series of comprehensive reviews of intervention efforts conducted during the 1970s, 1980s, and 1990s. These reviews offer insightful analyses of the efficacy studies conducted on children with disabilities and children who are at risk.

In most cases, the authors of these chapters conclude that high-quality programs delivered early in children's lives, and in some cases for extended periods, produce better immediate outcomes for children and families than if they had not participated in these programs:

- "High-quality, intensive programs that last for some years are the most likely to result in children's improvements in school or later real-life activities, but they are not a guarantee" (Bryant & Maxwell, 1997, p. 43).

- "There is, however, increasing recognition that both parent- and child-focused interventions can have beneficial impact" (Feldman, 1997, p. 188).

- "Early intervention for all types of communication disorders can be effective and almost certainly more efficient than intervention provided at later ages" (McLean & Woods Cripe, 1997, p. 418).

Most contributors to this volume were careful to note the methodological flaws of the reviewed studies, to qualify outcomes (e.g., initial differences in experimental and control groups that "washed out" over time), and to acknowledge the variability in study features that made drawing conclusions across investigations highly suspect.

It is also interesting to note that most contributors to this volume concluded that research addressing the effects of specific intervention features had just begun (second-generation research [Guralnick, 1997]) and that considerable work remains before interventionists can arrive at reliable conclusions about the effectiveness of carefully defined and described intervention content and procedures across populations of children and their families.

Since 1997, other comprehensive reviews that address the effectiveness of early intervention have appeared. Authors and contributors to these volumes have reviewed the effects of intervention on young children with disabilities and children who are at risk for disabilities. Conclusions from two influential volumes (i.e., *From Neurons to Neighborhoods* and *Handbook of Early Childhood Intervention*) reflect the comprehensive knowledge base about the effects of early intervention.

From Neurons to Neighborhoods contains the findings from a 2½-year project dedicated to the evaluation of the "current science of early childhood development" (Shonkoff & Phillips, 2000, p. ix). The study team of this project concluded that "more than three decades of developmental research and program evaluation have generated" a set of replicated findings. Several of these findings directly address the effectiveness of early intervention (pp. 342–343):

- "Well-designed and successfully implemented interventions can enhance the short-term performance of children living in poverty."

- "Well-designed and successfully implemented interventions can promote significant short-term gains on standardized cognitive and social measures for young children with documented developmental delays or disabilities."

- Short-term effects on cognitive performance for children at risk are greater when "intervention is goal-directed and child-focused."

- Short-term effects on cognitive and social performance for children with disabilities "are greater when the intervention is more structured and focused on the child–caregiver relationship."

- Longitudinal investigations focused on low-income populations indicate differences between experimental and control children in terms of high school graduation rates, subsequent income, welfare dependency, and criminal behavior.

- Longitudinal studies focused on young children with autism report "persistent benefits of intensive preschool interventions that are followed by continuing specialized services."

- Economic cost analyses find interventions directed to children at risk produce "benefits to families as well as savings in public expenditures."

It is important to note the specific qualifications that accompanied these conclusions (e.g., effects are short-term, focus is on specific behaviors, programs are well-designed and executed), as well as to note the general limitations of early intervention research (e.g., basic problems in research designs, significant variability across programs, focus is primarily on cognitive performance) discussed by Shonkoff and Phillips (2000).

The stated purpose of *Handbook of Early Childhood Intervention* (Shonkoff & Meisels, 2000) "is to provide a scholarly overview of the knowledge base and practice of early childhood intervention." In particular, the chapter by Farran (2000) provided a comprehensive analysis of the effects of intervention on vulnerable populations. Farran drew a number of sobering and well-supported conclusions based on her careful analysis of individual studies, for example,

- "Abecedarian and Project Care programs are perhaps the most scientifically controlled and thoroughly reported early intervention efforts in social science . . . Overall, their findings show modest success . . . " (2000, p. 515).

- High/Scope Perry Preschool Project's follow up of the target children at age 27 years suggested, "In many categories, there are significant differences favoring the program group as well as a fairly consistent trend in their favor" (2000, p. 517). However, Farran also identified concerns about the type of analyses used to arrive at these conclusions.

- The Infant Health and Development Program's initial findings on children reported mixed outcomes before age 3. By the fifth-year follow up, the experimental and control groups were not different on most measures. "The lack of effect for such an ambitious, well-run, and expensive program was unanticipated and troubling" (2000, p. 521).

Farran summarized the corpus of work on intervention treatment effects with risk groups suggesting that the intervention programs have not been shown to be better than doing nothing at all and that the more disadvantaged the children and families, the more compromised the intervention effects. She further suggested that intervention attempts have likely not been effective with low-income groups because the treatments do not take into account the ecological context of the families, as well as how to better prepare children for their subsequent public school experiences.

Farran also addressed intervention programs for children with disabilities. Again, her careful analysis led her to several troubling conclusions. First, there has been little attention given to the impact of programs on young children supported by the Individuals with Disabilities Education Act (IDEA) of 1990 (PL 101-476) and IDEA Amendments of 1997 (PL 105-17). "This review makes clear that the largest intervention effort for children with disabilities and their families [IDEA programs] has received little systematic attention concerning its effectiveness" (2000, p. 539). Second, the diversity across studies (e.g., population, design, and measurement variability) makes it difficult to arrive at general conclusions. "These studies [efficacy studies focused on children with disabilities] are so disparate that general conclusions are somewhat difficult to derive" (2000, p. 533). Third, future research should direct more of its attention to examining aptitude by treatment effects. "Providing the right intervention might not be so much finding a single approach to adopt . . . but in determining when in the developmental sequence it is appropriate and facilitating to administer certain forms of intervention" (2000, p. 540). She continues with the observation that "A more reasonable conclusion may be that we must look to the specific form of the intervention delivered at a particular time frame" (2000, p. 541).

What conclusions can be drawn from the efficacy investigations? First, quality intervention efforts have produced short-term effects, but most of these reported effects appear to dissipate over time. The dissipation may be, in part, the result of poor intervention received once children enter the public schools or, as Farran suggested, the lack of attention to children's and families' ecological contexts. Second, design and analyses flaws have compromised the results obtained from many of these investigations. The current scientific template, however, may be inappropriate to use to determine the effects of intervention efforts. Future success may be dependent on develop-

ing scientifically defensible but different standards for intervention research. Third, the diversity in populations, designs, measures, and intervention/treatments makes drawing general conclusions difficult. Again, this may be an inappropriate goal. An alternative is to accept the phenomena of treatment by aptitude effects and develop designs that accommodate this approach. The results would not be general conclusions but rather would establish specific relationships among children, their developmental trajectories, environmental context, and intervention/treatment efforts.

EFFECTS OF ACTIVITY-BASED INTERVENTION

Our attempts to study the effectiveness of activity-based intervention have faced the same problems (i.e., methodological constraints, target population, prohibitive costs). In particular, we have had little opportunity for random assignment to groups and significant difficulty in finding ways to establish legitimate control or comparison groups against which we can evaluate the effects of activity-based intervention. Even when locating contrast groups, their comparability as well as the comparability of other intervention approaches is often not established (e.g., Losardo & Bricker, 1994). Although confronted with these realities, we have collected information on child progress, parent satisfaction, and the general effectiveness of the approach since the early 1980s.

Although much of the collected information was formative and has been used internally to refine and improve the approach, we have published a series of outcome studies. These studies are reviewed next with an eye toward examining the effects of activity-based intervention. It should be pointed out that the early studies were primarily designed as evaluation studies, and descriptions of the intervention content and procedures are brief. The label *activity-based* was not used until the 1988 study; however, from the early 1980s the approach employed at the University of Oregon's Early Intervention Program was activity-based (see Bricker, 1986). Consequently, the evaluation studies described next were focused on determining the effectiveness of the activity-based approach.

Bricker and Sheehan (1981)

The first study addressing the effects of activity-based intervention was published in 1981 by Bricker and Sheehan. The article presented 2 years of program evaluation data on 63 children. The children ranged in age from 5 to 69 months and spanned the continuum from children without disabilities to those with severe disabilities. Children attended a center-based classroom 5 days per week; however, attendance varied across children. The intervention program focused on the children's IEP goals and objectives by embedding learning opportunities into routine, child-initiated, and planned activities. Parental involvement and participation was encouraged.

Standardized and criterion-referenced tests (i.e., the Bayley Scales of Infant Development [Bayley, 1969], McCarthy Scales of Children's Abilities [McCarthy, 1972], and Uniform Performance Assessment System [White, Edgar, & Haring, 1978]) were administered at the beginning and end of each school year. During both years, almost all pretest and posttest comparison on the standardized and criterion-referenced tests indicated that children's performances were significantly improved at posttest and that most changes were educationally significant (i.e., change exceeded 1 standard deviation). The fidelity of treatment was not monitored; therefore, we cannot be sure how faithfully the intervention staff implemented the elements of the activity-based approach. The program was, however, a field site for teaching graduate students, so there is reason to believe that the intervention closely adhered to the tenets of the activity-based approach. There were no control or comparison groups; however, the consistent findings of change across groups and tests suggest the intervention program had an impact. Nonetheless, the effects of maturation cannot be ruled out.

Bricker, Bruder, and Bailey (1982)

Bricker, Bruder, and Bailey (1982) reported an evaluation of the effects of developmental integration on 41 young children with disabilities assigned to three different classrooms that operated using the activity-based intervention approach. The children ranged in age from 10 months to 5 years and included those without disabilities and those with a variety of disabling conditions. This study also used standardized and criterion-referenced measures (i.e., Bayley Scales of Infant Development, McCarthy Scales of Children's Abilities, Uniform Performance Assessment System and Student Progress Record [Oregon State Mental Health Division, 1977]) and a pretest and posttest design. The study had no comparison group; however, standardized tests were included to provide some control through the use of the general cognitive index that is designed to examine performance change in proportion to chronological age. Interventionists were taught to embed learning opportunities related to children's goals and objectives into child-directed, routine, and planned activities—a key element of an activity-based approach to intervention. Parental involvement was a priority, although the form of involvement varied by family and child need.

The evaluation data reported on a subsample of the participating children indicated that statistically and educationally significant gains from pretest to posttest were made on the criterion-referenced tests. With the exception that no significant shift in the general cognitive index occurred for one of the groups, all other comparisons on the standardized tests were significant as well. These findings replicate the initial 1981 study outcomes but also suffer from the same limitations—no measures of treatment fidelity and no control group. Comparisons on the general cognitive index were used in lieu of control groups, and although better than no controls, these comparisons fall far short of accepted standards necessary for the objective demonstration of the value of an intervention effort.

Bailey and Bricker (1985)

In a similar study, the effects of activity-based intervention were examined on more than 80 children with mild to severe disabilities from infancy to 3 years old (Bailey & Bricker, 1985). Children attended either a home-based or a center-based program that employed an activity-based approach by embedding learning opportunities into a variety of meaningful activities, targeting functional responses, and providing contingent feedback to the children. Family participation remained a priority, although, as before, the nature of the participation varied across families. Standardized and criterion-referenced tests (i.e., Revised Gesell and Amatruda Developmental and Neurologic Examination [Knobloch, Stevens, & Malone, 1980] and Comprehensive Early Evaluation and Programming System [Bailey, 1983], the forerunner to the Assessment, Evaluation, and Programming System for Infants and Children (AEPS [Bricker, 2002]) were administered at the beginning and end of the school year.

An analysis of the pretest and posttest comparisons found significant gains for all children on the criterion-referenced measure. On the standardized measure, significant differences were found using maturity scores; however, no differences were found when using developmental quotients. This latter finding suggests that child change in proportion to age was not affected even if the children had gained a significant number of new skills over the year as indicated by the change on the criterion-referenced instrument and change in the maturity scores. Parent satisfaction with the program was reported to be high. This study did not have a comparison group nor were treatment fidelity data collected; however, once again this program served as a teaching site for graduate students learning to use activity-based intervention. There is little doubt that over time changes were introduced to the activity-based approach that may or may not have produced differential outcomes. Unfortunately, there is no objective documentation of how the approach changed over time and how that change might, in turn, be related to child change.

Bricker and Gumerlock (1988)

In a fourth study on the impact of activity-based intervention on child performance, Bricker and Gumerlock (1988) reported 2 years of outcome data on a sample of 46 infants and toddlers. These children had disabilities that ranged from mild to severe, and they attended a center-based program operated by trained interventionists. The elements of activity-based intervention were employed, and intervention content was determined by the children's IEP goals and objectives. As in the previous studies, the effects of activity-based intervention were measured using a pretest and posttest comparison of scores on criterion-referenced and standardized measures (i.e., Bayley Scales of Infant Development [Bayley, 1969], Revised Stanford-Binet [Thorndike, Hagen, & Sattler, 1986], Revised Gesell and Amatruda Developmental and Neurologic Examination [Knobloch et al., 1980], and Evaluation and Programming System [Bricker, Gentry, & Bailey, 1985], also a forerunner of AEPS). As in the previous studies, the analysis showed that the children's performance in general improved significantly from pretest to posttest on the standardized and criterion-referenced measures. In addition, this study reported children's progress on specific short-term and long-range educational goals. Again, this study did not measure treatment fidelity or provide controls.

In these four investigations, only limited attention was given to treatment by aptitude analysis. The Bricker and Sheehan (1981) study reported subgroup analysis for normal, at-risk, mild, moderate, and severe groups, and the Bricker and colleagues (1982) study reported separate findings for the groups of children with and without disabilities. These findings indicate that the intervention appears to have had a relatively positive effect across subgroups of children. More detailed analysis of treatment by aptitude effects will be useful to the design of future intervention efforts with young children with disabilities.

Losardo and Bricker (1994)

In 1994, Losardo and Bricker published a well-controlled study that compared the effects of activity-based intervention with a direct instruction approach. Six children who ranged in age from 47 to 66 months participated in this study. All children were attending a center-based intervention program for young children with disabilities. The control procedure was the use of an alternating treatment design so that the effects of direct instruction and activity-based intervention on vocabulary acquisition and generalization could be compared across the children. Vocabulary items were matched and then randomly assigned to either the activity-based or direct instruction treatment condition. The procedure was divided into a baseline and treatment phase for each child. Treatments were counterbalanced daily. During instruction, interventionists worked with the children following the stipulated elements of each approach. Fidelity of treatment data were collected and indicated that teachers systematically implemented the treatments over time. Study outcomes suggest that acquisition of vocabulary items occurred more quickly under the direct instruction condition but that generalization was significantly better for vocabulary items learned under the activity-based intervention condition. In addition, subsequent maintenance of the gains was significantly greater for the activity-based condition than for the direct instruction condition. In many ways the outcomes of this study make intuitive sense. That is, massed trials will produce more rapid acquisition, but meaningful embedded learning opportunities produce better generalization.

Bricker and Colleagues (1997)

From 1991 through 1996, funds provided by the U.S. Department of Education, Office of Special Education Programs, and awarded to the Early Intervention Program, University of Oregon, were used to develop a model demonstration program (Bricker, McComas, Pretti-Frontczak, Leve, Stieber, Losardo, & Scanlon, 1997). This model demonstration program had two phases. Phase one was designed to demonstrate the positive impact of activity-based intervention on young children with disabilities whereas phase two was a replication to verify that the findings reported for phase one could be reproduced at different sites. Phase one lasted 2 years and included three sites. Staff at each site were taught to use the four elements of activity-based intervention with the participating children. A total of 52 children participated, and they ranged in age from 7 to 27 months at the beginning of the project. Children at one site were classified as at risk (i.e., had teenage mothers), whereas the children at the other two sites had a range of disabilities. Fidelity of treatment data were collected for the duration of the project. Interventionists were found to consistently use the four elements of the approach. The Revised Gesell and Amatruda Developmental and Neurologic Examination (Gesell; Knobloch et al., 1980) and the AEPS (Bricker, 1993) were administered at the beginning, middle, and end of the school year.

A Proportional Change Index (PCI) is a numerical statement of the relationship between children's rate of development during intervention with the rate of development at the time intervention began and is used to compare developmental change over time. The PCI controls for differences between developmental age and chronological age at pretest. PCI data suggested that children progressed at their expected or better rate as measured by the Gesell. A within-group analysis of covariance was performed on participants' posttest AEPS scores (Bricker, 1993). The variate was the type of goals (i.e., target and nontarget). The covariate used was pretest scores on the AEPS. The analysis revealed that the greatest gains were made in target areas as compared with nontarget areas for both years of phase one. Parents were asked to complete a satisfaction questionnaire, and the results indicated high satisfaction with the program for both years.

Phase two was conducted over a 2-year period and involved eight replication sites in two states. Staff at each site was provided instruction on implementation of the four elements of the activity-based approach; however, the amount of instruction varied across sites. A total of 52 staff members participated. Fidelity of treatment data were collected on 36 teachers, and their performance did not vary over time. Children's performances were compared using the AEPS. The pretest–posttest comparisons indicated that the children ($N = 145$) made significant gains on all six domains of the test.

In April 1994, an external site visit of this demonstration project was conducted. Observations of the classrooms, interviews with staff, and reviews of the outcome data were undertaken. The site team's report indicated,

> We view this project as having substantial national significance to the field of early intervention. The project staff have done an excellent job of implementing the model in community programs that represent quite diverse populations served by early childhood programs. (Peck, Schwartz, & Warren, 1994)

The site team listed several project strengths and concluded with a set of recommendations that urge project staff to expand the current evaluation model "to include study of the contextual factors affecting the implementation of [activity-based intervention]."

The first phase of this model demonstration project was designed to examine the effects of activity-based intervention by collecting extensive child progress data. The second phase was designed to determine if outcomes could be replicated at other sites that were offered training in how to implement the activity-based approach. Child progress data from phase one and phase two are robust from the perspective of the large sample size and that the participants span the early childhood age range and disability continuum from children at risk to children with severe disabilities. Participants also came from different geographic sites and programs. In addition, phase two was able to demonstrate that interventionists can learn to use the activity-based approach with training. As noted by the site team, however, the outcomes from the project have done little to clarify the contextual factors that may affect the implementation of this approach.

Except for the Losardo and Bricker (1994) study, the investigations of activity-based intervention reviewed in this section are representative of first-generation early intervention efficacy research (Guralnick & Bennett, 1987). That is, the findings from such studies produce global outcomes that indicated early intervention, or in this case, activity-based intervention is effective in producing short-term change in children. The Losardo and Bricker study moved closer to what Guralnick (1997) calls second-generation research. This type of research is designed to study the effects of specific features rather than global effects.

If one accepts the significant constraints facing intervention researchers, we believe the general efficacy of activity-based intervention has been demonstrated. The work, however, can be criticized for its design and methodological flaws. The next step is to expand on the Losardo and Bricker study by examining specific features of activity-based intervention and by documenting their effects on child outcomes. Empirical work has begun that is focused on an important underlying process of activity-based intervention—embedding learning opportunities during daily activities (e.g., Pretti-Frontczak & Bricker, 2001).

A major role of interventionists, specialists, and caregivers is to provide opportunities for children to learn target goals and objectives as well as general curricular goals. A major feature of activity-based intervention and other naturalistic approaches is embedding learning opportunities into a range of authentic and therefore meaningful activities. The study of this important underlying process of activity-based intervention is an example of second-generation research and, therefore, is a step forward in beginning to bring better understanding to what specific parts, or portions, of global approaches produce change in children. An analysis of the work related to the approach is beyond the scope of this chapter, and many of the studies focused on the embedding of learning opportunities and instructional strategies have been reviewed elsewhere (e.g., Pretti-Frontczak, Barr, Macy, & Carter, 2003).

SUMMARY

We began this chapter by reminding the reader about the significant methodological, population, and cost constraints that face investigators interested in studying the effects of intervention on children who fall outside the typical distribution. As we noted, the barriers to the demonstration of intervention effects, particularly long-term effects, are sufficient to dissuade any but the most determined investigators. Intervention researchers face a serious dilemma between establishing sufficient control to make the outcomes defensible (i.e., establish external validity) and conducting the work in ways that at least minimally match what teachers, interventionists, and caregivers face on a daily basis (i.e., establish internal validity). Choosing either option creates daunting problems. One of the most significant challenges facing intervention researchers is the discovery or development of procedures that permit establishing sufficient scientific control but that can also accommodate the reality of field-based work.

The studies of global intervention efforts focused on populations of children at risk and with disabilities suggest that quality intervention efforts do produce at least short-term positive effects. That conclusion is reinforced by a study by Thomaidis, Kaderoglou, Stefou, Damianou, and Bakoula (2000) that employed a control group and found "that a well-structured early intervention program had a significant documented effect on the general developmental level of the treatment children as measured by DQ [developmental quotient] scores" (p. 20).

The study of the effects of activity-based intervention has been blessed with far fewer resources than many of the studies reviewed by Farran (2000). As one might expect, both the nature of the population and lack of resources have resulted in work that has serious methodological flaws. Nonetheless, we are willing to conclude that the implementation of the elements of activity-based intervention by well-prepared interventionists produces consistent positive change in children (e.g., Daugherty, Grisham-Brown, & Hemmeter, 2001; Grisham-Brown, Schuster, Hemmeter, & Collins, 2000; Horn, Lieber, Li, Sandall, & Schwartz, 2000; Kohler, Anthony, Steighner, & Hoyson, 2001; Kohler, Strain, Hoyson, & Jamieson, 1997; Losardo &

Bricker, 1994; Pretti-Frontczak & Bricker, 2001; Sewell et al., 1998; Wolery, 1994; Wolery, Anthony, Caldwell, Snyder, & Morgante, 2002; Wolery, Anthony, & Heckathorn, 1998).

As noted previously, the next step is to continue to study activity-based intervention not as a global entity but to parse its elements into manageable pieces for examination. We believe that studies focused on treatment by aptitude and specific intervention features will move the field toward better understanding of the effects of intervention. This valuable information will serve to improve activity-based intervention and enhance its effects on young children and their families.

REFERENCES

Baer, D. (1981). The nature of intervention research. In R. Schiefelbusch & D. Bricker (Eds.), *Early language: Acquisition and intervention*. Baltimore: University Park Press.

Bailey, D., Scarborough, A., & Hebbeler, K. (2003). National early intervention longitudinal study: Executive summary. *NEILS Data Report No. 2*. Menlo Park, CA: SRI International.

Bailey, E. (1983). *Psychometric evaluation of the Comprehensive Evaluation and Programming System*. Unpublished doctoral dissertation, University of Oregon, Eugene.

Bailey, E., & Bricker, D. (1985). Evaluation of a three-year early intervention demonstration project. *Topics in Early Childhood Special Education, 5*, 52–65.

Barnett, S.J., & Escobar, C.P. (1990). Economic costs and benefits of early intervention. In S.J. Meisels & J.P. Shonkoff (Eds.), *Handbook of early childhood intervention*. Cambridge: Cambridge University Press.

Bayley, N. (1969). *Bayley Scales of Infant Development*. New York: Psychological Corp.

Bricker, D. (1986). *Early education of at-risk and handicapped infants, toddlers, and preschool children*. Glenview, IL.: Scott, Foresman.

Bricker, D. (1989). *Early intervention for at-risk and handicapped infants, toddlers, and preschool children*. Palo Alto, CA: Vort Corp.

Bricker, D. (Ed.). (1993). *Assessment, Evaluation, and Programming System for Infants and Children*. Baltimore: Paul H. Brookes Publishing Co.

Bricker, D. (Series Ed.). (2002). *Assessment, Evaluation, and Programming System for Infants and Children* (2nd ed., Vols. 1–4). Baltimore: Paul H. Brookes Publishing Co.

Bricker, D., Bruder, M., & Bailey, E. (1982). Developmental integration of preschool children. *Analysis and Intervention in Developmental Disabilities, 2*, 207–222.

Bricker, D., Gentry, D., & Bailey, E. (1985). *Evaluation and Programming System: For Infants and Young Children—Assessment Level 1: Developmentally 1 Month to 3 Years*. Eugene: University of Oregon.

Bricker, D., & Gumerlock, S. (1988). Application of a three-level evaluation plan for monitoring child progress and program effects. *Journal of Special Education, 22*, 66–81.

Bricker, D., McComas, N., Pretti-Frontczak, K., Leve, C., Stieber, S., Losardo, A., & Scanlon, J. (1997). *Activity-based collaboration project: A nondirected model demonstration program for children who are at-risk and disabled and their families*. Unpublished report, University of Oregon, Center on Human Development, Early Intervention Program.

Bricker, D., & Sheehan, R. (1981). Effectiveness of an early intervention program as indexed by measures of child change. *Journal of the Division for Early Childhood, 4,* 11–28.

Bricker, W., & Bricker, D. (1976). The infant, toddler, and preschool research and intervention project. In T. Tjossem (Ed.), *Intervention strategies for high risk infants and young children.* Baltimore: University Park Press.

Bryant, D., & Maxwell, K. (1997). The effectiveness of early intervention for disadvantaged children. In M.J. Guralnick (Ed.), *The effectiveness of early intervention* (pp. 23–46). Baltimore: Paul H. Brookes Publishing Co.

Casto, G., & White, K. (1993). Longitudinal studies of alternative types of early intervention: Rationale and design. *Early Education and Development, 4,* 224–237.

Daugherty, S., Grisham-Brown, J., & Hemmeter, M.L. (2001). The effects of embedded instruction on the acquisition of target and nontarget skills in preschoolers with developmental delays. *Topics in Early Childhood Special Education, 21,* 213–221.

Escobar, C., Barnett, W., & Goetze, L. (1994). Cost analysis in early intervention. *Journal of Early Intervention, 18,* 48–63.

Farran, D. (2000). Another decade of intervention for children who are low income or disabled: What do we know now? In J.P. Shonkoff & S.J. Meisels (Eds.), *Handbook of early childhood intervention* (2nd ed.). Cambridge: Cambridge University Press.

Feldman, M. (1997). The effectiveness of early intervention for children of parents with mental retardation. In M.J. Guralnick (Ed.), *The effectiveness of early intervention* (pp. 171–192). Baltimore: Paul H. Brookes Publishing Co.

Gersten, R., Baker, S., & Lloyd, J. (2000). Designing high-quality research in special education: Group experimental design. *Journal of Special Education, 34,* 2–18.

Grisham-Brown, J., Schuster, J.W., Hemmeter, M.L., & Collins, B.C. (2000). Using an embedded strategy to teach preschoolers with significant disabilities. *Journal of Behavioral Education, 10,* 139–162.

Guralnick, M.J. (1997). Second-generation research in the field of early intervention. In M.J. Guralnick (Ed.), *The effectiveness of early intervention* (pp. 3–20). Baltimore: Paul H. Brookes Publishing Co.

Guralnick, M., & Bennett, F. (Eds.). (1987). *The effectiveness of early intervention for at-risk and handicapped children.* San Diego: Academic Press.

Horn, E., Lieber, J., Li, S.M., Sandall, S., & Schwartz, I. (2000). Supporting young children's IEP goals in inclusive settings through embedded learning opportunities. *Topics in Early Childhood Special Education, 20,* 208–223.

Infant Health and Development Program. (1990). Enhancing the outcomes of low-birth-weight, premature infants. *Journal of the American Medical Association, 263,* 3035–3042.

Kennedy, M. (1997). The connection between research and practice. *Educational Researcher, 26,* 4–12.

Knobloch, H., Stevens, F., & Malone, A. (1980). *Manual of developmental diagnosis: The administration and interpretation of the revised Gesell and Amatruda developmental and neurologic examination.* Hagerstown, MD: Harper & Row.

Kohler, F., Anthony, L., Steighner, S., & Hoyson, M. (2001). Teaching social interaction skills in integrated preschool: An examination of naturalistic tactics. *Topics in Early Childhood Special Education, 21,* 93–103, 113.

Kohler, F., Strain, P., Hoyson, M., & Jamieson, B. (1997). Merging naturalistic teaching and peer-based strategies to address the IEP objectives of preschoolers with autism: An examination of structural and child behavior outcomes. *Focus on Autism and Other Developmental Disabilities, 12,* 196–206.

Lerner, P., Hauser-Cram, P., & Miller, E. (1998). Assumptions and features of longitudinal designs. In B. Spodek, O. Saracho, & A. Pellegrini (Eds.), *Issues in early childhood educational research.* New York: Teachers College Press.

Lewis, M., & Wehren, A. (1982). The central tendency in study of the handicapped child. In D. Bricker (Ed.), *Intervention with at-risk and handicapped infants*. Baltimore: University Park Press.

Losardo, A., & Bricker, D. (1994). Activity-based intervention and direct instruction: A comparison study. *American Journal on Mental Retardation, 98*, 744–765.

McCarthy, D. (1972). *McCarthy scales of children's abilities*. New York: Psychological Corp.

McLean, L.K., & Woods Cripe, J. (1997). The effectiveness of early intervention for children with communication disorders. In M.J. Guralnick (Ed.), *The effectiveness of early intervention* (pp. 349–428). Baltimore: Paul H. Brookes Publishing Co.

Oregon State Mental Health Division. (1977). *The student progress record*. Salem, OR: Author.

Peck, C., Schwartz, I., & Warren, S. (1994). *Site Visit Report–April 27–28, 1994. A nondirected model demonstration program: Activity-based intervention*. Eugene: University of Oregon.

Pretti-Frontczak, K., Barr, D., Macy, M., & Carter, A. (2003). An annotated bibliography of research and resources related to activity-based intervention, embedded learning opportunities, and routines-based instruction. *Topics in Early Childhood Special Education, 23*, 29–39.

Pretti-Frontczak, K., & Bricker, D. (2001). Use of the embedding strategy by early childhood education and early childhood special education teachers. *Infant-Toddler Intervention: The Transciplinary Journal, 11*, 111–128.

Raver, C. (2002). Emotions matter: Making the case for the role of young children's emotional development for early school readiness. *Social Policy Report, XVI*, 3–18.

Sameroff, A. (1994). Ecological perspectives on longitudinal follow-up studies. In S. Friedman & H. Haywood (Eds.), *Concepts, domains, and methods*. San Diego: Academic Press.

Scruggs, T., & Mastropieri, M. (1994). Issues in conducting intervention research: Secondary students. In S. Vaughn & C. Bos (Eds.), *Research issues in learning disabilities: Theory, methodology, assessment, and ethics*. New York: Springer Verlag.

Sewell, T., Collins, B., Hemmeter, M., & Schuster, J. (1998). Using simultaneous prompting within an activity-based format to teach dressing skills to preschoolers with developmental disabilities. *Journal of Early Intervention, 21*, 132–145.

Shonkoff, J.P. & Meisels, S.J., (2000). *Handbook of early childhood intervention* (2nd ed.). Cambridge: Cambridge University Press.

Shonkoff, J.P., & Phillips, D.A. (Eds.). (2000). *From neurons to neighborhoods*. Washington, DC: National Academy Press.

Tarr, J., & Barnett, W. (2001). A cost analysis of Part C early intervention services in New Jersey. *Journal of Early Intervention, 24*, 45–54.

Thomaidis, L., Kaderoglou, E., Stefou, M., Damianou, S., & Bakoula, C. (2000). Does early intervention work? A controlled trial. *Infants and Young Children, 12*, 17–22.

Thorndike, R., Hagen, E., & Sattler, J. (1986). *The Stanford-Binet intelligence scale* (4th ed.). Chicago: Riverside.

Vincent, L., Salisbury, C., Strain, P., McCormick, C., & Tessier, A. (1990). A behavioral-ecological approach to early intervention: Focus on cultural diversity. In S.J. Meisels & J.P. Shonkoff (Eds.), *Handbook of early childhood intervention*. Cambridge: Cambridge University Press.

White, O., Edgar, E., & Haring, N. (1978). *Uniform performance assessment system*. Seattle: University of Washington, College of Education, Experimental Education Unit, Child Development and Mental Retardation Center.

Wolery, M. (1994). Implementing instruction for young children with special needs in early childhood classrooms. In M. Wolery & J.S. Wilbers (Eds.), *Including children with special needs in early childhood programs* (pp. 151–166). Washington, DC: National Association for the Education of Young Children.

Wolery, M., Anthony, L., Caldwell, N., Snyder, E., & Morgante, J. (2002). Embedding and distributing constant time delay in circle time and transitions. *Topics in Early Childhood Special Education, 22,* 14–25.

Wolery, M., Anthony, L., & Heckathorn, J. (1998). Transition-based teaching: Effects on transitions, teachers' behavior, and children's learning. *Journal of Early Intervention, 21,* 117–131.

10

Into the Future

The United States has seen a steady growth in the number of programs and services available to young children who have or are at risk for disabilities and their families. In part, this growth has been fueled by the national resurgence in the belief that early intervention has both preventive and curative powers that can offset the myriad of ills that beset today's young children and their families. Although those who are associated with early intervention/early childhood special education (EI/ECSE) and early childhood education (ECE) believe that intervention provided early in children's lives can be effective, we are aware that the problem is considerably more complicated than the delivery of services to young children and families.

Providing poorly organized, off-target programs, however early they are begun, will not produce the protective and positive outcomes politicians and voters are being led to expect from the investment of resources into early education programs. National "cure-all" expectations such as the Goals 2000: Educate America Act (PL 103-227) and the No Child Left Behind Act of 2001 (PL 107-110) place considerable pressure on the field to improve the quality of programs to ensure, to the extent possible, that children enter public schools with the necessary foundation for optimal learning. Indeed, expectations have expanded from preparing young children to learn to also preparing young children to have an emotionally and physically balanced life. Preparing children with disabilities and children who come from poor learning environments to learn effectively and to be emotionally well adjusted is a tall order. Meeting such challenges will require that researchers move forward in the exploration of methods to enhance early development, adjustment, and learning.

Our hope is that growth in numbers of programs serving young children will be paralleled by program staff's choice and use of the most effective intervention available. We believe that for most children and families, child-directed approaches such as activity-based intervention are the best choice. The success of these approaches in meeting national expectations for young children will be determined in part by our ability to describe and teach the elements and processes that compose them. That is, of course, the primary goal of this volume—to present a coherent and complete description of a comprehensive and coordinated approach to intervention.

Our teachings, writings, and discussions focused on activity-based intervention have led to important insights. Three of these insights have had a significant impact on our thinking and on how we will proceed in the future. First, program personnel do not tend to adopt an entire model or approach (e.g., Bricker, McComas, Pretti-Frontczak, Leve, Stieber, Losardo, & Scanlon, 1997). Rather, individuals appear to choose parts, elements, or pieces of an approach that are selected because they 1) match an individual's personal belief about how to teach or intervene, 2) are compatible with an individual's present style or approach, or 3) can be managed or integrated into an individual's present approach. Pieces or elements of an approach that do not fit personal beliefs, are not compatible with present approaches, or simply cannot be managed because of time and resources appear to be discarded and not adopted. The outcome, then, is anything but the straightforward application of an approach.

Second, interventionists require considerable time (e.g., months or even years) to consistently integrate a new element into their repertoires. We have found after instruction and conscientious follow-up that direct service delivery personnel experience considerable difficulty in increasing the frequency with which they embed learning opportunities that target children's goals and objectives into child-directed, routine, and planned activities. We believe these phenomena (i.e., piecemeal application of an approach and long latencies to improve intervention techniques) are not peculiar to activity-based intervention but rather reflect programmatic and personal realities that make change slow and arduous (Rogers, 1995).

Third, most learners of new concepts and strategies benefit from being exposed to multiple examples, particularly examples that parallel their circumstances. This insight has led to the development of many additional illustrations and examples of how to employ activity-based intervention that have been added to this volume. We are hopeful that the expansion of how to apply activity-based intervention will assist the reader in more quickly and effectively learning and applying the processes that compose activity-based intervention.

These observations on the willingness and ability of personnel to instigate change raise serious questions. The first set of questions is in regard to how to assist program personnel in learning about and adopting an approach or elements of an approach: How can instruction and follow-up consistently improve the services delivered to young children and their families? The second set of questions raises more difficult issues surrounding the integrity of the approach and measuring program effectiveness. For example, if an interventionist chooses to employ only two elements of activity-based intervention, then is he or she using activity-based intervention? Also, how does one address the impact or effectiveness of an approach if personnel employ only bits and pieces of the approach?

Part of the answer lies in the careful delineation of program features as we have discussed throughout this volume and as suggested by Guralnick (1997) in his proposal for second-generation research on program effectiveness. Another part of the answer appears to lie in our concepts or expectations about adopting models or approaches. The adoption of an entire approach or model is not a realistic expectation given what we know about human behavior. We will likely accomplish more if we change our expectations to asking personnel to consider the implementation of recommended practice features or processes. The manner and way of implementation will need to be varied in order to address the realities of specific settings, children, families, and direct service delivery personnel.

We expect activity-based intervention to be applied with thoughtful modification. We do not expect that all consultants, caregivers, and direct service personnel will understand, interpret, or apply the processes of the approach in the same way. We expect and value variation. We do hope, however, that the fundamental recommended practice features that underlie activity-based intervention are employed. We further hope that the articulation of the approach in this volume will assist personnel in that application. As we move into the future, feedback from the fields of EI/ECSE and ECE will tell us how well this hope has been realized.

REFERENCES

Bricker, D., McComas, N., Pretti-Frontczak, K., Leve, C., Stieber, S., Losardo, A., & Scanlon, J. (1997). *Activity-based collaboration project: A nondirected model demonstration program for children who are at-risk disabled and their families.* Unpublished report, University of Oregon, Center on Human Development, Early Intervention Program.

Goals 2000: Educate America Act, PL 103-227, 20 U.S.C. §§ 5801 *et seq.*

Guralnick, M.J. (Ed.). (1997). *The effectiveness of early intervention.* Baltimore: Paul H. Brookes Publishing Co.

No Child Left Behind Act of 2001, PL 107-110, 115 Stat. 1425, 20 U.S.C. §§ 6301 *et seq.*

Rogers, E. (1995). *Diffusion of innovations* (4th ed.). New York: The Free Press.

Appendix

Reproducible Forms

Intervention Guide

1. Basic information

Child's name: _____

Team members: _____

_____

Date intervention initiated: _____ Date intervention completed: _____

2. Goal, objectives/benchmarks, program steps

3. State standard(s) or IFSP outcome(s)

4. Multiple and varied learning opportunities, functional and generative goals, timely and integral feedback or consequences

Antecedents designed to provide learning opportunities	List of possible child responses: targeted (+) and nontargeted (–)	Feedback or consequences

5. Accommodations, modifications, and intervention strategies

6. Data collection procedures

Who (person responsible for collecting the data)	Where (which activities or locations)	When (how often or on which days)	How (which methods)

7. Decision rules

If adequate progress does not occur in _____ (specify time frame for when the team will review the data), then the team will (check all that apply):

_____ change which goals are targeted

_____ change selected antecedents or feedback/consequences

_____ change accommodations, modifications, or intervention strategies

_____ change how often learning opportunities are provided

_____ change where learning opportunities occur

_____ other (describe) _____

_____

Embedding Schedule

Child's name: _____

Team members: _____

_____

Dates schedule will be used: _____

Family routine or daily classroom activity	Target goal _____ _____ _____	Target goal _____ _____ _____
_____		
_____		
_____		
_____		

Group Embedding Schedule

Children's names: _____

Team members: _____

Dates schedule will be used: _____

Children and target goals	Daily classroom activities				
	____	____	____	____	____
Child's name: _____ 1.					
2.					
3.					
Child's name: _____ 1.					
2.					
3.					
Child's name: _____ 1.					
2.					
3.					

 **Activity Plan**

1. Activity name

2. Materials

3. Environmental arrangement

4. Sequence of steps

   Beginning

Middle

End

5. Embedded learning opportunities

6. Planned variations

7. Vocabulary

8. Peer interaction opportunities

9. Caregiver involvement

Index

Page numbers followed by *f* indicate figures; those followed by *t* indicate tables.